# FAULT LINES

# FAULT
# LINES

How Hidden Fractures Still
Threaten the World Economy

**RAGHURAM G. RAJAN**

PRINCETON UNIVERSITY PRESS

*Princeton and Oxford*

Published by Princeton University Press, 41 William Street, Princeton, New Jersey 08540
In the United Kingdom: Princeton University Press, 6 Oxford Street, Woodstock, Oxfordshire
OX20 1TW
press.princeton.edu

Library of Congress Cataloging-in-Publication Data

Rajan, Raghuram.
Fault lines : how hidden fractures still threaten the
world economy / Raghuram G. Rajan.
p.   cm.
Includes bibliographical references and index.
ISBN 978-0-691-14683-6 (hardcover : alk. paper)
1. Income distribution—United States—History—21st century.
2. United States—Social conditions—21st century.
3. Global Financial Crisis, 2008–2009.   4. Economic history—
21st century.   I. Title.
HC110.I5R36   2010
330.9'0511—dc22                    2010006031


British Library Cataloging-in-Publication Data is available


This book has been composed in Minion Pro and Knockout
by Princeton Editorial Associates Inc., Scottsdale, Arizona.


Printed on acid-free paper.

Printed in the United States of America


3 5 7 9 10 8 6 4 2

*To my parents*

# CONTENTS

## ACKNOWLEDGMENTS

A BOOK IS ALMOST ALWAYS a collective effort, even if it has only a single author. I owe many of the ideas in this book to the stimulating environment at the University of Chicago's Booth School of Business, where I have spent the best part of my academic life. The work I have coauthored with Douglas Diamond and Luigi Zingales is also central to some of my thinking here. Comments from Anil Kashyap, Richard Posner, Amit Seru, and Amir Sufi were very useful. I owe special thanks to Viral Acharya at New York University's Stern School of Business, who gave me very detailed comments on the chapters on finance. I have also benefited greatly from conversations with Marshall Bouton, John Cochrane, Arminio Fraga, Shrinivas Govindarajan, David Johnson, Randall Kroszner, Charles Prince, Edward Snyder, Joyce van Grondelle, Robert Vishny, Martin Wolf, and Naomi Woods. I thank Rishabh Sinha and Swapnil Sinha for their research assistance.

The time I spent at the International Monetary Fund between August 2003 and December 2006 taught me a lot about the politics of international finance. I learned a great deal from Anne Krueger and Rodrigo de Rato, as well as from my colleagues in the research department there, especially Timothy Callen, Charles Collyns, Kalpana Kochhar, Paolo Mauro, Gian Maria Milesi-Ferretti, Jonathan Ostry, Eswar Prasad, David Robinson, and Arvind Subramanian. Ken Rogoff, my predecessor at the Fund, has always been generous with his time and has been a source of very useful advice.

Seth Ditchik, my editor at Princeton University Press, has been invaluable in shaping my ideas into a coherent book. Peter Dougherty, the director, has been very supportive throughout the process. I also thank the other staff members of Princeton University Press and members of Princeton Editorial Associates who have helped bring the book to publication.

This book would not have been written without the support, encouragement, advice, and detailed comments I received from my wife, Radhika. She has been a true partner every step of the way. Finally, I thank my children, Tara and Akhil, for putting up with my work—maybe it was a relief to them because it prevented me from giving their lives my undivided attention. At any rate, they give me two great reasons to try to make the world better for the generations to come.

Chicago, February 2010

# FAULT LINES

# Introduction

THE FINANCIAL COLLAPSE of 2007 and the recession that followed left many economists on the defensive. News programs, magazines, pundits, and even the Queen of England all asked some variant of the question, why didn't you see it coming? Some in the economics community wrote articles or convened conferences to examine how they could have gotten it so wrong; others engaged in a full-throated defense of their profession.[1] For many who were hostile to the fundamental assumptions of mainstream economics, the crisis was proof that they had been right all along: the emperor was finally shown to have no clothes. Public confidence in authority was badly shaken.

Of course, it is incorrect to say that no one saw this crisis coming. Some hedge fund managers and traders in investment banks put their money instead of their mouths to work. A few government and Federal Reserve officials expressed deep concern. A number of economists, such as Kenneth Rogoff, Nouriel Roubini, Robert Shiller, and William White, repeatedly sounded warnings about the levels of U.S. house prices and household indebtedness. Niall Ferguson, a historian, drew parallels to past booms that ended poorly. The problem was not that no one warned about the dangers; it was that those who benefited from an overheated economy—which included a lot of people—had little incentive to listen. Critics were often written off as Cassandras or "permabears": predict a downturn long enough, the thinking went, and you would eventually be proved right, much as a broken clock is correct twice a day. I know, because I was one of those Cassandras.

Every year, the world's top central bankers get together for three days at Jackson Hole, Wyoming, along with private-sector analysts, economists, and financial journalists, to debate a set of topical papers commissioned for the event by the host, the Federal Reserve Bank of Kansas City. Following each day's presentations, participants go on long hikes in the beautiful Grand Teton National Park, where, amid the stunning mountain scenery, they talk central-banker shop: intense arguments about the Wicksellian rate of interest mingle with the sounds of rushing streams.

The 2005 Jackson Hole Conference was to be the last for the Federal Reserve Board chairman, Alan Greenspan, and the theme, therefore, was the legacy of the Greenspan era. I was the chief economist of the International Monetary Fund (IMF) at that time, on leave from the University of Chicago, where I have taught banking and finance for the best part of two decades. I was asked to present a paper on how the financial sector had evolved during Greenspan's term.

The typical paper on the financial sector at that time described in breathless prose the dramatic expansion of financial markets around the world. It emphasized the wonders of securitization, which allowed a bank to package its risky housing or credit card loans together and sell claims on the package in the financial market. Securitization allowed a bank to get the risky loans off its books. At the same time, it allowed long-term investors in the market, such as pension funds and insurance companies, to take on a small portion of the risky claims that they, by virtue of having longer horizons and holding a diverse portfolio of other assets, could hold more easily than the bank. In theory, with the risk better spread across sturdier shoulders, investors would demand a lower return for holding the risk, allowing the bank to charge lower loan rates and expand borrowers' access to finance.

In preparation for writing the paper, I had asked my staff to prepare graphs and tables. As we looked through them, I noted a few that seemed curious. They were plots of different measures of the riskiness of large U.S. banks, and they suggested that banks had become, if anything, more exposed to risk over the past decade. This was surprising, for if banks were getting risky loans off their balance sheets by selling them, they should have become safer. I eventually realized that I was committing the economist's cardinal sin of assuming *ceteris paribus*, that is, assuming that everything else but the phenomenon being studied, in this case securitization, remained the same. Typically, everything does not remain the same. Most important, deregulation and developments like securitization had increased competition, which increased the incentives for bankers (and financial managers more generally) to take on more complex forms of risk.

Once I saw this trend, the paper quickly wrote itself and was titled "Has Financial Development Made the World Riskier?" As the *Wall Street Journal* reported in 2009 in an article on my Jackson Hole presentation:

Incentives were horribly skewed in the financial sector, with workers reaping rich rewards for making money but being only lightly penalized for losses, Mr. Rajan argued. That encouraged financial firms to invest in complex products, with potentially big payoffs, which could on occasion fail spectacularly.

He pointed to "credit default swaps" which act as insurance against bond defaults. He said insurers and others were generating big returns selling these swaps with the appearance of taking on little risk, even though the pain could be immense if defaults actually occurred.

Mr. Rajan also argued that because banks were holding a portion of the credit securities they created on their books, if those securities ran into trouble, the banking system itself would be at risk. Banks would lose confidence in one another, he said. "The interbank market could freeze up, and one could well have a full-blown financial crisis."

Two years later, that's essentially what happened.[2]

Forecasting at that time did not require tremendous prescience: all I did was connect the dots using theoretical frameworks that my colleagues and I had developed. I did not, however, foresee the reaction from the normally polite conference audience. I exaggerate only a bit when I say I felt like an early Christian who had wandered into a convention of half-starved lions. As I walked away from the podium after being roundly criticized by a number of luminaries (with a few notable exceptions), I felt some unease. It was not caused by the criticism itself, for one develops a thick skin after years of lively debate in faculty seminars: if you took everything the audience said to heart, you would never publish anything. Rather it was because the critics seemed to be ignoring what was going on before their eyes.

In part, I was criticized because I was off message. Some of the papers in the conference, in keeping with the Greenspan-era theme, focused on whether Alan Greenspan was the best central banker in history, or just among the best. Someone raining on that parade, suggesting all was not well and calling for better regulation, was unlikely to attract encomiums, especially given Greenspan's known skepticism about the effectiveness of regulation. In part, the reaction was defensive, for if the financial sector had gone so far off track, were the regulators not at fault for being asleep at the switch? In part, it was hubris. The Federal Reserve had dealt successfully with the downturn caused by the dot-com bust in

2000–2001 and felt it knew how to rescue the system relatively painlessly if it got into trouble again.

Although I worried about banker incentives in my talk and regulatory motives in its aftermath, and although many more commentators and regulators have since come around to my point of view, I have come to believe that these issues are just the tip of the iceberg. The true sources of the crisis we have experienced are not only more widespread but also more hidden. We should resist the temptation to round up the most proximate suspects and pin the blame only on them. Greedy bankers can be regulated; lax government officials can be replaced. This is a convenient focus, because the villains are easily identified and measures can be taken against malfeasance and neglect. What's more, it absolves the rest of us of our responsibility for precipitating this crisis. But this is too facile a response.

We should also resist the view that this is just another crisis, similar to every financial crisis before it, with real estate and foreign capital flows at its center. Although there are broad similarities in the things that go wrong in every financial crisis, this one centered on what many would agree is the most sophisticated financial system in the world.[3] What happened to the usual regulatory checks and balances? What happened to the discipline imposed by markets? What happened to the private instinct for self-preservation? Is the free-enterprise system fundamentally broken? These questions would not arise if this were "just another" crisis in a developing country. And given the cost of this crisis, we cannot afford facile or wrong answers.

Although I believe that the basic ideas of the free-enterprise system are sound, the fault lines that precipitated this crisis are indeed systemic. They stem from more than just specific personalities or institutions. A much wider cast of characters shares responsibility for the crisis: it includes domestic politicians, foreign governments, economists like me, and people like you. Furthermore, what enveloped all of us was not some sort of collective hysteria or mania. Somewhat frighteningly, each one of us did what was sensible given the incentives we faced. Despite mounting evidence that things were going wrong, all of us clung to the hope that things would work out fine, for our interests lay in that outcome. Collectively, however, our actions took the world's economy to the brink of disaster, and they could do so again unless we recognize what went wrong and take the steps needed to correct it.

There are deep fault lines in the global economy, fault lines that have developed because in an integrated economy and in an integrated world, what is best for the individual actor or institution is not always best for the system. Responsibility for some of the more serious fault lines lies not in economics but in politics. Unfortunately, we did not know where all these fault lines ran until the crisis exposed them. We now know better, but the danger is that we will continue to ignore them. Politicians today vow, "Never again!" But they will naturally focus only on dealing with a few scapegoats, not just because the system is harder to change, but also because if politicians traced the fault lines, they would find a few running through themselves. Action will become particularly difficult if a more rapid recovery reinforces the incentives to settle for the status quo. This book is, therefore, an attempt to heed the warnings from this crisis, to develop a better understanding of what went wrong, and then to outline the hard policy choices that will tackle the true causes of this crisis and avert future ones.

Let us start with what are widely believed to be the roots of this crisis, which is, in part, a child of past crises.[4] In the late 1990s, a number of developing countries (in the interests of brevity, I use the term *developing* for countries that have relatively low per capita incomes and *industrial* for those that have high per capita incomes), which used to go on periodic spending binges fueled by foreign borrowing, decided to go cold turkey and save instead of spend. Japan, the second largest economy in the world, was also in a deepening slump. Someone else in the world had to consume or invest more to prevent the world economy from slowing down substantially. The good news for any country willing to spend more was that the now-plentiful surplus savings of the developing countries and Japan, soon to be augmented by the surpluses of Germany and the oil-rich countries, would be available to fund that spending.

In the late 1990s, that someone else was corporations in industrial countries that were on an investment spree, especially in the areas of information technology and communications. Unfortunately, this boom in investment, now called the dot-com bubble, was followed by a bust in early 2000, during which these corporations scaled back dramatically on investment.

As the U.S. economy slowed, the Federal Reserve went into overdrive, cutting interest rates sharply. By doing so, it sought to energize activity in sectors of the economy that are interest sensitive. Typically, such a move boosts corporate investment, but corporations had invested too much already during the dot-com boom and had little incentive to do more. Instead, the low interest rates prompted U.S. consumers to buy houses, which in turn raised house prices and led to a surge in housing investment. A significant portion of the additional demand came from segments of the population with low credit ratings or impaired credit histories—the so-called subprime and Alt-A segments—who now obtained access to credit that had hitherto been denied to them. Moreover, rising house prices gave subprime borrowers the ability to keep refinancing into low interest rate mortgages (thus avoiding default) even as they withdrew the home equity they had built up to buy more cars and TV sets. For many, the need to re-pay loans seemed remote and distant.

The flood of money lapping at the doors of borrowers originated, in part, from investors far away who had earned it by exporting to the United States and feeding the national consumption habit. But how did a dentist in Stuttgart, Germany, make mortgage loans to subprime borrowers in Las Vegas, Nevada? The German dentist would not be able to lend directly, because she would incur extremely high costs in investigating the Vegas borrower's creditworthiness, making the loan conform to all local legal requirements, collecting payments, and intervening in case of default. Moreover, any individual subprime homebuyer would have a high propensity to default, certainly higher than the level of risk with which a conservative private investor would be comfortable.

This is where the sophisticated U.S. financial sector stepped in. Securitization dealt with many of these concerns. If the mortgage was packaged together with mortgages from other areas, diversification would reduce the risk. Furthermore, the riskiest claims against the package could be sold to those who had the capacity to evaluate them and had an appetite for the risk, while the safest, AAA-rated portions could be sold directly to the foreign dentist or her bank.

The U.S. financial sector thus bridged the gap between an overconsuming and overstimulated United States and an underconsuming, understimulated rest of the world. But this entire edifice rested on the housing market. New housing construction and existing housing sales provided jobs in construction, real estate brokerage, and finance, while rising house prices provided the home equity to refinance old loans and finance new consumption. Foreign countries could emerge from their slump by exporting to the seemingly insatiable U.S. consumer, while also lending the United States the money to pay for these imports. The world was in a sweet but unsustainable spot.

The gravy train eventually came to a halt after the Federal Reserve raised interest rates and halted the house price rise that had underpinned the frenzied lending. Subprime mortgage-backed securities turned out to be backed by much riskier mortgages than previously advertised, and their value plummeted. The seemingly smart bankers turned out to have substantial portions of these highly rated but low-quality securities on their balance sheets, even though they must have known what they contained. And they had financed these holdings with enormous amounts of short-term debt. The result was that short-term creditors panicked and refused to refinance the banks when their debts came due. Some of the banks failed; others were bailed out even as the whole system tottered on the brink of collapse. Economies across the world went into a deep slump from which they are recovering slowly.

This narrative leaves many questions unanswered. Why was the flood of money that came in from outside the United States used for financing subprime credit? Why was the United States, unlike other economies like Germany and Japan, unable to export its way out of the 2001 recession? Why are poorer developing countries like China financing the unsustainable consumption of rich countries like the United States? Why did the Federal Reserve keep rates so low for so long? Why did financial firms make loans to people who had no income, no jobs, and no assets—a practice so ubiquitous that it attracted its own acronym, NINJA loans? Why did the banks—the sausage makers, so to speak— hold so many of the sausages for their own consumption when they knew what went into them?

I attempt to address all these questions in this book. Let me start by saying that I do not have a single explanation for this crisis, and so no single silver bullet to prevent a future one. Any single explanation would be too simplistic. I use the metaphor of *fault lines*. In geology, fault lines are breaks in the Earth's surface where tectonic plates come in contact or collide. Enormous stresses build up around these fault lines. I describe the fault lines that have emerged in the global economy and explain how these fault lines affect the financial sector.

One set of fault lines stems from domestic political stresses, especially in the United States. Almost every financial crisis has political roots, which no doubt differ in each case but are political nevertheless, for strong political forces are needed to overcome the checks and balances that most industrial countries have established to contain financial exuberance. The second set of fault lines emanates from trade imbalances between countries stemming from prior patterns of growth. The final set of fault lines develops when different types of financial systems come into contact to finance the trade imbalances: specifically, when the transparent, contractually based, arm's-length financial systems in countries like the United States and the United Kingdom finance, or are financed by, less transparent financial systems in much of the rest of the world. Because different financial systems work on different principles and involve different forms of government intervention, they tend to distort each other's functioning whenever they come into close contact. All these fault lines affect financial-sector behavior and are central to our understanding of the recent crisis.

## Rising Inequality and the Push for Housing Credit

The most important example of the first kind of fault line, which is the theme of Chapter 1, is rising income inequality in the United States and the political pressure it has created for easy credit. Clearly, the highly visible incomes at the very top have gone up. The top 1 percent of households accounted for only 8.9 percent of income in 1976, but this share grew to 23.5 percent of the total income generated in the United States in 2007. Put differently, of every dollar of real income growth that was generated between 1976 and 2007, 58 cents went to the top 1 percent of households.[5] In 2007 the hedge fund manager John Paulson earned $3.7 billion, about 74,000 times the median household income in the United States.[6]

But although the gargantuan incomes at the very top excite public interest and enrage middle-class columnists, most Americans rarely meet a billionaire hedge fund manager. More relevant to their experience is the fact that since the 1980s, the wages of workers at the 90th percentile of the wage distribution in the United States—such as office managers—have grown much faster than the wage of the 50th percentile worker (the median worker)—typically factory workers and office assistants. A number of factors are responsible for the growth in the 90/50 differential. Perhaps the most important is that although in the United States technological progress requires the labor force to have ever-greater skills—a high school diploma was sufficient for our parents, whereas an undergraduate degree is barely sufficient for the office worker today—the education system has been unable to provide enough of the labor force with the necessary education. The problems are rooted in indifferent nutrition, socialization, and learning in early childhood, and in dysfunctional primary and secondary schools that leave too many Americans unprepared for college.

The everyday consequence for the middle class is a stagnant paycheck as well as growing job insecurity. Politicians feel their constituents' pain, but it is very hard to improve the quality of education, for improvement requires real and effective policy change in an area where too many vested interests favor the status quo. Moreover, any change will require years to take effect and therefore will not address the current anxiety of the electorate. Thus politicians have looked, or been steered into looking, for other, quicker ways to mollify their constituents. We have long understood that it is not income that matters but consumption. Stripped to its essentials, the argument is that if somehow the consumption of middle-class householders keeps up, if they can afford a new car every few years and the occasional exotic holiday, perhaps they will pay less attention to their stagnant monthly paychecks.

Therefore, the political response to rising inequality—whether carefully planned or an unpremeditated reaction to constituent demands—was to expand lending to households, especially low-income ones. The benefits—growing consumption and more jobs—were immediate, whereas paying the inevitable bill could be postponed into the future. Cynical as it may seem, easy credit has been used as a palliative throughout history by governments that are unable to address the deeper anxieties of the middle class directly. Politicians, however, want to couch the objective in more uplifting and persuasive terms than that of crassly increasing consumption. In the United States, the expansion of home ownership—a key element of the American dream—to low- and middle-income households was the defensible linchpin for the broader aims of expanding credit and consumption. But when easy money pushed by a deep-pocketed government comes into contact with the profit motive of a sophisticated, competitive, and amoral financial sector, a deep fault line develops.

This is not, of course, the first time in history when credit expansion has been used to assuage the concerns of a group that is being left behind, nor will it be the last. In fact, one does not even need to look outside the United States for examples. The deregulation and rapid expansion of banking in the United States in the early years of the twentieth century was in many ways a response to the Populist movement, backed by small and medium-sized farmers who found themselves falling behind the growing numbers of industrial workers and demanded easier credit. Excessive rural credit was one of the important causes of bank failure during the Great Depression.

### Export-Led Growth and Dependency

There are usually limits to debt-fueled consumption, especially in a large country like the United States. The strong demand for consumer goods and services tends to push up prices and inflation. A worried central bank then raises interest rates, curbing both households' ability to borrow and their desire to consume. Through the late 1990s and the 2000s, though, a significant portion of the increase in U.S. household demand was met from abroad, from countries such as Germany, Japan, and, increasingly, China, which have traditionally relied on exports for growth and had plenty of spare capacity to make more. But, as I argue in Chapter 2, the ability of these countries to supply the goods reflects a serious weakness in the growth path they have followed—excessive dependence on the foreign consumer. This dependence is the source of the second fault line.

The global economy is fragile because low domestic demand from traditional exporters puts pressure on other countries to step up spending. Because the exporters have excess goods to supply, countries like Spain, the United Kingdom, and the United States—which ignore growing household indebtedness and even actively encourage it—and countries like Greece—which lack the political will to control government populism and union demands—tend to get a long rope. Eventually, high household or government indebtedness in these countries limits further demand expansion and leads to a wrenching adjustment all around. But so long as large countries like Germany and Japan are structurally inclined—indeed required—to export, global supply washes around the world looking for countries that have the weakest policies or the least discipline, tempting them to spend until they simply cannot afford it and succumb to crisis.

Why are so many economies dependent on consumption elsewhere? Their dependence stems from the path they chose toward rapid growth, out of the destruction created by World War II or out of poverty. Governments (and banks) intervened extensively in these economies to create strong firms and competitive exporters, typically at the expense of household consumption in their own country.

Over time, these countries created a very efficient export-oriented manufacturing sector—firms like Canon, Toyota, Samsung, and Formosa Plastics are world leaders. The need to be competitive in foreign markets kept the exporters on their toes. But although global competition limited the deleterious effects of government intervention in the export sector, there were no such restraints in the domestic-oriented production sector. Banks, retailers, restaurants, and construction companies, through their influence over government policies, have managed to limit domestic competition in their respective sectors. As a result, these sectors are very inefficient. There are no large Japanese banks, for example, that rival HSBC in its global reach, no Japanese retailers that approach Walmart in size or cost competitiveness, and no Japanese restaurant chains that rival McDonald's in its number of franchises.

Therefore, even though these economies grew extraordinarily fast to reach the ranks of the rich, as their initial advantage of low wages disappeared and exports became more difficult, their politically strong but very inefficient domestic-oriented sector began to impose serious constraints on internally generated growth. Not only is it hard for these economies to grow on their own in normal times, but it is even harder for them to stimulate domestic growth in downturns without tremendously wasteful spending. The natural impulse of the government, when urged to spend, is to favor influential but inefficient domestic producers, which does little for long-run growth. Therefore, these countries have become dependent on foreign demand to pull them out of economic troughs.

The future does not look much brighter. As populations in these countries age, not only will change become more difficult, but their dependencies will also worsen. And China, which is likely to be the world's largest economy in the not too distant future, is following a dangerously similar path. It has to make substantial policy changes if it is not to join this group as an encumbrance on, rather than an engine of, world economic growth.

## The Clash of Systems

In the past, fast-growing developing countries were typically not net exporters, even though their factories focused on producing to meet demand elsewhere. The fast pace of growth of countries like Korea and Malaysia in the 1980s and early 1990s entailed substantial investment in machinery and equipment, which were often imported from Germany and Japan. This meant they ran trade deficits and had to borrow money on net from world capital markets to finance their investment.

Even export-led developing countries thus initially helped absorb the excess supply from the rich exporters. But developing countries experienced a series of financial crises in the 1990s that made them realize that borrowing large amounts from industrial countries to fund investment was a recipe for trouble. In Chapter 3, I explain why these economies moved from helping to absorb global excess supply to becoming net exporters themselves and contributing to the problem: essentially, their own financial systems were based on fundamentally different principles from those of their financiers, and the incompatibility between the two, the source of the fault line, made it extremely risky for them to borrow from abroad to support investment and growth.

In the competitive financial systems in countries like the United States and the United Kingdom, the accent is on transparency and easy enforceability of contracts through the legal system: because business transactions do not depend on propinquity, these are referred to as "arm's-length" systems. Financiers gain confidence because of their ability to obtain publicly available information and understand the borrower's operations and because they know that their claims will be protected and enforced by the courts. As a result, they are willing to hold long-term claims, such as equity and long-term debt, and to finance the final user directly rather than going through intermediaries like banks. Every transaction has to be justified on its own and is conducted through competitive bidding. This description is clearly a caricature—transparency was missing during the recent crisis—but it reflects the essentials of the system.

The financial systems in countries where government and bank intervention was important during the process of growth are quite different. Public financial information is very limited, perhaps because the government and banks directed the flow of financing during the growth phase and did not need, or want, public oversight then. Even though in most of these countries the government has withdrawn from directing financial flows, banks still play an important role, and information is still closely guarded within a group of insiders. Because of the paucity of public information, enforcement of contractual claims largely depends on long-term business relationships. The borrower repays the lender or renegotiates in good faith to avoid the loss of the relationship, and the adverse consequences it would have, in a system where relationships are the currency of exchange. This means that outside financiers, especially foreigners, have little access to the system. Indeed, this barrier is what makes the system work, because if borrowers could play one lender off against another, as in the arm's-length competitive system, enforcement would break down.

So what happens when arm's-length, industrial-country private investors are asked to finance corporate investment in a developing country with a relationship system, as was the case in the early 1990s? Foreign investors who do not understand the murky insider relationships do three things. They minimize risks by offering only short-term loans so that they can pull their money out at short notice. They denominate payments in foreign currency so that their claims cannot be reduced by domestic inflation or a currency devaluation. And they lend through the local banks so that if they pull their money and the banks cannot repay it, the government will be drawn into supporting its banks to avoid widespread economic damage. Thus foreign investors get an implicit government guarantee. The threat of inflicting collateral damage is what makes arm's-length foreign investors willing to entrust their money to the opaque relationship system.

The problem in the mid-1990s in East Asia was that foreign investors, protected by such measures, had little incentive to screen the quality of ventures financed. And the domestic banking system, whose lending was until recently directed and guaranteed by the government, had little ability to exercise careful judgment, especially when borrowers were climbing the ladder of technological sophistication and investing in complex, capital-intensive projects. Borrowers were obviously happy with the free flow of credit and had no desire to ask questions. But when the projects financed by this poorly directed lending started underperforming, foreign investors were quick to pull their money out. Therefore, developing countries that relied substantially on foreign money to finance their investments suffered periodic booms and busts, culminating in the crises of the late 1990s.

Those crises were both devastating and humiliating. For example, the fall in Indonesian GDP from peak to trough was close to 25 percent, similar to the fall experienced by the United States during the Great Depression. But Indonesia's fall occurred in the span of only a year or so. As the economy tipped into free fall, with millions of workers becoming unemployed without any form of support, Indonesia experienced race riots and political turmoil. To cap it all, a proud country that felt it had liberated itself from its colonial masters and had achieved some measure of economic independence had to go hat in hand to the IMF for a loan and, in order to get it, was forced to submit to a plethora of conditions. Some of these were dictated directly by industrial countries to favor their own interests, leaving Indonesians seething about their perceived loss of sovereignty.

It should come as no surprise, then, that a number of developing countries decided to never leave themselves at the mercy of international financial markets (or the IMF) again. Rather than borrow from abroad to finance their investment, their governments and corporations decided to abandon grand investment projects and debt-fueled expansion. Moreover, a number decided to boost exports by maintaining an undervalued currency. In buying foreign currency to keep their exchange rate down, they also built large foreign-exchange reserves, which could serve as a rainy-day fund if foreign lenders ever panicked again. Thus in the late 1990s, developing countries cut back on investment and turned from being net importers to becoming net exporters of both goods and capital, adding to the global supply glut.

Investment by industrial-country corporations also collapsed soon after, in the dot-com bust, and the world fell into recession in the early years of the new millennium. With countries like Germany and Japan unable to pull their weight because of their export orientation, the burden of stimulating growth fell on the United States.

## Jobless Recoveries and the Pressure to Stimulate

As I argue above, the United States was politically predisposed toward stimulating consumption. But even as it delivered the necessary stimulus for the world to emerge from the 2001 recession, it discovered, much as in the 1991 recovery, that jobs were not being created. Given the short duration of unemployment benefits in the United States, this created enormous additional political pressure to continue injecting stimulus into the economy. As I argue in Chapter 4, jobless recoveries are not necessarily a thing of the past in the United States— indeed, the current recovery is proving slow thus far in generating jobs. Jobless recoveries are particularly detrimental because the prolonged stimulus aimed at forcing an unwilling private sector to create jobs tends to warp incentives, especially in the financial sector. This constitutes yet another fault line stemming from the interaction between politics and the financial sector, this time one that varies over the business cycle.

From 1960 until the 1991 recession, recoveries from recessions in the United States were typically rapid. From the trough of the recession, the average time taken by the economy to recover to pre-recession output levels was less than two quarters, and the lost jobs were recovered within eight months.[7]

The recoveries from the recessions of 1991 and 2000–2001 were very different. Although production recovered within three quarters in 1991 and just one quarter in 2001, it took 23 months from the trough of the recession to recover the lost jobs in 1991 recession and 38 months in the 2001 recession.[8] Indeed, job losses continued well into the recovery, so that these recoveries were deservedly called jobless recoveries.

Unfortunately, the United States is singularly unprepared for jobless recoveries. Typically, unemployment benefits last only six months. Moreover, because health care benefits have historically been tied to jobs, an unemployed worker also risks losing access to affordable health care.

Short-duration benefits may have been appropriate when recoveries were fast and jobs plentiful. The fear of losing benefits before finding a job may have given workers an incentive to look harder and make better matches with employers. But with few jobs being created, a positive incentive has turned into a source of great uncertainty and anxiety—and not just for the unemployed. Even those who have jobs fear they could lose them and be cast adrift.

Politicians ignore popular anxiety at their peril. The first President Bush is widely believed to have lost his reelection campaign, despite winning a popular war in Iraq, because he seemed out of touch with public concerns about the jobless recovery following the 1991 recession. That lesson has been fully internalized by politicians. In politics, economic recovery is all about jobs, not output, and politicians are willing to add stimulus, both fiscal (government spending and lower taxes) and monetary (lower short-term interest rates), to the economy until the jobs start reappearing.

In theory, such action reflects democracy at its best. In practice, though, the public pressure to do something quickly enables politicians to run roughshod over the usual checks and balances on government policy making in the United States. Long-term policies are enacted under the shadow of an emergency, with the party that happens to be in power at the time of the downturn getting to push its pet agenda. This leads to greater fluctuations in policy making than might be desired by the electorate. It also tends to promote excess spending and impairs the government's long-term financial health.

In Chapter 5, I explore the precise ways in which U.S. monetary policy is influenced by these political considerations. Monetary policy is, of course, the domain of the ostensibly independent Federal Reserve, but it would be a brave Federal Reserve chairman who defied politicians by raising interest rates before jobs started reappearing. Indeed, part of the Federal Reserve's mandate is to maintain high employment. Moreover, when unemployment stays high, wage inflation, the primary concern of central bankers today, is unlikely, so the Fed feels justified in its policy of maintaining low interest rates. But there are consequences: one problem is that a variety of other markets, including those abroad, react to easy policy. For instance, prices of commodities such as oil and metals are likely to rise. And the prices of assets, such as houses and stocks and bonds, are also likely to inflate as investors escape low short-term interest rates to invest in anything that offers a decent return.

More problematic still, the financial sector is also prone to take greater risks at such times. In the period 2003–2006, low interest rates added to the incentives already provided by government support for low-income housing and fueled an extraordinary housing boom as well as increasing indebtedness. In an attempt to advance corporate investment and hiring, the Fed added fuel to the fire by trying to reassure the economy that interest rates would stay low for a sustained period. Such assurances only pushed asset prices even higher and increased financial-sector risk taking. Finally, in a regulatory coup de grâce, the Fed chairman, Alan Greenspan, effectively told the markets in 2002 that the Fed would not intervene to burst asset-price bubbles but would intervene to ease the way to a new expansion if the markets imploded. If ever financial markets needed a license to go overboard, this was it.

By focusing only on jobs and inflation—and, in effect, only on the former—the Fed behaved myopically, indeed politically. It is in danger of doing so again, even while being entirely true to the letter of its mandate. Although the Fed has a limited set of tools and therefore pleads that it should not be given many potentially competing objectives, it cannot ignore the wider consequences to the economy of its narrow focus: in particular, low interest rates and the liquidity infused by the Fed have widespread effects on financial-sector behavior. As with the push for low-income housing, the fault line that emerges when politically motivated stimulus comes into contact with a financial sector looking for any edge is an immense source of danger.

## The Consequences to the U.S. Financial Sector

How did tremors on all the fault lines come together in the U.S. financial sector to nearly destroy it? I focus on two important ways this happened. First, an enormous quantity of money flowed into low-income housing in the United States, both from abroad and from government-sponsored mortgage agencies such as Fannie Mae and Freddie Mac. This led to both unsustainable house price increases and a steady deterioration in the quality of mortgage loans made. Second, both commercial and investment banks took on an enormous quantity of risk, including buying large quantities of the low-quality securities issued to finance subprime housing mortgages, even while borrowing extremely short term to finance these purchases.

Let me be more specific. In the early 2000s, the savings generated by the export-dependent developing countries were drawn into financing the United States, where fiscal and monetary stimulus created enormous additional demand for goods and services, especially in home construction. Foreign investors looked for safety. Their money flowed into securities issued by government-sponsored mortgage agencies like Fannie Mae and Freddie Mac, thus furthering the U.S. government's low-income housing goals. The investors, many from developing countries, implicitly assumed that the U.S. government would back these agencies, much as industrial-country investors had assumed that developing-country governments would back them before the crises in those countries. Even though Fannie and Freddie were taking enormous risks, they were no longer subject to the discipline of the market.

Other funds, from the foreign private sector, flowed into highly rated subprime mortgage-backed securities. Here, the unsuspecting foreign investors relied a little too naively on the institutions of the arm's-length system. They believed in the ratings and the market prices produced by the system, not realizing that the huge quantity of money flowing into subprime lending, both from the agencies and from other foreign investors, had corrupted the institutions. For one of the weaknesses of the arm's-length system, as I explain in Chapter 6, is that it relies on prices being accurate: but when a flood of money from un-questioning investors has to be absorbed, prices can be significantly distorted. Here again, the contact between the two different financial systems created fragilities.

However, the central cause for the financial panic was not so much that the banks packaged and distributed low-quality subprime mortgage-backed secu-rities but that they held on to substantial quantities themselves, either on or off their balance sheets, financing these holdings with short-term debt. This brings us full circle to the theme of my Jackson Hole speech. What went wrong? Why did so many banks in the United States hold on to so much of the risk?

The problem, as I describe in Chapter 7, has to do with the special character of these risks. The substantial amount of money pouring in from unquestion-ing investors to finance subprime lending, as well as the significant government involvement in housing, suggested that matters could go on for some time with-out homeowners defaulting. Similarly, the Fed's willingness to maintain easy conditions for a sustained period, given the persistent high level of unemploy-ment, made the risk of a funding squeeze seem remote. Under such circum-stances, the modern financial system tends to overdose on these risks.

A bank that exposes itself to such risks tends to produce above-par profits most of the time. There is some probability that it will produce truly horrible losses. From society's perspective, these risks should not be taken because of the enormous costs if the losses materialize. Unfortunately, the nature of the reward structure in the financial system, whether implicit or explicit, emphasizes short-term advantages and may predispose bankers to take these risks.

Particularly detrimental, the actual or prospective intervention of the gov-ernment or the central bank in certain markets to further political objectives, or to avoid political pain, creates an enormous force coordinating the numerous entities in the financial sector into taking the same risks. As they do so, they make the realization of losses much more likely. The financial sector is clearly centrally responsible for the risks it takes. Among its failings in the recent crisis include distorted incentives, hubris, envy, misplaced faith, and herd behavior. But the government helped make those risks look more attractive than they should have been and kept the market from exercising discipline, perhaps even making it applaud such behavior. Government interventions in the aftermath of

*TBTF*

*Moral hazard*

the crisis have, unfortunately, fulfilled the beliefs of the financial sector. Political moral hazard came together with financial-sector moral hazard in this crisis. The worrisome reality is that it could all happen again.

Put differently, the central problem of free-enterprise capitalism in a modern democracy has always been how to balance the role of the government and that of the market. While much intellectual energy has been focused on defining the appropriate activities of each, it is the interaction between the two that is a central source of fragility. In a democracy, the government (or central bank) simply cannot allow ordinary people to suffer collateral damage as the harsh logic of the market is allowed to play out. A modern, sophisticated financial sector understands this and therefore seeks ways to exploit government decency, whether it is the government's concern about inequality, unemployment, or the stability of the country's banks. The problem stems from the fundamental incompatibility between the goals of capitalism and those of democracy. And yet the two go together, because each of these systems softens the deficiencies of the other.

I do not seek to be an apologist for bankers, whose hankering for bonuses in the aftermath of a public rescue is not just morally outrageous but also politically myopic. But outrage does not drive good policy. Though it was by no means an innocent victim, the financial sector was at the center of a number of fault lines that affected its behavior. Each of the actors—bankers, politicians, the poor, foreign investors, economists, and central bankers—did what they thought was right. Indeed, a very real possibility is that key actors like politicians and bankers were guided unintentionally, by voting patterns and market approval respectively, into behavior that led inexorably toward the crisis. Yet the absence of villains, and the fact that each of these actors failed to bridge the fault lines makes finding solutions more, rather than less, difficult. Regulating bankers' bonus pay is only a very partial solution, especially if many bankers did not realize the risks they were taking.

## The Challenges That Face Us

If such a devastating crisis results from actors' undertaking reasonable actions, at least from their own perspective, we have considerable work to do. Much of the work lies outside the financial sector; how do we give the people falling behind in the United States a real chance to succeed? Should we create a stronger safety net to protect households during recessions in the United States, or can we find other ways to make workers more resilient? How can large countries around the world wean themselves off their dependence on exports? How can they develop their financial sectors so that they can allocate resources and risks efficiently? And, of course, how can the United States reform its financial system so that it does not devastate the world economy once again?

In structuring reforms, we have to recognize that the only truly safe financial system is a system that does not take risks, that does not finance innovation or growth, that does not help draw people out of poverty, and that gives consumers little choice. It is a system that reinforces the incremental and thus the status quo. In the long run, though, especially given the enormous challenges the world faces—climate change, an aging population, and poverty, to name just a few—settling for the status quo may be the greatest risk of all, for it will make us unable to adapt to meet the coming challenges. We do not want to return to the bad old days and just make banking boring again: it is easy to forget that under a rigidly regulated system, consumers and firms had little choice. We want innovative, dynamic finance, but without the excess risk and the outrageous behavior. That will be hard to achieve, but it will be really worthwhile.

We also have to recognize that good economics cannot be divorced from good politics: this is perhaps a reason why the field of economics was known as political economy. The mistake economists made was to believe that once countries had developed a steel frame of institutions, political influences would be tempered: countries would graduate permanently from developing-country status. We should now recognize that institutions such as regulators have influence only so long as politics is reasonably well balanced. Deep imbalances such as inequality can create the political groundswell that can overcome any constraining institutions. Countries can return to developing-country status if their politics become imbalanced, no matter how well developed their institutions.

There are no silver bullets. Reforms will require careful analysis and sometimes tedious attention to detail. I discuss possible reforms in Chapters 8 to 10, focusing on broad approaches. I hope my proposals are less simplistic and more constructive than the calls to tar and feather bankers or their regulators. If implemented, they will transform the world we live in quite fundamentally and move it away from the path of deepening crises to one of greater economic and political stability as well as cooperation. We will be able to make progress toward overcoming the important challenges the world faces. Such reforms will require societies to change the way they live, the way they grow, and the way they make choices. They will involve significant short-term pain in return for more diffuse but enormous long-term gain. Such reforms are always difficult to sell to the public and hence have little appeal to politicians. But the cost of doing nothing is perhaps worse turmoil than what we have experienced recently, for, unchecked, the fault lines will only deepen.

The picture is not all gloom. There are two powerful reasons for hope today: technological progress is solving problems that have eluded resolution for centuries, and economic reforms are bringing enormous numbers of the poor directly from medieval living conditions into the modern economy. Much can be gained if we can draw the right lessons from this crisis and stabilize the world economy. Equally, much could be lost if we draw the wrong lessons. Let me now lay out both the fault lines and the hard choices that confront us, with the hope that collectively we will make the right difference. For our own sakes, we must.

# CHAPTER ONE

# Let Them Eat Credit

J ANE IS AN ASSISTANT in a large nonprofit research organization, where she has worked for the past thirty-two years. She was an excellent typist in school and took a few courses in business practice. After spending a semester in college, she decided that the cost of an undergraduate education was not worth the benefits; jobs for typists were plentiful, and the money seemed attractive. Her first job was with the nonprofit, where she initially worked for two bosses. Her primary tasks were to type up reports and research papers, file the enormous amount of paperwork that kept accumulating, and answer the phones.

Over the years, many of those who started in positions similar to Jane's have lost their jobs. The advent of the computer—first the mainframe, then the personal computer—eliminated much of the routine work of assistants. Midlevel supervisors and managers learned to type their own documents. Presentations and basic analysis were outsourced, sometimes to far-off countries, where workers did what was necessary overnight. Most files became electronic, stored on disks rather than in physical cabinets. And as Jane's bosses turned to communicating by e-mail, phone calls became rarer and rarer: they were not in a fast-moving business requiring constant verbal contact with their clients. As a result, Jane's secretarial job too became endangered, and eventually she was laid off.

Jane, however, survived the onslaught of the machines, largely by reinventing herself. She quickly found another job within the organization. She has become a sort of "fixer" for her new bosses, taking on tasks that they have little time or capacity to handle—such as picking the restaurant and ordering the menu for an office dinner, inviting speakers to the organization and managing their schedules, heading off irate clients and ensuring their problems are dealt with, or following up with an obdurate office accountant questioning a bill submitted by one of her bosses. Because Jane has transformed herself into one who takes care of the unusual tasks, ones that machines cannot handle, she has to report to more bosses—nine at last count. Work is exhausting, because demands come from all sides, but Jane is thankful she still has a job. And it is more interesting now.

Jane's bosses have benefited hugely from the revolution in computers and communications. The research papers and articles they write receive much wider circulation. In the past they had to be photocopied and sent by mail to a small list of the truly interested, but today they are uploaded to a website and quickly seen by many. Their presentations are more colorful and their seminars more interesting, which means that their audiences pay closer attention when they speak. They routinely field requests from strangers who have come across their work somewhere on the Web, to speak, consult, or give expert testimony.

Thus advances in technology have wide-ranging effects across the population. The routine tasks done by secretarial and clerical workers like Jane, typically those with a high school education and perhaps even with some college experience, have been automated. But the nonroutine, creative tasks typically undertaken by those with advanced degrees have been aided by technology. From CEOs, who can see their firm's latest inventory position by tapping on a few keys, to analysts and consultants, whose reports can be accessed around the world, the influence and reach of the skilled and the creative has increased.[1] Technology has increased their productivity even while rendering others redundant.

Typically, however, technological advance is a good thing for everyone in the long run. It eliminates drudgery while giving the worker the time and capacity to make use of her finer talents. We are surely better off posting a document on an accessible website than asking a clerical worker to affix thousands of stamps and destroy so many trees to send physical mail that will ultimately be thrown away. But in the short run, technological advances can be extremely disruptive, and the disruption can persist into the long run if people do not have the means to adapt.

America has adapted to technological change before. As agriculture gave way to manufacturing in the mid-1800s, the elementary school movement in the United States created the most highly educated population in the world. As factory work became more sophisticated, and as demand grew for office workers to handle myriad activities in the emerging large, multidivision firms, the demand for workers with high school training increased. The high school movement took off in the early part of the twentieth century and provided the flexible, trained workers who would staff America's factories and offices. In 1910, fewer than one-tenth of U.S. workers had a high school diploma; in the 1970s, when Jane started her career, more than three-quarters did.[2]

Although earlier episodes of adaptation were very successful, the next phase of the race between technology and education, as the Harvard economists Claudia Goldin and Lawrence Katz have put it, has been far less satisfactory in the United States. Recent technological advances now require many workers to have a college degree to carry out their tasks. But the supply of college-educated workers has not kept pace with demand—indeed, the fraction of high school graduates in every age cohort has stopped rising, having fallen slightly since the 1970s.[3] Those who are fortunate enough to have bachelor's and advanced degrees have seen their incomes grow rapidly as the demand for graduates exceeds supply. But those who don't—seven out of ten Americans, according to the 2008 census—have seen relatively stagnant or even falling incomes.[4]

Faced with a weak safety net and continuing uncertainty about jobs that could easily be eliminated by the next technological advance or wave of outsourcing, many Americans find it hard to feel optimistic about the future. Although Americans have, by and large, been flexible in their search for opportunity —willing to uproot themselves and travel across the continent to take a new job—the demands on them are far greater now. Many have to go back to school to remedy a deficient high school education before they can derive the full benefit of further education, all for distant and uncertain job prospects. Some lack the fortitude and strength of purpose to do so; others simply do not have the resources. For a single mother of two, for example, who is barely making ends meet with two low-paying jobs, further education is simply not a feasible option.

The gap between the growing technological demand for skilled workers and the lagging supply because of deficiencies in the quantity and quality of education is just one, albeit perhaps the most important, reason for growing inequality. The reasons for rising inequality are, of course, a matter of much debate, with both the Left and the Right adhering to their own favored explanations. Other factors, such as the widespread deregulation in recent decades and the resulting increases in competition including for resources (such as talent), the changes in tax rates, the decrease in unionization, and the increase in both legal and illegal immigration, have no doubt all played a part.[5] Regardless of how the inequality has arisen, it has led to widespread anxiety.

Many have lost faith in the narrative of America as the land of unbounded opportunity, which in the past created the public support that made the United States a bastion of economic freedom. Politicians, always sensitive to their constituents, have responded to these worrisome developments with an attempt at a panacea: facilitating the flow of easy credit to those left behind by growth and technological progress. And so America's failings in education and, more generally, the growing anxiety of its citizenry about access to opportunity have led in indirect ways to unsustainable household debt, which is at the center of this crisis. That most observers have not noted these links suggests this fault line is well hidden and therefore particularly dangerous.

### The Growing Inequality of Incomes

Incomes in the United States, of which wages constitute the most important component, have been growing more unequal. The wages of a 90th-percentile earner—that is, a person earning more than 90 percent of the general population—increased by about 65 percent more over the period 1975–2005 than the wages of a 10th-percentile earner. (This difference is known as the 90/10 differential.) In 1975, the 90th percentile earned, on average, about three times more than the 10th percentile; by 2005 they earned five times more.[6] All of this growth was concentrated at the top: the wages of those in the middle relative to those at the 10th percentile have not gone up anywhere near as much as the wages of the 90th percentile have grown relative to those in the middle.

Many commentators, both in academia and in the popular press, have focused on the income gains made by the top 1 percent or even the top 0.01 percent of earners, perhaps because it is more customary to look up than down. I believe the more troublesome trend for the United States is the 90/10 or 90/50 differential, which reflects the changes most Americans experience.

Much of the 90/10 differential can be attributed to what economists call the "college premium." The ratio of the wages of those who have only a bachelor's degree to those who only have a high school degree has risen steadily since 1980. The 2008 Current Population Survey by the Census Bureau indicated that the median wage of a high school graduate was $27,963, while the median wage of someone with an undergraduate degree was $48,097—about 72 percent more. Those with professional degrees (like an MD or MBA) earn even more, with a median wage of $87,775.[7] That the 90/10 differential is largely due to the college premium also explains why the 50/10 differential has not moved as much—neither the 50th percentile earner nor the 10th percentile earner has been to college. In fact, the 50th percentile typically consists of white-collar workers like Jane and her colleagues, who have been most squeezed by the technological change.

Why has the college premium increased? One view is that it is because technology has become even more demanding of skills, reflecting what economists term "skill-biased technical change." But Goldin and Katz argue that the pace of technological change and its demand for greater skills has been relatively steady: the automobile and the airplane were as disruptive to lifestyles in the beginning of the twentieth century as the Internet and organizational change were at the end. Rather, what has changed is the supply of the educated. Between 1930 and 1980, the average years of schooling among Americans age 30 or older increased by about one year every decade. Americans in 1980 had 4.7 years more schooling on average than Americans in 1930. But between 1980 and 2005, the pace of increase in educational attainments was truly glacial—only 0.8 years over the entire quarter century.[8]

In part, the reason for the slower increase in supply has been the relative stagnation of high school graduation rates. Although the United States has led historically in the fraction of the population with high school degrees, that fraction has not increased since 1980, and other countries have caught up and surpassed the United States. Moreover, while more and more Americans in the 20–24 age group are going to college (61 percent in 2003, up from 44 percent in 1980), no doubt in part attracted by the potential boost to wages, college graduation rates have not kept pace: too many students like Jane are dropping out of college despite an increasing college premium over time. College graduation rates for young men born in the 1970s are no higher than for men born in the 1940s—a shocking fact when one considers how much greater demand there is now for workers with college degrees.[9]

One possible explanation of the relative stagnation in education is that there might be a natural limit to how much education a population can absorb. After all, not everyone has the aptitude or inclination to write a PhD thesis. If that is the case in the United States, however, the rest of the world does not seem to sense such a limit. Despite leading the world in the past, the United States has fallen behind twelve other rich countries in four-year-college graduation rates.[10] When we also note that its high school graduation rates put it in the bottom third among rich countries, we can see why the United States is falling behind both its own historical record and its competitors.

Finally, wages are not the only component of income. Income from property such as stocks and bonds also adds to overall income, while taxes subtract from it. Interestingly, even for the richest 0.01 percent of Americans toward the end of the twentieth century, 80 percent of income consisted of wages and income from self-owned businesses, and only 20 percent consisted of income from arm's-length financial investments.[11] This ratio is in stark contrast to the pattern in the early part of the century, when the richest derived most of their income from property. The rich are now the working rich—whether they are entrepreneurs like Bill Gates or bankers like Lloyd Blankfein of Goldman Sachs—instead of the idle rich. At a time when wealth seems to be within the grasp of anyone who can get a good job, it is all the more unfortunate that so many Americans, by dint of their poor education, are locked out of the productive jobs that would make them better off.

I have used the term *education* so far, even when I refer to employability, but a better term is *human capital*, which refers to the broad set of capabilities, including health, knowledge and intelligence, attitude, social aptitude, and empathy that make a person a productive member of society. Formal education plays perhaps the most important role in forming an individual's human capital, but family, community, and employers also play important parts. In what follows, I focus on education, but I also refer to these other elements, especially in Chapter 9 when I turn to remedies.

Education plays a far greater role than simply improving an individual's income and career prospects: it has intrinsic worth of its own, allowing us to make use of our finer faculties. In addition, studies show that the educated typically take better care of their own health, are less prone to indulging in criminal activities, and are more likely to participate in civic and political activities. Moreover, they influence their children to do the same, so that their education has beneficial effects on future generations also. So as it falls behind in education, America is diminishing the quality of its society.

## Why Is the United States Falling Behind?

Why is the educational system failing the United States? With a university system that is still considered the best in the world, and which attracts students from every corner of the globe, the failure clearly does not lie in the quality of university education. Instead, there are three obvious problems that my earlier discussion suggests. First, the quality of the learning experience in schools is so poor that far too many students drop out before completing high school. Second, in a related vein, even among those who graduate from high school, many are unprepared for the rigors of university education. Finally, as the college premium increases, the cost of higher education also increases: it is a service that is provided by the well-educated with very small increases in productivity over the years (college class sizes have not increased dramatically at my university despite all the improvements in communications technology, though the learning experience has probably improved). Despite attempts to expand financial aid, a quality education at a private university is passing beyond the reach of even middle-class families. And with tight state budgets, even state schools are raising fees significantly.

Of course, learning does not take place only in the classroom. Differences in aptitude for education emerge in early childhood as a result of varying nutrition, learning environments, and behavioral expectations. The family matters immensely, as do the kind of role models children want to emulate and the attitudes their friends have. At my daughter's university-affiliated school, the smartest kid in class is pushed to excel and is secretly admired even if she does not belong to the popular set. Advanced students take university courses in high school and even sign up for research projects with professors. However, in too many schools in America, being smart can be positively dangerous, as children resent and set upon those who dare to try to escape the trap of low expectations. Here again, advantage breeds more advantage. The rich can afford to live in better neighborhoods, can give their children the health care and nutrition that allow them to grow up healthy, and can hire tutors and learning aides if their children fall behind. Even dysfunctionality hurts children less if their parents are rich. As the political analysts Ross Douthat and Reihan Salam put it: "The kids in Connecticut prep schools smoked pot and went on to college like their parents; kids in rural Indiana smoked meth and dropped out; kids in the South Bronx smoked crack and died in gang wars."[12]

Family instability, too, is harder on poor children. Poor, less well-educated couples are more likely to break up, and when that happens the economic consequences are more severe than for the well-off: the cost of maintaining two establishments, shuttling children between the two parents, and child care eat up a much bigger fraction of the poor parents' income, leaving less for other basic necessities, let alone counseling and remedial tuition to help devastated children cope with the breakup. Divorce therefore affects the children's health and schooling far more in a poor family than in a rich family. Inequality tends to further perpetuate itself through the social environment.

We do not need to get into the moral issues surrounding extreme inequality to understand that it is a thoroughly undesirable state of affairs. To the extent that it is caused by a significant part of the population's not being able to improve themselves because of lack of access to quality education, it signifies tremendous inefficiency. A mind is a terrible thing to waste, and the United States is wasting too many of them.

## Other Reasons for Inequality

Differences in educational attainment in the face of rising technological demand for skills are, of course, only one reason for the growing inequality. There are other reasons why measured inequality might rise.[13] Rising inequality in the United States in the past three decades coincides with a period of deregulation. Increasing competition does increase the demand for talented employees, thus increasing the dispersion of wages within any segment of the population. In general, this would increase inequality, although by increasing the costs of discriminating against the poor but talented, it could reduce inequality. Deregulation can also lead to more entry and exit of firms, which increases the volatility of each worker's earnings: an entrepreneur who earns nothing for a few years and then makes millions adds to both the bottom and the top of the distribution curve in different years. (So does a penurious graduate student before becoming a well-paid professor!) These effects may account for up to one-third of the increase in measured inequality.[14]

Greater immigration and trade have also played a part because immigrants, competing directly for unskilled jobs, and unskilled workers far away, competing through trade, have both served to hold down wages of unskilled U.S. workers. Most studies see the magnitude of these effects as small.[15] Unskilled immigrants have, however, contributed to inequality in a different way. They typically occupy the bottom of the income distribution and thus contribute to measured inequality.[16] Paradoxically, although their incomes are often higher than their incomes in the home country, they swell the ranks of those who appear down and out in America.

The reduction in the punitive postwar marginal tax on high incomes (from a top rate of 91 percent through much of the 1950s and the 1960s, through a number of ups and downs, to 35 percent at the time of writing) has increased incentives to earn higher incomes and may thus have contributed to the growing entrepreneurship and inequality.[17] The weakness of unions may also have reduced moderately educated workers' bargaining power, though the loss of high-paying unionized jobs probably has more to do with increased competition and entry as a result of deregulation, as well as competition from imports. A relatively stagnant minimum wage has certainly allowed the lowest real wages to fall (thereby also ensuring that some people who would otherwise be unemployed do have a job), though only a small percentage of American workers are paid the minimum wage. Finally, the entry of women into the workforce has also affected inequality. Because the well-connected and the highly educated tend to mate more often with each other, "assortative" mating has also helped increase household income inequality.

The reasons for growing income inequality are, undoubtedly, a matter of heated debate. To my mind, the evidence is most persuasive that the growing inequality I think the most worrisome, the increasing 90/10 differential, stems primarily from the gap between the demand for the highly educated and their supply. Progressives, no doubt, attribute substantial weight to the antilabor policies followed by Republican governments since Ronald Reagan, whereas conservatives attribute much of the earlier wage compression to anticompetitive policies followed since Franklin Roosevelt. Neither side would, however, deny the importance of differential educational attainments in fostering inequality.

## Attitudes toward Inequality

Americans have historically not been too concerned about economic inequality except when it becomes extreme—as it did toward the end of the nineteenth century. Through a variety of means such as antitrust laws and estate taxes, they have ensured that wealth generated from corporate ownership does not become so highly concentrated that it upsets the distribution of political power. The government has repeatedly intervened to limit the power of banks—as in Andrew Jackson's fight to close the Second Bank of the United States (after he accused it of political meddling), the creation of the Federal Reserve in 1913 so that banks had an alternative to J. P. Morgan as the lender of last resort, and the Glass-Steagall Act of 1933, which broke up the most powerful banks. Similarly, through antitrust investigations, most famously against John D. Rockefeller's Standard Oil and Bill Gates's Microsoft, the government has sought to rein in the power of big business. But with the exception of some episodes—for example, during the Great Depression—the government and the public have not been strongly predisposed toward punitive taxation of the rich to achieve a more equitable distribution of income.

"Soak the rich" policies have seldom been popular among the less well-off in America, not necessarily because they have great sympathy for the rich but perhaps because the poor see themselves eventually becoming rich: Horatio Alger's stories of ordinary people attaining great success in the land of limitless opportunity had broad appeal.[18] Although such optimism may always have been unrealistic, the gulf between the possible and the practical might have been small enough in the past that Americans could continue dreaming. According to the World Values Survey, 71 percent of Americans believe the poor have a good chance of escaping poverty, while only 40 percent of Europeans share this be-lief.[19] These differences are particularly surprising because cross-country stud-ies suggest that people in the United States are not much more mobile across income classes than in European countries, and indeed the bottom 20 percent of earners may be unusually immobile in the United States.[20] Nevertheless, the idea of income mobility was deeply ingrained in the past. That great observer of America, Alexis de Tocqueville, remarked that in America, "wealth circulates with astounding rapidity and experience shows it is rare to find two successive generations in the full enjoyment of it."[21]

Over the past 25 years, though, more and more Americans have come face to face with the bitter reality that they are trapped by educational underachieve-ment. The *Newsweek* columnist Robert Samuelson has argued that "on the whole, Americans care less about inequality—the precise gap between the rich and the poor—than about opportunity and achievement: are people getting ahead?"[22] Yet inequality in education is particularly insidious because it reduces opportu-nity. Someone who has had an indifferent high school education cannot even dream of getting a range of jobs that the new economy has thrown up. For Amer-icans, many of whom "define political freedom as strict equality but economic freedom as an equal chance to become unequal," inequality of access to quality education shakes the very foundation of their support for economic freedom, for they no longer have an equal chance.[23]

If Americans no longer have the chance to be upwardly mobile, they are less likely to be optimistic about the future or to be tolerant of the mobility of others —because the immobile are hurt when others move up. When others in town become richer, the cost of everything goes up, and the real income—the income in terms of its purchasing power—of the economically immobile falls. Matters are even worse if the immobile measure their worth in terms of their posses-sions: my Chevrolet becomes much less pleasurable when my neighbor up-grades from a Honda to a Maserati.[24] Envy has historically been un-American, largely because it was checked by self-confidence. As self-confidence withers, can envy, and its close cousin, hatred, be far behind?

As more and more Americans realize they are simply not equipped to com-pete, and as they come to terms with their own diminished expectations, the words *economic freedom* do not conjure open vistas of unlimited opportunity. Instead they offer a nightmare vision of great and continuing insecurity, and growing envy as the have-nots increasingly become the have-nevers. Without some change in this trend, destructive class warfare is no longer impossible to contemplate.

## The Political Reaction

Politicians have recognized the problem posed by rising inequality. Because African Americans and Hispanics have been harder hit by poor schooling than other groups, their lack of progress is also conflated with race. Nevertheless, politicians have understood that better education is part of the solution. A number of presidents have taken up the cause, but without making much of a dent. Moreover, even if they could make a difference, the changes would take effect too late to alter the lives of today's adults.

Taxation and redistribution could be an alternative; but, as the political scientists Nolan McCarthy, Keith Poole, and Howard Rosenthal argue, growing income inequality has made Congress much more polarized and much less likely to come together on matters of taxation and redistribution.[25] Even as I write this, the Senate is divided completely along party lines in its attitude toward health care reform, with Democrats unanimous in support, and Republicans equally unanimous in opposition. Politicians are coming to terms with something Aristotle pointed out: that although quarrels are more likely in an unequal society, striving to rectify the inequality may precipitate the very conflict that the citizenry wants to avoid.[26]

Politicians have therefore looked for other ways to improve the lives of their voters. Since the early 1980s, the most seductive answer has been easier credit. In some ways, it is the path of least resistance. Government-supported credit does not arouse as many concerns from the Right at the outset as outright income redistribution would—though, as we have experienced, it may end up as a very costly way to redistribute, imposing harm on the recipient and costs on the taxpayer.

Politicians love to have banks expand housing credit, for credit achieves many goals at the same time. It pushes up house prices, making households feel wealthier, and allows them to finance more consumption. It creates more profits and jobs in the financial sector as well as in real estate brokerage and housing construction. And everything is safe—as safe as houses—at least for a while.

Easy credit has large, positive, immediate, and widely distributed benefits, whereas the costs all lie in the future. It has a payoff structure that is precisely the one desired by politicians, which is why so many countries have succumbed to its lure. Rich countries have, over time, built institutions such as financial-sector regulators and supervisors, which can stand up to politicians and deflect such short-term myopia. The problem in the United States this time was that the politicians found a way around these regulatory structures, and eventually public support for housing credit was so widespread that few regulators, if any, dared oppose it.

## A Short History of Housing Credit

The period leading up to the Great Depression was also a time of great credit expansion and, perhaps not coincidentally, one of substantial income inequality. Mortgages were different then. Residential mortgages were offered by banks and thrift companies (also known as savings and loans associations). Mortgages were available for only a short term, about five years, and featured a single capital repayment at maturity, unless the borrower could refinance the loan. Moreover, most loans were at variable rates, so the borrower bore the risk that interest rates would change; and lenders did not typically lend more than 50 percent of value, so homeowners bore much of the risk of house-price fluctuations.[27]

In the 1930s, as the Depression worsened, refinancing dried up, valuations plummeted, and homeowners, strapped for the cash to repay maturing loans, started defaulting in droves. With 10 percent of the nation's housing stock in foreclosure, the government intervened in the housing market to save it from free fall. Among the institutions it created initially were the Home Owner's Loan Corporation (HOLC) and the Federal Housing Administration (FHA).

HOLC's role was to buy defaulted mortgages from banks and thrifts and restructure them into fixed-rate, 20-year fully amortizing mortgages (in which the principal is paid over the term of the loan). The long maturity and the fully amortizing payment structure meant that homeowners were not confronted with the disastrous refinancing problem. The government was willing to hold these mortgages for a while, but it did not see itself in the loan business in the long term and had to find a way of making the mortgages palatable to private-sector lenders. Private lenders, historically averse to making long-term loans, had to be persuaded to trust borrowers.

The solution was that the FHA would bear the default risk by providing mortgage insurance—essentially assuring lenders that it would repay the loan if the homeowner defaulted. The FHA protected itself by charging an insurance premium, setting strict limits on the maximum loan it would finance (initially 80 percent of the property value), and the amount of the loan it would insure. This restriction also ensured that a private market emerged for the mortgages, or portions thereof, that the government would not insure.

Thus the banks and the thrifts that bought FHA-insured mortgages had to bear only the interest-rate risk—the risk stemming from the fact that they were financing fixed-rate long-term mortgages with short-term, effectively variable-rate deposits. So long as short-term rates did not spike, this was a profitable business.

The HOLC was wound down in 1936. To provide a financing alternative to banks, the Federal National Mortgage Association (FNMA, later Fannie Mae) was set up to draw private long-term financing into the mortgage market once again. Essentially, FNMA bought FHA-insured mortgages and financed them by issuing long-term bonds to investors like insurance companies and pension funds. Unlike the banks and thrifts, FNMA had longer-term fixed-rate financing and therefore did not bear much interest-rate risk even if it held the mortgages on its books.

The system worked well until rising short-term interest rates in the late 1960s caused deposits to flow out of banks and thrifts—because regulatory deposit-rate ceilings introduced during the Depression to prevent excessive competition did not permit them to match the higher market interest rates. Financing for mortgages dried up. To compensate, the government tried to bring more direct financing capacity into the market by splitting Fannie into two in 1968—creating a Government National Mortgage Association (GNMA or Ginnie Mae) to continue insuring, packaging, and securitizing mortgages, and a new, privatized Fannie Mae that would finance mortgages by issuing bonds or securitized claims to the public. At a time when President Lyndon Johnson needed funds to pay for the growing costs of the Vietnam War, privatization conveniently removed Fannie Mae's debt from counting as a government liability, making the government's balance sheet look a lot healthier. Soon after, Freddie Mac (or the Federal Home Loan Mortgage Corporation, to go by its full name) was created to help securitize mortgages made by the thrifts, and eventually it too was privatized.

As inflation rose in the late 1970s and early 1980s, the Federal Reserve chairman, Paul Volcker, increased short-term interest rates to hitherto unimagined levels to try to tame it. With much of their portfolio invested in fixed long-term interest-rate mortgages, made when interest rates were low, and much of their financing tied to sky-high short-term interest rates, the savings and loan or thrift industry essentially went bankrupt. The political reaction was not to shut the thrifts down: housing was too important, the industry too well connected, and the hole that the taxpayer would have to fill too embarrassing to own up to.

Instead, the political system reacted with the Depository Institutions Deregulation and Monetary Control Act of 1980 and Garn–St. Germain Depository Institutions Act of 1982, which liberalized the range of loans that thrifts could make, including mortgages, and the ways they could borrow, to help the industry earn its way back to stability. The sorry history of ensuing developments, in particular the immensely risky and ultimately disastrous gambles that thrifts took in commercial real estate, backed with taxpayer money, has been told elsewhere.[28] A sizeable loss for thrifts was converted into a gigantic loss for taxpayers, aided and abetted by politicians. Suffice it to say that as a consequence, the insurers Fannie and Freddie, rather than the thrifts, played an increasing role in mortgage financing.

## Fannie and Freddie

Fannie and Freddie, variously known as government-sponsored enterprises (GSEs) or agencies, were curious beasts. They were not quite private, though they had private shareholders to whom their profits belonged. And they certainly were not public, in that they were not owned by the government, but they had both government benefits and public duties. Among their perks, they were exempted from state and local income taxes, they had government appointees on their boards, and they had a line of credit from the U.S. Treasury. For the investing public, these links to the government indicated that the full faith and credit of the United States stood behind these organizations. Fannie and Freddie could thus raise money at a cost that was barely above the rate paid by the Treasury. These perks came with a public mandate—to support housing finance.

Fannie and Freddie did two things to fulfill their mandate. They bought mortgages that conformed to certain size limits and credit standards they had set out, thus allowing the banks they bought from to go out and make more mortgage loans. The agencies then packaged pools of loans together and issued mortgage-backed securities against the package after guaranteeing the mortgages against default. They also started borrowing directly from the market and investing in mortgage-backed securities underwritten by other banks. Because the mortgages were sound, these were fairly safe and extremely profitable activities. But much of the profit stemmed from their low cost of financing, deriving from the implicit government guarantee, and this was a critical political vulnerability.

## The Affordable-Housing Mandate

As evidence mounted in the early 1990s that more and more Americans faced stagnant or declining incomes, the political establishment started looking for ways to help them with fast-acting measures—certainly faster than education reform, which would take decades to produce results. Affordable housing for low-income groups was the obvious answer, and Fannie and Freddie were the

obvious channels. Congress knew it could use Fannie and Freddie as vehicles
for its designs because they benefited so much from government largesse, and
their managers' arms could be twisted without any of the agencies' activities in-
conveniently showing up as an expenditure in government budgets.

In 1992, the U.S. Congress passed the Federal Housing Enterprise Safety and
Soundness Act, partly to reform the regulation of the agencies and partly to promote homeownership for low-income and minority groups explicitly. The act
instructed the Department of Housing and Urban Development (HUD) to develop affordable-housing goals for the agencies and to monitor progress toward
these goals. Whenever Congress includes the words *safety and soundness* in any
bill, there is a distinct possibility that it will achieve exactly the opposite, and
that is precisely what this piece of legislation did.

Even though the agencies could not head off legislation, they could shape it
to their advantage. They ensured that the legislation allowed them to hold less
capital than other regulated financial institutions and that their new regulator,
an office within HUD—which itself had no experience in financial-services
regulation—was subject to congressional appropriation.[29] This meant that if
the regulator actually started constraining the behavior of the agencies, the
agencies' friends in Congress could cut the regulator's budget. The combination
of an activist Congress, government-supported private firms hungry for profits,
and a weak and pliant regulator proved disastrous.

At first Fannie and Freddie were not eager to put their profitable franchise at
risk. But seeing the political writing on the wall, they complied. Steven Holmes,
a reporter for the *New York Times,* offered a prescient warning in the 1990s: "In
moving, even tentatively, into this new area of lending, Fannie Mae is taking on
significantly more risk, which may not pose any difficulty in flush economic
times. . . . But the government sponsored entity may run into trouble in an economic downturn, prompting a government rescue similar to that of the Savings
and Loan industry in the 1980s."[30] As housing boomed, the agencies found
the high rates available on low-income lending particularly attractive, and the
benign environment and the lack of historical experience with low-income
lending allowed them to ignore the additional risk.

Under the Clinton administration, HUD steadily increased the amount of
funding it required the agencies to allocate to low-income housing. The agencies complied, almost too eagerly: sometimes it appeared as if they were egging
the administration on to increase their mandate so that they would be able to
justify their higher risk taking (and not coincidentally, management's higher
bonuses) to their shareholders. After being set initially at 42 percent of assets in

1995, the mandate for low-income lending was increased to 50 percent of assets in 2000 (in the last year of the Clinton administration).

Some critics worried that the agencies were turning a blind eye to predatory lending to those who could not afford a mortgage. But reflecting the nexus between the regulator and the regulated, HUD acknowledged in a report in 2000 that the agencies "objected" to disclosure requirements "related to their purchase of high-cost mortgages," so HUD decided against imposing "an additional undue burden"![31]

### The National Homeownership Strategy

Congress was joined by the Clinton administration in its efforts. In 1995, in a preamble to a document laying out a strategy to expand home ownership, President Clinton wrote: "This past year, I directed HUD Secretary Henry G. Cisneros . . . to develop a plan to boost homeownership in America to an all-time high by the end of this century. . . . Expanding homeownership will strengthen our nation's families and communities, strengthen our economy, and expand this country's great middle class. Rekindling the dream of homeownership for America's working families can prepare our nation to embrace the rich possibilities of the twenty-first century." What did this mean in practice? The strategy document went on to say: "For many potential homebuyers, the lack of cash available to accumulate the required down payment and closing costs is the major impediment to purchasing a home. Other households do not have sufficient available income to make the monthly payments on mortgages financed at market interest rates for standard loan terms. Financing strategies, *fueled by the creativity and resources of the private and public sectors* [italics mine], should address both of these financial barriers to homeownership."[32]

 Simply put, the Clinton administration was arguing that the financial sector should find creative ways of getting people who could not afford homes into them, and the government would help or push wherever it could. Although there was some distance between this strategy and the NINJA loans and "liar" loans (loans for which borrowers could come up with creative representations of their income because no documentation was required) that featured so prominently in this crisis, the course was set.

 The Clinton administration pushed hard in other ways. The Community Reinvestment Act (CRA) passed in 1977 required banks to lend in their local markets, especially in lower-income, predominantly minority areas. But CRA did not set explicit lending goals, and its enforcement was left to regulators. The Clinton administration increased the pressure on regulators to enforce CRA through investigations of banks and threats of fines.[33] A careful study of bank mortgage lending shows that lending went up as CRA enforcement increased over the 1990s, especially in the highly visible and politically sensitive metropolitan areas where banks were most likely to be scrutinized.[34]

Recall also that the Federal Housing Administration guaranteed mortgages. It typically focused on riskier mortgages that the agencies were reluctant to touch. Here was a vehicle that was directly under political control, and it was fully utilized. In 2000, the Clinton administration dramatically cut the minimum down payment required for a borrower to qualify for an FHA guarantee to 3 percent, increased the maximum size of mortgage it would guarantee, and halved the premiums it charged borrowers for the guarantee. All these actions set the stage for a boom in low-income housing construction and lending.

## The Ownership Society

The housing boom came to fruition in the administration of George W. Bush, who also recognized the dangers of significant segments of the population not participating in the benefits of growth. As he put it: "If you own something, you have a vital stake in the future of our country. The more ownership there is in America, the more vitality there is in America, and the more people have a vital stake in the future of this country."[35] In a 2002 speech to HUD, Bush said:

> But I believe owning something is a part of the American Dream, as
> well. I believe when somebody owns their own home, they're realizing
> the American Dream. . . . And we saw that yesterday in Atlanta, when
> we went to the new homes of the new homeowners. And I saw with
> pride firsthand, the man say, welcome to my home. He didn't say, wel-
> come to government's home; he didn't say, welcome to my neighbor's
> home; he said, welcome to my home. . . . He was a proud man. . . .
> And I want that pride to extend all throughout our country.[36]

Later, explaining how his administration would go about achieving its goals, he said: "And I'm proud to report that Fannie Mae has heard the call and, as I understand, it's about $440 billion over a period of time. They've used their influence to create that much capital available for the type of home buyer we're talking about here. It's in their charter; it now needs to be implemented. Freddie Mac is interested in helping. I appreciate both of those agencies providing the underpinnings of good capital."[37]

The Bush administration pushed up the low-income lending mandate on Fannie and Freddie to 56 percent of their assets in 2004, even as the Fed started increasing interest rates and expressing worries about the housing boom. Peter Wallison of the American Enterprise Institute and Charles Calomiris of Columbia University argue that Fannie and Freddie moved into even higher gear at this time not so much because of altruism, but because the accounting scandals that were exposed in those agencies in 2004 made them much more pliant to Congress's demands for more low-income lending.[38]

How much lending flowed from these sources, and when? It is not easy to get a sense of the true magnitude of subprime and Alt-A lending by Fannie, Freddie, and the FHA, partly because as Edward Pinto, a former chief credit officer of Fannie Mae, has argued, many loans on each of these entities' books were subprime in nature but not classified as such.[39] For instance, Fannie Mae classified a loan as subprime only if the originator itself specialized in the subprime business. Many risky loans to low-credit-quality borrowers thus escaped classification as subprime or Alt-A loans. When the loans are appropriately classified, Pinto finds that subprime lending alone (including financing through the purchase of mortgage-backed securities) by the mortgage giants and the FHA started at about $85 billion in 1997 and went up to $446 billion in 2003, after which it stabilized at between $300 and $400 billion a year until 2007, the last year of his study.[40] On average, these entities accounted for 54 percent of the market across the years, with a high of 70 percent in 2007. He estimates that in June 2008, the mortgage giants, the FHA, and various other government programs were exposed to about $2.7 trillion in subprime and Alt-A loans, approximately 59 percent of total loans to these categories. It is very difficult to reach any other conclusion than that this was a market driven largely by government, or government-influenced, money.

## Lending Goes Berserk

As more money from the government-sponsored agencies flooded into financing or supporting low-income housing, the private sector joined the party. After all, they could do the math, and they understood that the political compulsions behind government actions would not disappear quickly. With agency support, subprime mortgages would be liquid, and low-cost housing would increase in price. Low risk and high return—what more could the private sector desire? Unfortunately, the private sector, aided and abetted by agency money, converted the good intentions behind the affordable-housing mandate and the push to an ownership society into a financial disaster.

Both Clinton and Bush were right in worrying that growth was leaving large segments of the population behind, and their solution—expanded home ownership—was a reasonable short-term fix. The problem with using the might of the government is rarely one of intent; rather, it is that the gap between intent and outcome is often large, typically because the organizations and people the government uses to achieve its aims do not share them. This lesson from recent history, including the savings and loans crisis, should have been clear to the politicians: the consequences of the government's pressing an agile financial sector to act in certain ways are often unintended and extremely costly. Yet the political demand for action, any action, to satisfy the multitudes who believe the government has all the answers, is often impossible for even the sensible politician to deny.

Also, it is easy to be cynical about political motives but hard to establish intent, especially when the intent is something the actors would want to deny—in this case, politicians using easy housing credit as a palliative. As I argue repeatedly in this book, it may well be that many of the parts played by the key actors were guided by the preferences and applause of the audience, rather than by well-thought-out intent. Even if no politicians dreamed up a Machiavellian plan to assuage anxious voters with easy loans, their actions—and there is plenty of evidence that politicians pushed for easier housing credit—could have been guided by the voters they cared about.[41] Put differently, politicians may have tried different messages until one resonated with voters. That message—promising affordable housing, for example—became part of their platform. It could well be that voters shaped political action (much as markets shape corporate action) rather than the other way around. Whether the action was driven by conscious intent or unintentional guidance is immaterial to its broader consequences.

A very interesting study by two of my colleagues at the University of Chicago's Booth School, Atif Mian and Amir Sufi, details the consequences in the lead-up to the crisis.[42] They use ZIP codes to identify areas that had a disproportionately large share of potential subprime borrowers (borrowers with low incomes and low credit ratings) and show that these ZIP codes experienced credit growth over the period 2002–2005 that was more than twice as high as that in the prime ZIP codes. More interesting, the number of mortgages obtained in a ZIP code over that period is *negatively* correlated with household income growth: that is,

ZIP codes with lower income growth received more mortgage loans in 2002–2005, the only period over the entire span of the authors' study in which they saw this phenomenon. This finding should not be surprising given the earlier discussion: there was a government-orchestrated attempt to lend to the less well-off.

The greater expansion in mortgage lending to subprime ZIP codes is associated with higher house-price growth in those ZIP codes. Indeed, over the period 2002–2005 and across ZIP codes, house-price growth was higher in areas that had lower income growth (because this is where the lending was focused). Unfortunately, therefore, all this lending was driving house prices further away from the fundamental ability of household income to support repayment. The consequence of all this lending was more default. Subprime ZIP codes experienced an increase in default rates after 2006 that was three times that of prime ZIP codes, and much larger than the default rates these areas had experienced in the past.

Could the increased borrowing by low-income households have been driven by need? After all, I have argued that their incomes were stagnating or even falling. It is hard, though, to imagine that strapped households would go out and borrow to buy houses. The borrowing was not driven by a surge in demand: instead it came from a greater willingness to supply credit to low-income households, the impetus for which came in significant measure from the government.

Not all the frenzied lending in the run-up to the recent crisis was related to low-income housing: many unviable loans were made to large corporate buyouts also. Nevertheless, subprime lending and the associated subprime mortgage-backed securities were central to this crisis. Without any intent of absolving the brokers and the banks who originated the bad loans or the borrowers who lied about their incomes, we should acknowledge the evidence suggesting that government actions, however well intended, contributed significantly to the crisis. And the agencies did not escape the fallout. With the losses on the agencies' mortgage portfolios growing and hints that investors in agency debt were getting worried, on Sunday, September 7, 2008, Henry J. Paulson, secretary of the treasury, announced what the market had always assumed: the government would take control of Fannie and Freddie and effectively stand behind their debt. Conservative estimates of the costs to the taxpayer of bailing out the agencies amount to hundreds of billions of dollars. Moreover, having taken over the agencies, the government fully owned the housing problem. Even as I write, the government-controlled agencies are increasing their exposure to the housing market, attempting to prop up prices at unrealistic levels, which will mean higher costs to the taxpayer down the line.

The agencies are not the only government-related organizations to have problems. As the crisis worsened in 2007 and 2008, the FHA also continued to guarantee loans to low-income borrowers. Delinquency rates on those mortgages exceed 20 percent today.[43] It is perhaps understandable (though not necessarily wise) that government departments will attempt to support lending in bad times, as they play a countercyclical role. As Peter Wallison of the American Enterprise Institute has pointed out, it is less understandable why the FHA added to the subprime frenzy in 2005 and 2006, thus exacerbating the boom and the eventual fall.[44] Delinquencies on guaranteed loans offered then also exceed 20 percent. The FHA will likely need taxpayer assistance. The overall cost to the taxpayer of government attempts to increase low-income lending continue to mount and perhaps will never be fully tallied up.

### Interesting Differences in the United States

As house prices rose between 1999 and 2007, households borrowed against the home equity they had built up. The extent of such borrowing was so great that the distribution of loan-to-value ratios of existing mortgages in the United States barely budged over this period, despite double-digit increases in house prices.[45] House-price appreciation also enabled low-income households to obtain other forms of nonmortgage credit. For instance, according to the Survey of Consumer Finances conducted by the Federal Reserve Board, between 1989 and 2004 the fraction of low-income families (families in the bottom quartile of income distribution) that had mortgages outstanding doubled, while those that had credit card debt outstanding grew by 75 percent.[46] By contrast, the fraction of high-income families (families in the top quartile of income distribution) that had mortgages or credit card debt outstanding fell slightly over this period, suggesting that the rapid spread of indebtedness was concentrated in poorer segments of the population.

Indeed, although housing booms took place around the world, driven by low interest rates, the boom in the United States was especially pronounced among borrowers who had not had prior easy access to credit, the subprime and Alt-A segments of the market. Detailed studies indicate that this housing boom was different because house prices for the low-income segment of the population rose by more and fell by more than they did for the high-income segments. By contrast, in previous U.S. housing booms, house prices for the high-income segment were always more volatile than for the low-income segment.[47] Relative to other industrial countries like Ireland, Spain, and the United Kingdom, all of which had house-price booms that turned to busts, U.S. house prices overall were nowhere as high relative to fundamentals.[48] But the boom was concentrated in those least able to afford the bust. The U.S. boom was different, at least in its details.

Some progressive economists dispute whether the recent crisis was at all related to government intervention in low-income housing credit.[49] This certainly was not the only factor at play, and to argue that it was is misleading. But it is equally misleading to say it played no part. The private financial sector did not suddenly take up low-income housing loans in the early 2000s out of the goodness of its heart, or because financial innovation permitted it to do so—after all, securitization has been around for a long time. To ignore the role played by politicians, the government, and the quasi-government agencies is to ignore the elephant in the room.

I have argued that an important political response to inequality was populist credit expansion, which allowed people the consumption possibilities that their stagnant incomes otherwise could not support. There were clearly special circumstances in the United States that made this response more likely—in particular, the many controls the government had over housing finance and the difficulty, given the increasing polarization of U.S. politics, of enacting direct income redistribution. Moreover, the objective of expanding home ownership drew on the politically persuasive historical symbolism of small entrepreneurs and farmers in the United States, all owning their property and having a stake in society and progress. These specific circumstances would not necessarily apply in other industrial countries.

That said, there are a number of parallels, both in U.S. history and in the contemporary experience of emerging markets, for the use of credit as a populist palliative. A previous episode of high income inequality in the United States came toward the end of the nineteenth century and the beginning of the twentieth century. As small and medium-sized farmers perceived that they were falling behind, their grievances about the lack of access to credit and the need for banking reforms were articulated by the Populist Party. Pressure from such quarters helped accelerate the deregulation of banking and the explosion of banks in the early part of the twentieth century. Indeed, in North Dakota, after a Populist candidate won the 1916 gubernatorial race with the support of small farmers, the Populist Party created the United States' first state-owned bank, the Bank of North Dakota.[50] The explosion in rural bank credit was followed in the 1920s by a steady decline in the prices of agricultural produce, widespread farmer distress, and the failure of a large number of small rural banks. As in the recent crisis, populist credit expansion went too far.

The tradition of using government-linked financial institutions to expand credit to politically important constituencies of moderate creditworthiness is also well established in emerging markets. For example, Shawn Cole, a professor at Harvard Business School, finds that Indian state-owned banks increase their lending to the politically important but relatively poor constituency of farmers by about 5 to 10 percentage points in election years.[51] The effect is most pronounced in districts with close elections. The consequences of the lending are greater loan defaults and no measurable increase in agricultural output, which suggest that it really serves as a costly form of income redistribution. Most recently, the coalition United Progressive Alliance (UPA) government waived the repayment of loans made to small and medium-sized farmers just before the 2009 elections, an act that some commentators believed helped the coalition get reelected. Populism and credit are familiar bedfellows around the world.

## Summary and Conclusion

Growing income inequality in the United States stemming from unequal access to quality education led to political pressure for more housing credit. This pressure created a serious fault line that distorted lending in the financial sector. Broadening access to housing loans and home ownership was an easy, popular, and quick way to address perceptions of inequality. Politicians set about achieving it through the agencies and departments they had set up to deal with the housing-debt disasters during the Great Depression. Ironically, the same organizations may have helped precipitate the ongoing housing catastrophe.

This is not to fault their intent. Both the Clinton administration's attempt to make housing affordable to the less well-off and the Bush administration's attempt to expand home ownership were laudable. They were also politically astute in that they focused on alleviating the concerns of those being left behind while buying time for more direct policies to work. But the gap between government intent and outcomes can be very wide indeed, especially when action is mediated through the private sector. More always seems better to the impatient politician. But any instrument of government policy has its limitations, and what works in small doses can become a nightmare when scaled up, especially when scaled up quickly. Some support to low-income housing might have had benefits and prompted little private-sector reaction. But support at a scale that distorted housing prices and private-sector incentives was too much. Furthermore, the private sector's objectives are not the government's objectives, and all too often policies are set without taking this disparity into account. Serious unintended consequences can result.

Successive governments pushed Fannie and Freddie to support low-income lending. Given their historical focus on prime mortgages, these agencies had no direct way of originating or buying subprime loans in the quantities that were being prescribed. So in the years of the greatest excess, they bought subprime mortgage-backed securities, but without adjusting for the significantly higher risks that were involved. And the early rewards from taking these risks were higher profits. That there also were very few defaults initially emboldened the agencies to plunge further, and their weak and politically influenced regulator did little to restrain them. At the same time, as brokers came to know that someone out there was willing to buy subprime mortgage-backed securities without asking too many questions, they rushed to originate loans without checking the borrowers' creditworthiness, and credit quality deteriorated. But for a while, the problems were hidden by growing house prices and low defaults—easy credit masked the problems caused by easy credit—until house prices stopped rising and the flood of defaults burst forth.

On net, easy credit, as is typically the case, proved an extremely costly way to redistribute. Too many poor families who should never have been lured into buying a house have been evicted after losing their meager savings and are now homeless; too many houses have been built that will not be lived in; and too many financial institutions have incurred enormous losses that the taxpayer will have to absorb for years to come. Although home ownership rates did go up— from 64.2 percent of households in 1994 to 69.2 percent in 2004—too many households that could not afford to borrow were induced to do so, and since 2004, even home ownership has declined steadily (to 67.2 percent as of the fourth quarter of 2009), with the rate likely to fall further as many households face foreclosure.[52]

This is a lesson that needs to be more widely absorbed. Few "solutions" hold more support and promise up front, and lead to more recrimination after the fact, than opening the spigot of lending. For poor countries there is a strong parallel with the past enthusiasm for foreign aid. Now we know that aid leads to dependency, indebtedness, and poor governance and rarely leads to growth.[53] The new miracle solution is microcredit—lending to the poor through group loans, a system in which peer pressure from the group makes individuals more likely to repay. Although it has promise on a small scale, history suggests that when scaled up, and especially when used as an instrument of government policy, it will likely create significant problems.

So what should the United States do to deal with the waning of the American dream, with the shrinking of opportunities for the large mass of the American people? Ignoring the problem will only make matters worse. Inequality feeds on itself. Moreover, it will precipitate a backlash. When people see a dim economic future in a democracy, they work through political channels to obtain redress, and if the political channel does not respond, they resort to other means. The first victims of a political search for scapegoats are those who are visible and easily demonized, but powerless to defend themselves. Illegal immigrants and foreign workers do not vote, but they are essential to the economy—the former because they often do jobs no one else will touch in normal times, and the latter because they are the source of the cheap imports that have raised the standard of living for all, but especially those with low incomes. There has to be a better way than simply finding scapegoats, and I examine possible solutions in subsequent chapters.

At this point, though, I want to turn to a problem that was growing in magnitude elsewhere in the world. Even as political compulsions in the United States were pushing it to become more favorable to boosting consumption, countries like Germany and Japan, which were extremely dependent on exports for growth, were accounting for a larger share of the world economy. Why they, and a growing number of emerging markets, have become dependent in this way, and the consequences of such dependence for countries like the United States, are the issues I turn to now.

# CHAPTER TWO

# Exporting to Grow

I GREW UP IN DIFFERENT PARTS of the world because my father was an Indian diplomat. My first real memories of India are from my early teens, in the mid-1970s, when he returned to work in Delhi. It was not an easy time. We were not poor, but my parents had to bring up four children on my father's government salary. More problematic, there was very little to buy, especially for children who had grown used to the plentiful choices in European supermarkets. Every evening, one of us children trudged around the local markets looking for bread. The government was trying to limit the production of "unnecessary" consumer goods, of which bread was deemed one. Moreover, because the government also regulated the official sale price for bread, the little that was produced was diverted to favored clients and sold at black-market prices. So we went around the empty stores, trying to ingratiate ourselves with the shopkeepers in the hope that one would sell us half a loaf of bread from his hidden stock—at twice the fixed price. I remember the joy we felt when a friend's brother bought a shop in the market. My new connections ensured our bread supply, allowing us to stop haunting the market.

We were not so lucky in our quest for a car. High import duties made foreign cars unaffordable. The government allowed only three domestic firms to produce cars, and only in limited quantities, for cars were deemed unnecessary as well. The only Indian-made car that could accommodate our large family was the Ambassador—a local version of the 1954 Oxford Morris, virtually unchanged from the original. But the waiting list for an Ambassador, which in most other countries would be deemed an antique, was years. So my father settled for a scooter that he rode to work. Because public transport was unreliable, family outings were rare.

The government wanted to limit consumption and encourage savings, and households did save a lot. But there were also unintended consequences. Because goods were in short supply and prices were fixed at ludicrously low levels, little was available in the open market. Black markets flourished: everything could be obtained if you had cash or connections. Few jobs were created: the production of more cars would have meant more demand for restaurants and cinemas and thus more jobs not only for auto workers but also for waiters and ticket clerks. I thought there might be some grand design I did not understand, but the government's policy clearly was not working, because India was still poor. I was determined to learn more, so I became interested in economics. This book is another unintended consequence of the government's policies.

Thirty-five years later, it is relatively easy to describe the typical path that successful countries have followed in the search for growth. It has emphasized both substantial government intervention in the early stages—which is why I broadly refer to it as *relationship* or *managed* capitalism—and a focus on exports. Although easy to describe, it is much harder to implement. At key junctures, the government has to take steps that go against its natural inclinations; the India of my youth muffed the game plan. Perhaps this is one reason why only a handful of countries have grown rapidly out of poverty in recent years.

The export-led managed-growth strategy, when implemented well, has been the primary path out of poverty in the postwar era. In the early days of this strategy, the exporters were small enough to allow the rest of the world to boost its spending and absorb the exports easily. Unfortunately, even as exporters like Germany and Japan have become large and rich, the habits and institutions they acquired while growing have left them unable to generate strong, sustainable domestic demand and become more balanced in their growth.

The surpluses they put out into the global goods markets have circled the world, looking for those who have the creditworthiness to buy the goods, and tempting countries, companies, and households around the world into spending. In the 1990s, developing countries ran the trade deficits necessary to absorb these goods: the next chapter shows how many of them suffered deep financial crises and forswore further deficits and borrowing. Even as developing countries dropped the hot potato of foreign-debt-financed spending in the late 1990s, the United States, as well as European countries such as Greece, Spain, and the United Kingdom, picked it up. First, though, I want to describe the export-led managed growth strategy and why it worked.

## The Elusive Search for Growth

Few people realize that many of today's wealthy nations are rich today because they grew steadily for a long time, not because they grew particularly fast. Between 1820 and 1870, the per capita incomes of Australia and the United States, *then or now?*

the fast-growing emerging markets of their time (I refer to them as *early developers*), grew annually at 1.8 percent and 1.3 percent, respectively.[1] By contrast, *late developers* like Chile, South Korea, and Taiwan, which joined the ranks of wealthier nations only in recent decades, grew at multiples of these rates over a shorter period. Japan was not quite a poor country in 1950 (though in 1950 its per capita income was lower than Mexico's). However, between 1950 and 1973, Japanese per capita income grew at a rate of around 8 percent a year. These late developers have set the aspirational level for today's developing countries, but theirs is a very different path from that of the early developers especially with respect to the speed of their growth.

How did the late developers grow so fast? In the entire history of humankind, no country had grown as fast as Japan did between 1950 and 1973. But since then, South Korea, Malaysia, Taiwan, and China have approached and even exceeded this rate of growth. To understand these developments, we have to understand why countries are poor in the first place and how they attempt to climb out of poverty.

## Is More Capital the Key to Growth?

A difference obvious to anyone who travels from a rich country to a poor country is the varying levels of physical capital. In rich countries, vast airports accommodating big planes, enormous factories packed with high-tech machinery, huge combines in well-irrigated fields, and households with appliances and gadgets for every imaginable use suggest to us that far more physical capital is in use than in poor countries. Physical capital increases income because it makes everyone more productive. A single construction worker with a backhoe can shift far more mud than several workers with shovels and wheelbarrows.

If, however, the only difference between the rich and the poor countries is physical capital, the obvious question, posed by the University of Chicago Nobel laureate Robert Lucas in a seminal paper in 1990, is, Why does more money not flow from rich countries to poor countries so as to enable the poor countries to buy the physical capital they need?[2] After all, poor countries would gain enormously from a little more capital investment: in some parts of Africa, it is easier to get to a city a few hundred miles away by taking a flight to London or Paris and taking another flight back to the African destination than to try to go there directly. Commerce would be vastly increased in Africa if good roads were built between cities, whereas an additional road would not make an iota of difference in already overconnected Japan. Indeed, Lucas calculated that a dollar's worth of physical capital in India would produce 58 times the returns available in the United States. Global financial markets, he argued, could not be so blind as to ignore these enormous differences in returns, even taking into account the greater risk of investing in India.

Perhaps, Lucas concluded, the explanation is that the returns in poor countries are lower than suggested by these simple calculations because these countries lack other factors necessary to produce returns: perhaps education or, more broadly, human capital. It may seem that an Egyptian farmer, using the ox and plow that his ancestors used five thousand years ago, could increase his efficiency enormously by using a tractor. By comparison, it would seem likely that a farmer in Iowa who already owns an array of agricultural machinery would improve his yield only marginally by buying an additional tractor. But the Egyptian farmer is likely to be far less educated than the farmer in Iowa and to know less about the kinds of fertilizers and pesticides that are needed or when they should be applied to maximize crop yields. As a result, the additional income the Egyptian farmer could generate with a single tractor might be far less than what the Iowa farmer could generate by buying one more machine to add to the many he already has.

However, even accounting for differences in human capital between rich and poor countries, Lucas surmised that capital should still be far more productive in the latter. Moreover, evidence suggests that the enormous investments in education around the world in recent years have not made a great difference to growth.[3] Something else seems to be missing in poor countries that keeps machines and educated people from maximizing productivity and the countries from growing rich—something that dollops of foreign aid cannot readily supply.

## Organizational Capital

The real problem, in my view, is that developing countries, certainly in the early stages of growth, do not have the organizational structure to deploy large quantities of physical capital effectively.[4] You cannot simply buy a complicated, high-speed machine tool and hire a smart operator to run it: you need a whole organization surrounding that operator if the machine is to be put to productive use. You need reliable suppliers to provide the raw materials, buyers to take the output from the tool and use it in their production lines, managers to decide the mix of products that will be made, a maintenance team to take care of repairs, a purchasing team to deal with suppliers, a marketing team to deal with buyers, a security outfit to guard the facility at night, and so on. The organizational differences between a small car repair shop and Toyota, or between a medical dispensary housed in a shed and the Mayo Clinic, are enormous, and determine their ability to use large modern sophisticated machines effectively.

Of course, these complex organizations do not operate in a vacuum either. They need other complex organizations to provide inputs and sometimes to buy their output. Equally important, they need finance, infrastructure—for example, electric power, and transport and communication networks—and governance institutions to provide security to property and life as well as to facilitate business transactions.

## How the Early Developers Built Organizational Capital

The great Austrian economist Joseph Schumpeter argued that capitalism grew through innovation, with newcomers bringing in creative new processes and techniques that destroyed the businesses of old incumbents. Much of capitalism's dynamism in industrial countries does reflect this process: in the past few years, for example, the whole business of film photography has been almost completely eclipsed by the digital photography revolution. Film makers such as Kodak, which did not anticipate the speed of this change, have had to struggle to remake themselves.

With this kind of growth process in mind, what is loosely termed the institutional school of economists has argued that the role of the government in business is to create the institutional environment for competition and innovation —to establish secure property rights, strengthen patent laws, reduce barriers to entry, and reduce taxes—and then let the private sector take charge. There is a small problem with this view. No large country has ever grown rapidly from poverty to riches with this kind of strategy, in part because poor countries do not have the necessary private organizations to take advantage of such an environment, and the environment, in turn, is not conducive to creating the organizations quickly.

For example, British India had many of the qualities that these economists advocate: a small and fairly honest government, low taxes, low tariffs, a focus on building infrastructure like railways, and a laissez-faire attitude (even toward famines).[5] However, between 1820 and 1950, per capita incomes in India were virtually stagnant, growing at just 0.1 percent per year because the British did little to nurture local industry. Instead they encouraged imports of both goods and management, especially from Britain: India had among the lowest import tariffs in the world in 1880. As a result, India's private sector simply did not have the encouragement or the requisite cover behind which to develop organizational capital.

Indeed, economists may overplay the role of institutions in growth. History suggests that institutional change often does not predate but rather accompanies the process of growth.[6] For example, sensible governments of developing countries do not have strong laws protecting intellectual-property rights when their industrial sector is starting out: such laws would put an end to the rampant copying from foreigners that is often the basis for initial growth. Instead, they enact property-rights legislation when domestic firms have become strong enough to innovate and demand protection. Generally, institutions seem to develop along with, and in response to, the need for them. They are then refined through use and kept from exercising authority arbitrarily by the complex organizations that use them and pay for their upkeep. In many ways, the real challenge for developing countries is, again, to create effective complex organizations.

Rich early developers such as Australia, Canada, and the United States built their complex organizations over time. New industries often started with many small firms, some of which were exceptionally innovative or well managed. These generated larger profits than their competitors, hired more employees, and, over time, built effective and stable organizational structures. Initially, these firms grew slowly, both because it takes time to build the social relationships, the organizational norms, and the organizational procedures that allow the firm to function efficiently and because the availability of outside finance to an untried, unproven organization is limited. Eventually, some firms gained reputation and wealth: many of these were family firms like Anheuser-Busch or Cargill in the United States, whose reputation could transfer down through generations.[7] Because banks would accept these firms' reputation and wealth as collateral for financing, they could grow faster. All in all, however, growth was slow and steady, with many firms falling by the wayside; failure rates for small, new firms are spectacularly high even today.[8]

Governments of early developers, in general, simply did not have much capacity to intervene to create a nurturing environment, even if they wanted to. Before the dramatic increase in spending during the Great Depression, the total outlays of the U.S. government in 1930 were only 3.4 percent of GDP.[9] The primary roles of the government were thought to be defense and maintaining law and order. However, wealth was a source of military power, and wealthier people were happy and did not foment trouble. Governments, therefore, did try to foster growth, typically through the strategic use of trade barriers and tariffs.

Daniel Defoe, the businessman, journalist, pamphleteer, and author of *Robinson Crusoe*, among other books, describes in detail in *A Plan of the English Commerce* one of the earliest documented instances of government-aided development: the way the Tudor monarchs transformed England from a country reliant on raw-wool exports to one that exported manufactured woolens.[10] Prior to his coronation following the War of the Roses, Henry VII spent time as a refugee in the Low Countries. Impressed by the prosperity in those lands, derived from wool manufacturing, he decided to encourage manufacturing in England.

The measures he took included identifying locations suitable for manufacturing, poaching skilled workers from the Low Countries, increasing duties on or even banning the export of raw wool, and banning the export of unfinished cloth. The monarchy also started promoting the export of finished woolen garments, with Elizabeth I dispatching trade envoys to the Russian, Mogul, and Persian empires. The calibrated and measured support afforded to industry is best reflected in the fact that raw-wool exports were permanently banned only when the monarchy was confident that domestic manufacturers could use all the raw wool available and were competitive enough internationally to export the additional production. Such managed competition eventually drove manufacturers in the Low Countries to ruin.

Governments also tried to create private monopolies in banking or trade (recall the East India Company, which was granted certain monopoly rights over trade with India and ended up ruling much of the subcontinent). But citizens saw these as indirect forms of taxation and, as democratic rights expanded, fought hard to curb them. So competition within the domestic market was typically unfettered, with governments rarely intervening. The extent of government intervention is the critical difference between the early developers and many of the late developers.

## The Strategy of Late Developers

The late developers, especially nations that became independent just after World War II, started out with organizational deficiencies similar to those of the early developers. Indian politicians like to recall that when India became independent in 1947, it had to import even sewing needles.[11] Their governments were, however, much more impatient for growth, especially given the expectations of their newly free citizens. Moreover, when they started out, they faced much

fiercer competition from firms in developed countries than the early developers had faced initially. In the century or so between when the early developers
began industrializing and when the late developers started, the cost of trans-
portation had fallen tremendously, and the extent of potential competition from
firms in richer countries was commensurately much higher.

Their strategy for advancement, though, was clear: climb the same ladder the
rich countries had done, step by step, moving from the least sophisticated technologies to the frontier of innovation, using low labor costs to stay competitive
until technologies improved and the available capital stock, including human
capital, increased.

The organizational path was less well laid out. Given that the late developers
had little faith that their small and underdeveloped private-sector firms could
lead growth at a pace that would satisfy their needs, they had two options: they
could create government enterprises to undertake business activity, or they
could intervene in the functioning of markets to create space for a favored few
private firms to grow relatively unhindered by competition. In either situation,
the country's savings were directed through a largely captive financial system to
the favored few firms. Governments also typically protected their domestic market from foreign imports through high tariffs and import restrictions, allowing
domestic firms the space to flourish.

## The Commanding Heights

Consider first the strategy of creating state-owned enterprises. In a developing
country, the government typically is the best-developed organization, apart
from the army. It is tempting for it to use its existing organizational templates—
often put in place by a colonial power—to create additional departments to
manage investment and production. Indeed, Lenin, in a famous speech in 1922,
pointed the way (ironically while defending his New Economic Policies, which
allowed more freedom to farmers and traders) when he declared that the state
must control the most important sectors of the economy—the "commanding
heights," as he called them.[12]

Some countries have grown rich from substantial contributions made by
government-owned firms—France and Taiwan are examples—but there aren't
many. The fundamental problem with the government's implementing projects
such as building schools, roads, and dams, let alone running complex firms, is
that incentives in the government are not aimed at using resources efficiently.

The primary role of the government is to ensure that the superstructure that facilitates private activity—including public security, the functioning of markets, and the enforcement of contracts—functions efficiently. Typically, this means a neutral and transparent exercise of power with the public interest in mind, not power that can be bought by the highest bidder. The sociologist Max Weber postulated that a bureaucrat's rewards should come from long-term career progress, status, and the knowledge that he has served the public interest, rather than from the spoils of office. In other words, he believed that the absence of monetary incentives for performance accorded well with the nature of the bureaucrat's work.

Moreover, because performance in many government activities is hard to measure, government officials are typically not given monetary incentives for fear that they might focus on the measurable (for example, the number of files cleared) rather than the useful (the quality of decisions made). Instead, a plethora of rules guide their behavior. Because large organizations find it hard to manage the intra-organizational frictions and jealousies that arise when compensation structures differ considerably within them, it is probably not surprising that even bureaucrats undertaking measurable tasks, such as implementing clear, time-bound projects, are not given strong monetary incentives. As a result, government projects take too long, and administrators do not adapt flexibly to circumstances. Such flexibility would typically mean the bureaucrat's exercising initiative and violating some rule.

Inefficiency arising from poor incentives within the organization is compounded by the fact that the government is a monopoly and has little fear of running out of resources so long as the taxpayer can be squeezed. The combination of poor incentives and little competition typically results in poor outcomes when governments undertake activities that should belong to the private domain. For instance, Argentina's telephone system under state ownership in the 1980s was notorious for its inefficiency—the waiting period for a phone line was more than six years, and some businesses employed staff who sole job was to hold a telephone handset for hours on end until they heard a dial tone.[13]

History does offer some examples of strong state-owned-enterprise-led growth. Under Stalin, the Soviet Union grew rapidly while the rest of the world was mired in the Great Depression. Indeed, much as Japan was the role model for East Asian economies like South Korea, the Soviet Union, with its state-led growth, was the role model for leaders like Jawaharlal Nehru and Mao Zedong.[14] Unfortunately, the imitators did not realize that the incentive for bureaucrats to perform in the Soviet Union at that time might have come initially from revolutionary and patriotic fervor, fortified with a dose of terror: if failure to complete a project on time is met with accusations of sabotage and a firing squad, bureaucrats can become surprisingly energetic. However, such incentives cannot be maintained over sustained periods of time: fervor turns to cynicism, and terror eventually turns on itself.

Moreover, even if the incentives within government-owned firms can be maintained, the relationships between the firms become far more complicated over time, as poor economies finish catching up on the essential. Growth eventually requires not only more steel but also much more detailed information—which grade of steel is needed, how much, when, and where. The Nobel Laureate Friedrich von Hayek recognized that this information is diffused in society: it is possessed by the various consumers and distributors of steel products around the country. It could be aggregated in the planning ministry if everyone is asked to file reports, but a lot of tacit information would be lost on the way as the respondents' feel for a market was converted into a hard number. Furthermore, the reported numbers would be distorted by each one's incentives—with consumers wanting to shade demand numbers up so as to encourage production and producers wanting lower numbers so as to ease the pressure on them.

Hayek's fundamental contribution was to recognize that market prices can play a role in aggregating information in a way that is not biased by organizational disabilities or biases. The market prices of various grades of steel, for instance, are established every day—sometimes on organized exchanges—by the forces of demand and supply for this product. Producers and consumers do not write reports but simply express their interest—which reflects their unbiased and informed expectations of the future—through the price at which they are willing to sell or buy steel. Most important, they do so not to fulfill a bureaucratic requirement, but from the purest of motives, self-interest. No matter how qualitative each one's information is, no matter how detrimental it is to some people, so long as the market functions, its prices aggregate all these individuals' information. In the Soviet Union, the system eventually failed in part because the information on which central planning was based was a fantasy that bore no correspondence to ground realities; but this information was so carefully manipulated that even the CIA had no idea of the true weakness of the Soviet economy.

In sum, there are indeed some well-run state-owned firms. But the best state-run firms typically distance themselves from government norms, procedures, and interference and are often private in all but ownership.

## Favoring the Few

Instead of relying on state-owned firms to propel growth, a number of governments have tried to remedy private-sector organizational deficiencies and build domestic champions, even while relying on some market signals to allocate resources. The process of playing midwife, often derided as crony capitalism but better termed relationship or managed capitalism, involved a judicious mix of the government's giving firms some protection from foreign competition and special privileges so that they could generate the profits around which they could build their organizational capital, while maintaining some incentives for firms to be efficient.

One example is Taiwan's efforts in the early 1950s to promote its textile industry.[15] The first textile manufacturers in Taiwan were mainland Chinese, who put their machines on board ships when the Communists took over in 1949 and relocated on the other side of the straits. Soon after, in the early 1950s, the Taiwanese government imposed restrictions on the entry of any new yarn producers to prevent "excessive competition." It then supported incumbents by supplying raw cotton to mills directly, advancing them working capital, and buying up the entire production of yarn. It followed a similar approach toward weavers. It also imposed tariffs on imported yarn and cloth and even banned imports when tariffs proved insufficient. As the textile industry boomed, the government encouraged firms to merge so that they could realize economies of scale.

More generally, the tools used by governments have included erecting barriers to entry, offering tax breaks so that private firms can generate larger profits and use their retained earnings to fund investment, encouraging close ties between banks and favored firms so that the former lend abundantly (and cheaply) to the latter, providing raw materials at a subsidized price, and imposing tariffs so that foreign competition is not a threat. With subsidies and protection from the government, some favored champions have grown rapidly and profitably, acquiring technology, wealth, organizational capabilities, and stability.

Government intervention has sometimes gone much further. K. Y. Yin, an electrical engineer who was also a voracious reader of economic texts (including Adam Smith), was Taiwan's chief economic planner in the 1950s and is often referred to as the father of Taiwan's industrial development.[16] He commissioned a study in 1953 that identified plastics as an important area for Taiwan to enter. According to a possibly apocryphal story, Yin used his access to information on bank deposits to identify an individual, Y. C. Wang, as someone who had both enough savings and the entrepreneurial zest to undertake a plastics project, and instructed Wang to do it.[17] The first Taiwanese plant for polyvinyl chloride (PVC) was built under government supervision and transferred to Wang in running order in 1957. He went on to build the Formosa Plastics Group, Taiwan's largest business.

There are, however, a number of problems with government intervention that favors a few. Nothing prevents a corrupt government from distributing favors to incompetent friends or relatives, a problem that has plagued countries like the Philippines. Even if a government starts out with the best intentions and carefully screens incumbents, government protection means that those who become lazy and inefficient are not forced to shut down. A key conundrum for governments therefore has been how to retain the disciplinary incentives provided by the market while still allowing firms the room to make profits and build organizational capabilities.

Some governments tried to instill a sense of efficiency and quality directly. For instance, the Taiwanese planner, Yin, ordered the destruction of twenty thousand substandard light bulbs at a public demonstration in Taipei and confiscated tons of substandard monosodium glutamate, the food additive.[18] In those cases, the message to producers got through. But governments need a source of discipline more systematic than the whims of bureaucrats, one that would be applied without sparing the favored few.

A second problem with favoring producers in developing countries is that households get a raw deal, and so consumption tends to be low. For starters, wages tend to be low because the many workers in low-productivity agriculture constitute a reserve army, waiting to take up factory jobs at low wages, and keep industrial wages from rising rapidly. But over time governments can also interfere in the wage-setting process, favoring manufacturers over workers so as to keep firms competitive and profitable. Also, the favored firms may pay low prices for government-controlled natural resources such as energy and minerals. Governments make up the shortfall in their revenue by taxing households more, even while the firms charge high prices for the goods they sell to those same households in the cartelized domestic markets.[19] To add insult to injury, banks offer low government-set deposit rates for household savings, thus cutting further into household income, even while making subsidized loans to businesses.

In sum, the need to create strong firms may lead the state to favor the producer and the financier at the expense of the citizens. As a result, consumption is unnaturally constrained in such economies. The India of my youth was not dissimilar to the Korea that my Korean friends still remember, where wages

were low, work hours long, and consumption frowned on. Indeed, many of them recollect how dim Seoul was at night, because bright neon lights advertising consumer goods were prohibited. Midnight curfews both ensured security and prevented young workers from wasting their energy on an unproductive night life. So a second problem of managed capitalism is that because consumption is repressed, firms are deprived of large domestic markets.

### Export-Led Growth and Managed Capitalism

 One way to both discipline inefficient firms and expand the market for goods is to encourage the country's large firms to export. Not only are firms forced to make attractive cost-competitive products that can win market share internationally, but the larger international markets offer them the possibility of scale economies. Moreover, because they are no longer constrained by the size of the domestic market, they can pick the products for which they have the greatest comparative advantage.

Often, the starter sector in developing countries is easy-to-make but labor-intensive consumer goods like garments and textiles. Having consolidated the protected textile sector as described earlier, the Taiwanese government started putting in place incentives to export. By 1961, Taiwanese textile exports had become a big enough threat that the United States imposed quotas on them— a sure sign that Taiwan's textile industry had come of age.

Once industry learned the basics of production in textiles, it started moving up the technological ladder to produce more complicated goods. As late as 1970, textiles were still Korea's leading export, followed by plywood and, curiously, wigs, whereas its major exports today include cars, chips (silicon, not potato), and cell phones.[20] Today, it is China, Vietnam, and Cambodia that compete to export textiles.

Developing-country governments tried to enhance incentives even further by offering greater benefits to firms that managed to increase exports. For instance, because foreign exchange was scarce in the early days of growth, imports were severely restricted. Successful exporters were, however, given licenses to import, and the prospect of making money by selling these licenses gave them strong incentives to expand their foreign market share. In situations where foreign countries imposed import quotas, or where raw materials were scarce, the government also allocated a greater share of these to the more successful exporters. So both indirectly and directly, the efficient were encouraged.

The export-led growth strategy does not mean that government reduces its support to industry. Indeed, exports may initially require more support if domestic firms are to be competitive globally. Some countries have provided a general subsidy by maintaining an undervalued exchange rate or holding down wages by suppressing or co-opting unions; such strategies are more easily followed by authoritarian governments. Others have provided a specific targeted subsidy by underpricing key raw material or energy inputs to exporters or by directly providing cash rebates for exports or for importing manufacturing equipment intended to produce exports.

What is clear is that a necessary concomitant to the strategy of government intervention to create strong domestic firms is to push them to prove their mettle by exporting. Managed capitalism has proved enormously successful in its immediate objective of getting countries out of poverty. It is not, however, an easy strategy to implement.

## Missing the Turn

Managed capitalism initially requires a producer bias that is not easy to sustain in populist democracies. Then the government, despite coddling firms in their early years, has to turn and push them toward exports. For small nations like Taiwan, limited domestic markets made the second step virtually a necessity. But for countries with large domestic markets like Brazil, that second transformation was long delayed.

One country that flubbed this move was India. Under its first prime minister, Jawaharlal Nehru, India did strive to build organizational capacity. Although Nehru reserved industries like steel and heavy machinery for the state sector, he never actively suppressed the private sector. Instead, a system of licensing—the infamous "license-permit raj"—was put in place, ostensibly to use the country's savings carefully. This meant guiding investment away from industries that bureaucrats thought were making unnecessary consumer goods (even durable ones such as cars), and instead into areas that could lay the basis for future growth, such as heavy machinery. The result, however, was that incumbents, typically firms owned by established families that were well enough connected to procure license early, were protected from competition. Barriers were also erected against foreign competition in order to provide a nurturing environment to India's infant industries until they matured and became competitive.

The protection India offered these industries, however, became an excuse for the companies to become "Peter Pans"—companies that never grew up. Car manufacturing is a case in point. Over nearly four decades, only five different models of the Ambassador car were produced, and the sole differences between them seemed to be the headlights and the shape of the grill. After growing rapidly just after independence, the Indian economy got stuck at a per capita real growth rate of about 1 percent—dubbed the "Hindu" rate of growth.

Like Korea or Taiwan, India should have made the switch toward exports and a more open economy in the early 1960s. But because the protected Indian domestic market was large, at least relative to that of the typical late developer, firms were perfectly happy exploiting their home base despite government attempts to encourage exports. This is not to say that government efforts to change were particularly strenuous, especially given that protected firms were an important source of revenue to the ruling party for fighting elections. Democracy at this stage may well have seemed a source of weakness: leaders like Park Chung Hee in Korea and Lee Kuan Yew in Singapore did not have to worry about such niceties. As a result, India stayed closed, poor, and uncompetitive long after the economies of countries like Korea, which were at similar levels of per capita income in the early 1960s, had taken off.

### What Happens When the Exporters Get Rich: Germany and Japan

Not every country has been able to succeed with an export-led growth strategy. Moreover, this strategy also has weaknesses that may become clear only gradually, as countries grow rich. To understand these weaknesses, we should take a closer look at Germany and Japan. Neither was really poor after World War II— their people were educated, these countries had the blueprints to create the necessary organizations, and some of their institutional infrastructure survived— but both had devastated, bombed-out economies, with their capital stock substantially destroyed, large firms and combines broken up or suppressed by the occupation authorities, and households too downtrodden to be an important source of consumption. Exports were the obvious answer to their problems.

With a large number of workers still in agriculture, and with labor organizations docile, postwar wages initially did not keep pace with the extraordinary rate of productivity growth (a measure of the growth in efficiency with which inputs are used and thus a measure of the profit margins that can be distributed to workers through higher wages). As a result, corporations were able to generate substantial profits for a while.

In both countries, the mature banking sector took on part of the role that was played by the government in the countries discussed earlier. Close cooperation between firms and universal banks in Germany, cemented by share holdings by firms and banks in one another, led to domestic cartels and diminished domestic competition, allowing corporations to focus their energies on competing in foreign markets. Similarly, in Japan, the ties between firms and banks in the bank-centered networks called *keiretsus*, which were overseen by the powerful Ministry of Finance and the Ministry of International Trade and Industry (MITI), resulted in a canonical version of managed capitalism.

Once the excess labor in agriculture was fully drawn in to the manufacturing sector, however, wages inexorably increased to keep pace with productivity growth in the efficient export sector. By 1975, hourly wage rates in manufacturing in Germany had caught up with those in the United States, and Japan caught up in the early 1990s. Low wages therefore no longer offered a competitive advantage for the exporters. More problematic, once the initial phase of catch-up was over and Germany and Japan approached the levels of capital per worker that existed in advanced economies such as the United States, the growth rate of investment slowed considerably, and so did imports of capital goods. With the postwar households conditioned to limit consumption, and successive governments intent on disciplined macroeconomic policies, both Germany and Japan started running large trade surpluses. These initially helped them repay foreign borrowing but eventually resulted in increasing pressure on the currency to appreciate.[21]

To stay competitive, both countries had to move up the value chain of production and to the frontiers of innovation, making more and more high-tech, skill-intensive products. More important, they also had to improve productivity steadily. They certainly managed to do this in the sectors that exported or competed with imports, the so-called tradable sector. But problems eventually emerged in the domestic nontradable sector, in areas like construction, retail, and hotels, where foreign competition was often naturally absent and sometimes deliberately kept out. Although the extent of government intervention to support exporters was naturally disciplined by international competition—after all, regardless of how much the government helps, if you produce a shoddy product at too high a cost, you will lose export market share—there were no such constraints in the nontradable sector. Productivity growth eventually lagged because the market forces that would force the inefficient to shrink or close were suppressed.

Japan has fared worse than Germany in this respect. As a part of the European Union (EU), Germany is subject to the EU's rules on fostering domestic competition—though because it has substantial power in the union, it plays a big role in watering them down. Japan has not found any equivalent external discipline in Asia. As a result, the close relationship between government and incumbents has been particularly detrimental to efficiency in the domestic-oriented production sector.

Many a visitor to Japan is surprised at the sight of elevator ladies in hotels—women whose job it is to usher guests into the next available elevator, even though bright lights and buzzers clearly indicate, to anyone who can hear or see, which elevator is next. Perhaps these women had a function when elevators were a new invention, when spotting the next elevator was a challenge, and elderly guests had to be coaxed to get in. That the job has not been done away with over the years, or transformed to retain its essential functions (greeting visitors) while allowing the women to do some useful work, suggests an uncompetitive service sector.

Indeed, when an upstart haircutting firm in Japan recently started opening salons rapidly and undercutting existing barber shops by offering quick, cheap haircuts, a nationwide association of barbershops took note.[22] It called for more regulation, protesting that it was unhygienic to cut hair without a shampoo beforehand, and had an ordinance passed requiring all barbershops to have expensive shampooing facilities. This immediately slowed the upstart and hit directly at its low-price strategy.

More generally, as rising wages in the productive export sector pulled up wages elsewhere in the economy, high wages (relative to productivity) and the resulting high prices of nontraded goods such as haircuts, restaurant meals, and hotel rooms reduced domestic demand for them. So the export-oriented miracle economies started looking oddly misshapen, much like someone who exercises only the limbs on one side of the body: a superefficient manufacturing sector existed side by side with a moribund services sector; a focus on foreign demand persisted even while domestic demand lay dormant.

## The Fault Line: The Case of Japan

Japan's and Germany's dependence on exports for growth did not matter much in the early years, when they were small relative to the rest of the world. But as they became the second and third largest economies in the world, it put a substantially greater burden on other countries to create excess demand.

What is particularly alarming for the future of countries following this path is that Japan did try to change, but without success. In the Plaza Accord of 1985,

Japan agreed, under U.S. pressure, to allow its exchange rate to appreciate against the dollar. As Japanese exports came under pressure, the Bank of Japan cut interest rates sharply. According to a high-ranking Bank of Japan official: "We intended first to boost both the stock and property markets. Supported by this safety net—rising markets—export-oriented industries were supposed to reshape themselves so they could adapt to a domestically-led economy. This step then was supposed to bring about enormous growth of assets over every economic sector. This wealth-effect would in turn touch off personal consumption and residential investment, followed by an increase of investment in plant and equipment. In the end, loosened monetary policy would boost real economic growth."[23]

What the loose monetary policy instead triggered was a massive stock market and real estate bubble that led to the widely circulated, although exaggerated, claim that the land on which the Imperial Palace stood in Tokyo was worth more than the state of California. Corporate investment did pick up. But instead of reorienting themselves toward manufacturing for domestic demand, Japanese firms started investing much more in East Asian countries where labor costs were substantially cheaper, again with the intent of exporting. Construction and consumption in Japan did boom, but these were temporary spikes. When the alarmed central bank started raising rates in the early 1990s, the collapse in stock and real estate prices led to an economic meltdown whose effects are still being felt.

So, far from automatically becoming more balanced in their growth as they become rich, export-led economies have found it extremely hard to boost their growth on their own, because the typical channels through which they can increase final consumption tend to atrophy during the period of emphasis on exports. As banks grow used to protected markets and instructions on whom to lend to, they have little capacity to lend carefully when given the freedom to do so. Also, given the strong ties between the government and producers, it is far more convenient for the government to channel spending through domestic producers that are influential but not necessarily efficient. In Japan, more government spending generally results in more bridges and roads to nowhere as the powerful construction lobby secures stimulus funds. Even as Japan has been covered with stimulus-induced concrete, the economy has remained moribund.

As a result, not only are countries like Japan unable to help the global economy recover from a slump, but they are themselves dependent on outside stimulus to pull them out of it. This is a serious fault line. Indeed, an important source of Japan's malaise in the early 1990s was that the United States did not pull out all the customary stops in combating the 1990–91 U.S. recession, and thus did not provide the demand that historically had helped Japan out of its downturns. It was not until the early 2000s, after a number of failed Japanese attempts to pull itself out of its decade-long slump, that the massive U.S. stimulus in response to the dot-com bust helped Japan export its way out of trouble yet again.[24]

There is no natural, smooth, and painless movement away from export dependence to becoming a balanced economy. Even ignoring the clout of the export sector, which would like to preserve its benefits, the costs of changing emphasis are substantial, and the tools the government has for redressing past distortions are limited. For instance, wages in the domestic sector are often too high relative to productivity in those sectors. To allow greater differentiation of wages, as will be necessary to allow the service sector to flourish, existing service-sector workers must suffer a steep drop in incomes. They have strong incentives to fight against such change. Moreover, foreign entry into the service sector could boost productivity. But years of protection and overregulation are hard to overcome, and strong incumbent interests, like those of the Japanese barbers, will fight against competition and entry.

Similarly, consumers have been trained to be cautious about spending, and retail finance is not well developed. Japanese households, unlike those in the United States, do not readily borrow to spend. It is hard for older people to forget the experiences of postwar deprivation and insecurity or the subsequent period of growth when saving was considered patriotic, and it is the older generations who have more spending power and still determine the overall pattern of consumption. For a while, younger consumers in Japan were thought to offer the answer. But after years of depressing economic outcomes, they too seem to be retreating into their shells, perhaps further depressed by the enormous public debt and underfunded pension schemes they will have to shoulder.[25] Economic reform in Japan requires tremendous political will, a commodity in short supply when the status quo is perfectly comfortable and the pace of relative decline gentle.

### Will China Deepen the Fault Line or Bridge It?

Will the world become more balanced in the future as the late developers continue to grow? The experiences of Germany and Japan offer grim portents for the future. A number of late developers will be joining the ranks of the middle-income nations, if not the rich, in the near future. Will they continue to depend excessively on exports, or will they be able to reform their economies, making the needed transformation back to balanced growth, once they have become rich? Of especial importance is China, which barring untoward incidents, is likely to become the world's largest economy in a decade or two. Although China has a huge domestic economy, it too has followed the path of export-led growth.

Chinese households consume even less as a share of the country's income than the typical low average in export-oriented economies. Because economic data from China, as in many developing countries, are not entirely reliable, economists constantly attribute any Chinese aberration to data problems. But assuming the data are broadly right, why is Chinese household consumption so extraordinarily low? In part, it is because Chinese households cannot rely on the traditional old-age safety net in Asia, namely children. As a result of the government's policy of allowing most couples only one child, six adults (four grandparents and two parents) now depend on one child for future support.[26] No wonder adults, especially older ones, are attempting to increase their savings quickly. To make matters worse, many of them have lost the cradle-to-grave benefits that once came with jobs with state-owned firms, and the costs of needed services like health care are rising quickly as the economy develops. China is trying to improve its pension and social security system, but countries typically take decades to convince citizens that they will get what is promised from such schemes.

China also faces a more traditional problem related to export-led growth strategies. As a proportion of the total income generated in the Chinese economy, household incomes are low. Wages are low because they are held down by the large supply of workers still trying to move from agriculture to industry. Household income is further limited because the subsidized inputs to state-owned firms, like low interest rates, also mean households receive low rates on their bank deposits. Moreover, a number of benefits such as education and health care are no longer provided for free by the state, eating further into discretionary spending.

Finally, consumption may be low because Chinese households feel poorer than they actually are. State-owned firms do not pay dividends to the state and because households do not own their shares directly, they do not see the extremely high profits made at state-owned firms as part of their own wealth. Of course, in the long run, it is hard to believe that the wealth created by these state-owned firms will not be recaptured for the public good. For now, though, households believe they have no part in it, and they consume less than they might if they believed they were richer.

Low domestic consumption, of course, makes the economy excessively reliant on foreign demand. Moreover, even if the Chinese can find ways to boost household consumption in a crisis, it constitutes only a small share of overall demand, and thus the effect on growth is small. Therefore, the Chinese authorities typically try to stimulate investment when they need to keep up growth in the face of a global slowdown—and they do need strong growth to keep up with the expectations of the people. They push loans from the state-owned banking system to local governments and state-owned firms, who then do more of what they were already doing, without regard to long-run profitability. Thus far China has successfully followed the principle "Build it and they will come." But rapid investment in fixed assets carries many dangers, especially once the basic infrastructure is in place. As Yasheng Huang of MIT points out, Chinese bureaucrats have a penchant for glamour projects—vast airports, fancy modern buildings (typically housing the bureaucrats themselves), and enormous malls. It is not clear that this way of stimulating the economy will remain sustainable. China's leadership has adapted in the past when necessary. Can they step away from the seductions of export-led growth and fixed-asset investment before it is too late? Only time will tell whether China will deepen or mend this fault line.

## Summary and Conclusion

The late developers were not innovators initially: they had no need to innovate because rich countries had already developed the necessary technology, and the technology could be licensed or "borrowed." Instead, they tried to remedy a fundamental deficiency: the weakness of existing organizations—even while tackling more traditional development problems like the lack of basic education and skills in the workforce and deficiencies in the health care system. The process of strengthening organizations, in their view, required massive but careful government intervention. Infant firms had to be nurtured. The very real danger, as evidenced in India's stagnation during the 1960s and 1970s, was that the infant firms would demand permanent protection and then strangle growth.

One option was to increase internal competition by reducing barriers to entry and eliminating various subsidies. But governments thought this would waste resources and be potentially harmful to the incumbents who had only recently become profitable. Moreover, the internal market was small, made even smaller by the repression of households in favor of producers. The solution instead was to use the disciplinary power, as well as the attractiveness, of the large global market. Governments forced the now-healthy firms to compete to export, using the threat of opening up the economy to foreign investment to keep firms on their toes.

There were considerable pressures on the government to prevent it from forcing this change. Businesses would have loved protection to continue so that they
could lead a quiet, profitable, life. But a few governments, typically authoritarian ones that managed to avoid the influence from the private sector that comes
with having to fight elections, drove the transformation to an export orientation.[27] Those are the growth miracles that we celebrate today.

Unfortunately, their growth is still strongly dependent on exports. Government policies, domestic vested interests, and household habits formed during
the years of catch-up growth conspire to keep them dependent. The world has
thus become imbalanced in a way that markets cannot fix easily: much of my
tenure at the International Monetary Fund was spent warning not about finance
but about global trade imbalances. The two are linked, for the global trade surpluses produced by the exporters search out countries with weak policies that
are disposed to spend but also have the credibility to borrow to finance the
spending—at least for a while. In the 1990s, developing countries, especially
those in Latin America and East Asia, spent their way into distress. How and
why this happened is what I turn to next.

# CHAPTER THREE

# Flighty Foreign Financing

I N THE 1980S AND 1990S, surpluses produced by exporters like Germany and Japan were looking for markets.[1] Poorer developing countries, with low levels of per capita consumption and investment, were ideal candidates for boosting their spending, provided they could get financing. In fact, even though they too focused on producing for export markets, a number of developing countries, like Korea, invested a lot as they grew, importing substantial quantities of raw material, capital goods, and machinery. In doing so, they ran large trade deficits and helped absorb the surpluses.

Developing countries had to borrow from abroad to finance the difference between what they spent (their consumption plus their investment) and what they produced, as well as to pay interest and principal on prior borrowings. In the 1950s and 1960s, much of this borrowing came from other countries or from multilateral institutions like the World Bank.[2] However, in the 1970s and 1980s, Western banks, recycling the mounting petrodollar surpluses of Middle Eastern countries, assumed more of the lending to developing countries. In the 1990s, foreign arm's-length investors such as mutual funds and pension funds increased their share of lending to developing countries by buying their government and corporate bonds. Thus foreign financing of developing countries became increasingly private and arm's-length.

Unfortunately, few countries have the discipline to borrow and spend carefully while running large trade deficits. Indeed, large amounts of foreign financing tend to encourage wasteful spending decisions. Many developing countries learned from terrible crises in the 1980s and 1990s that it was very risky to expand domestic spending rapidly through a foreign-debt-financed binge, whether the expansion was through consumption or investment.

The boom in busts in the 1990s had varied effects on the behavior of developing countries.[3] For those like Brazil and India, which were consuming too much, the financial difficulties made them liberalize their economies and cut back on excessive and populist government spending, leading to more stable and faster growth. The busts led exporters, like the East Asian economies that had been borrowing to fund investment, to curtail investment so as to reduce their dependence on foreign borrowing. They started intervening in their exchange rates, building up exchange reserves, and in the process pumping their savings out into the global economy, ready to finance anyone who wanted to spend more. With the East Asian economies absorbing fewer imports, the surpluses searching for markets elsewhere increased, making the global economy yet more imbalanced. The fault line described in the previous chapter deepened.

## Savings and Investment

In the perfect world envisioned by economists, a country's investments should not depend on its savings. After all, countries should be able to borrow as much as they need from international financial markets if their investment opportunities are good, and their own domestic savings should be irrelevant. So there should be a low correlation between a country's investment and its savings. In a seminal paper in 1980, Martin Feldstein from Harvard University and Charles Horioka from Osaka University showed that this assumption was incorrect: there was a much higher positive correlation between a country's investment and its savings than one might expect if capital flowed freely across countries.[4]

The interpretation of these findings was that countries, especially poor ones like Burundi and Ecuador, could not get as much foreign financing as they needed, so they had to cut their coats to fit the cloth. However, there is another explanation, not necessarily incompatible with the first. Countries might also have chosen to limit their foreign borrowing, thus inducing a strong correspondence between their investment and their savings. But why would they do so if their investment opportunities, once they overcame the organizational deficiencies noted in the previous chapter, were high?

To try to understand this question, some years ago I undertook a study with Arvind Subramanian, now at the Peterson Institute, and Eswar Prasad, now at Cornell University, in which we looked at the correlation between the average current-account surpluses of developing countries and their growth over recent decades. The current account is just the difference between a country's savings and its investment. A surplus indicates that the country contributes savings to the global pool, while a deficit indicates that it borrows from the rest of the world to finance its investment. A current-account surplus typically also means a trade surplus: the country exports more than it imports.

We found a positive correlation for developing countries: the more a country finances its investment through its own domestic savings, the faster it grows. Conversely, the more foreign financing it uses, the more slowly it grows. Of course, a country might need foreign financing either because it saves very little relative to the norm or because it invests a lot. We found that the more a country invests, the more it grows, which is natural: by investing, it increases its roads and machines, all of which go to make its workers more productive. However, the more its investment was financed from foreign sources as opposed to domestic savings, the slower its growth. Interestingly, these relationships did not hold for developed countries. Developing countries, at least the ones that grew fast on a sustained basis, seemed to avoid significant foreign financing.

In creating a bias in favor of producers, developing countries have stunted the development of their financial systems. This makes it hard for them to use foreign financing to expand domestic demand for goods and services effectively. Indeed, with the exception of foreign direct investment—for instance, Toyota's setting up its own factory in China—foreign financing ultimately relies, either directly or indirectly, on the willingness of the developing-country government to support domestic expansion, rather than on the ability of its private sector to do so. Because foreign lenders focus on the creditworthiness of the country and its government rather than on the specific attributes of the project being financed, and because they effectively obtain seniority over domestic lenders, foreign lending tends to be more permissive than it ought to be, given the benefits of the project. Furthermore, because political compulsions invariably force governments to press hard on the accelerator, countries tend to overuse foreign finance until they are yanked back by a sudden stop in foreign inflows. The ensuing bust tends to set back growth tremendously.

### The Financial Sector in a Producer-Biased Economy

A government-directed, producer-biased strategy of growth tends to stunt the development of that country's financial sector. Because banks are told whom to lend to, and because domestic competition among producers is limited anyway, banks tend not to seek out information or develop their credit-evaluation skills. The legal infrastructure to close down weak borrowers, or to enforce repayment from recalcitrant ones, is virtually nonexistent.

As we saw earlier, the government does try to help producers by setting deposit rates low in order to lower the cost of credit. However, because interbank competition is limited, banks tend to become very inefficient, with bloated staffs and excessively bureaucratic procedures. Anyone who wishes to cash a check at a public-sector bank in a developing country would do well to develop an attitude of resignation while watching the check crawl from desk to desk, adding signature upon signature, before it finally appears at the cashier's window. These inefficiencies as well as limited competition result in an enormous interest spread (the difference between the bank's lending rate and its cost of funds): in Brazil, the spread routinely has been more than 10 percentage points even for short-term loans to corporations in good standing, whereas it is a fraction of a percent in industrial countries. Thus much of the cost of capital advantage obtained by setting deposit rates for households very low is lost through inefficiencies in the banking sector.

Not only do households get little for their savings, but they also find it very difficult to borrow. Lending to households is very risky even in a modern financial system like that of the United States, and doubly so in an underdeveloped financial system. Mechanisms to track credit histories simply do not exist. Because few people have jobs in the formal documented sector, and a significant portion of incomes—such as remittances sent by workers to their parents—are not based on formal contracts, banks have little information on which to base lending decisions. And because the judicial system does not allow easy enforcement of claims against assets, banks cannot lend easily against houses or washing machines.

Households do borrow from moneylenders, with kneecaps sometimes serving as collateral against default, but such borrowing takes place at astronomical rates of interest. The formal banking system could charge high interest rates to compensate for the risk of default (but lower rates than the informal system), but such practices are typically blocked by politicians, who "fight" for citizens by capping formal-sector interest rates at low levels, thus making lending unprofitable and driving households to the informal and unregulated moneylenders. Everything changes as the financial system develops, but this is a reasonable description of many developing countries' financial systems in the 1990s.

I said earlier that there were broadly two reasons a developing country could need foreign financing: if it saved little relative to the norm or invested significantly more than the norm. Let us now consider circumstances in which a country saved too little.

### Saving Little and the 1994 Mexican Crisis

Given that developing-country households find it hard to obtain retail credit, they typically cannot overrun their budgets. Instead, they save for a rainy day, anticipating the difficulties they will experience when times get tough. Unlike its counterpart in the United States, therefore, the underdeveloped financial sector in a developing country makes it difficult for the government to use easy credit as an instrument to carry out populist policies. Instead, the developing country's government performs the role of the financial sector, borrowing and offering transfers and subsidies to favored constituencies so as to allow households to spend more. So the primary reason a developing country saves little is that the government runs large deficits and borrows to finance them. Usually, these deficits are caused by overspending on transfers and subsidies to politically favored segments of the population—by political logic rather than economic rationale.

For example, Kenya, a country that survives on international aid and had an annual per capita income of US$463 in 2006, paid its legislators a base compensation of about $81,000 a year, tax free, plus a variety of allowances and perks that effectively doubled their take-home pay.[5] In a year of widespread drought, a favored car for legislators was the Mercedes-Benz E class, supported by a "basic" monthly car allowance of $4,719. The legislators had the gall to hold up a drought-relief bill as they demanded a higher car allowance, citing the shoddy condition of the roads in their constituencies as justification. Unsurprisingly, the public's demand that the legislators fix the roads had little effect, but the raise went through. These "public servants" earned significantly more than most Kenyan corporate executives and more than their counterparts in the developed world.

When the government's borrowing exceeds available domestic resources, and it does not have access to official government-to-government aid, it turns to foreign private lenders. Because governments command some credibility, and have some access to borrowing from multilateral institutions like the IMF, lenders are willing to finance them for a while. Knowing, however, the temptations that face an opportunistic government—to inflate away debt if denominated in the domestic currency or to pile on more and more debt on existing debt, thus eroding its value—foreign lenders take precautions. They demand repayment in foreign currency (which is not affected by the country's ability to inflate or devalue its currency), and they shorten the terms of their loans in proportion to the country's indebtedness, so that they can pull their loans at short notice.

Instead of controlling its spending, therefore, the populist government that has exhausted its ability to borrow domestically turns to foreign lenders to finance it. Thus the circumstances in which foreign loans are made are not propitious. Knowing this, foreign lenders demand protection, which the government can typically give only by eroding the rights of existing domestic creditors—for instance, the more the overindebted government borrows in foreign currency, the higher the inflation it will eventually have to generate to erode domestic-debt claims on it. Moreover, because foreign investors make short-term loans, any adverse political development may scare them into refusing to refinance the government. Even more problematic, a substantial improvement in opportunities in their home countries—such as a rise in interest rates—can cause foreign investors to pull their money out en masse.[6]

All these factors were at play in the Mexican crisis of 1994. The *sexenio*, or  six-year administration, of President Carlos Salinas de Gortari was coming to an end. In the traditional fashion of the dominant party, the Partido Revolucionario Institucional (PRI), he launched a spending splurge to keep voters happy. Domestic savings dropped by 3.3 percent of GDP between 1991 and 1994, with much of it accounted for by an increase in government spending, leading to a current-account deficit that touched 7 percent of GDP in 2004. Even while the need for foreign financing mounted, political developments took a turn for the worse. In Chiapas, aggrieved peasants rose up in an armed rebellion against the government, and later in the year, the PRI's presidential candidate, Donaldo Colosio, was assassinated. Moreover, the Federal Reserve of the United States raised interest rates throughout 1994, from 3 percent to 5.5 percent, giving investors the incentive to bring their money back to the United States.

As foreign investors became more worried about financing the Mexican current-account deficit, the government started converting its short-term peso-denominated debt into *tesobonos*—short-term bonds that were indexed to the dollar-peso exchange rate and would protect investors from a devaluation. But as political uncertainty increased, even this was not protection enough. Investors started selling out, converting their pesos into dollars, and departing the country. The central bank's exchange reserves became depleted, and the new president, Ernesto Zedillo, had a full-blown crisis on his hands when he entered office. Eventually, an enormous loan was put together by the U.S. Treasury and the IMF to prevent Mexico from defaulting on its debts. Investors in the *tesobonos* were paid back, but the country went through a wrenching crisis, and those who held on to peso-denominated debt suffered heavy losses.

The 1994 Mexican crisis was a classic populist emerging-market crisis, driven by excessive government spending. The 1998 East Asian crisis was different, first because the crisis stemmed from excessive investment by countries that did save considerable amounts, and second because in many countries, the domestic private sector was centrally at fault. To understand what happened, we need to examine corporate investment in a producer-biased economy.

## Corporate Investment and Managed Capitalism

I argue above that bank funds are costly in a producer-biased economy, despite the subsidies offered to favored borrowers. In these economies, new corporate investment is most easily financed by resources that are produced by the corporations themselves—funds generated by growth in sales and profitability. For existing corporations that are well connected to the banks, this practice saves on costly borrowing. For corporations that are young and do not have strong bank relationships—such as the fast-growing but underfunded private sector in China —it may be the only option. Therefore corporations typically invest substantially more only when they grow faster, with their saved profits financing investment. The producer-biased strategy facilitates this kind of growth because the surplus value generated by the economy is allocated directly to producers, enhancing their profits and their ability to invest, instead of winding its way circuitously through households and a financial system that is incapable of lending effectively.

This kind of resource allocation is beneficial in some respects. Profitable corporations, which presumably have better investment opportunities, have more resources to invest in their existing businesses: profitability therefore drives investment, improving on the politicized investment decisions the state or the banking system would otherwise make. The danger, of course, is that profitable firms continue doing more of the same until they build overcapacity and extinguish the profits. For small countries focused on exports, the world market is typically large enough to make this possibility remote. For a large country like China, overcapacity is a clear and present danger.

Corporations mitigate such problems by diversifying. South Korea's *chaebols* —conglomerates with businesses in areas as diverse as construction and electronics—or India's family-owned conglomerates, like the Tatas or the Birlas, essentially try to replicate the role of the financial system by creating an internal capital market within the conglomerate. Although the loss of corporate focus in conglomerates has often been found to be a problem in developed countries, resulting in storied corporations like ITT or Litton Industries being broken up, conglomerates have proved very valuable in developing countries because the alternative—relying on the financial system for funds—is so inferior.[7]

Of course, if corporations want to grow really fast, internal funds may not be enough. Also, new entrants into emerging industries need financing. Fast-growing young industries may therefore move to borrowing from domestic banks. And if domestic savings are not enough, they have to borrow from foreign investors. This is what corporations in East Asian countries did in the early 1990s.

## Investing Too Much and the 1998 East Asian Crisis

We are already familiar with the export-led growth path followed by the East Asian economies. Having enjoyed a period of rapid growth, these economies started increasing their investment, financed with sizeable capital inflows from abroad in the early 1990s. Investment as a fraction of GDP, averaged across Korea, Malaysia, and Thailand, increased from an already high level of 29 percent in 1988 to an extraordinarily high 42 percent in 1996.

Yet these economies simply did not have the capacity to undertake this level of investment effectively. Ambitious corporations dreamed of silicon-wafer fabrication facilities, petrochemical complexes, and integrated steel plants. A $1.2 billion semiconductor plant started in Thailand in December 1995 as a joint venture between Texas Instruments and the Alphatec group was typical.[8] The fabrication facility was state-of-the-art, intended to produce 16- and 64-megabit dynamic random-access memory chips, with the output to be purchased by Texas Instruments. The eventual aim was to build a 4,000-acre high-tech park, called Alpha Technopolis, to rival Taiwan's famous Hsinchu Science-Based Industrial Park. The vision was grand, perhaps overly so.

After their initial role in directing credit and creating strong national champions, East Asian governments withdrew from the business of allocating credit, a task that had become much more difficult as businesses moved up the ladder of development into more complicated technologies. The task of credit allocation then devolved to domestic banks.

Domestic banks historically had overcome the impediments to lending— such as the difficulties of enforcing repayment—by developing near-incestuous, long-term relationships with firms. Regular visits and meetings with clients gave them access to information that was not public, as did cross-shareholdings and membership on the companies' boards. Furthermore, given the difficulty that outsiders had in accessing such information, the banks had a hold over their borrowers. Borrowers repaid for fear that their bank would cut them off from further funds and no one else would step up to lend.

Such relationships carried costs. Banks could not lend easily outside their existing circle of relationships, and they risked supporting client firms long after they should have been closed down. Outsiders had little idea of what was really going on in firms. Corporate practices were not transparent; nor were cash flows within or between the extensive corporate pyramids and cross-holdings. It was difficult to assess the extent to which a corporation was close to banks or the government and the extent of implicit or explicit support it could count on. Furthermore, the relative priority of other investors in claims to corporate assets in case of liquidation was uncertain, and the absence of a clear, effectively implemented bankruptcy code further reduced investor confidence.

As corporations invested at a faster rate than could be financed by domestic savings, they had to turn to foreign capital. But foreign investors, many of whom were banks, did not know much about domestic corporations and had little confidence that they would be able to enforce their rights in court. Unlike domestic banks, which enjoyed close relationships with firms, foreigners were not willing to lend long term and leave themselves exposed to potential malfeasance by corporations.

Instead, foreign creditors lent short term, in foreign currency, and often not to the corporation directly but to the domestic bank, which then lent to the corporations. Lending to the domestic bank effectively placed the government on the hook. Unless it was willing to see its banks fail, the betting was that the government, which was in fine health, would bail out a distressed bank, and hence its foreign lenders. Other foreign investors came in through the equity markets as portfolio investors, confident that they could sell and depart at the first sign of trouble.

The loans that domestic corporations took from their relationship banks were also typically denominated in foreign currency. Banks wanted to offload currency risk onto firms. The firms were willing to bear this risk because loans denominated in foreign currencies had lower interest rates, and the domestic currency had been relatively stable against foreign currencies.

The problem, therefore, was that managed capitalism was not equipped to deal with a plentiful supply of arm's-length money from outside. When money was scarce and the government directed lending, large projects were scrutinized carefully by the government before it directed certain banks to finance them. Although those close to the government benefited excessively from this privileged access to finance, there was at least a layer of oversight. Moreover, corporations had been careful because defaults against their traditional lenders could mean a permanent cutoff of funding. But now, with money plentifully supplied by foreign investors who themselves exercised little scrutiny because they thought they were well protected, competition to make loans heated up, and domestic corporations' fear of being cut off by domestic banks became remote. Corporations became less careful, and domestic banks, flooded with money that had to be lent, did not compensate by increasing their own diligence.

The East Asian crisis was thus largely a result of corporate overinvestment, in commercial real estate as well as manufacturing. And although the well-connected elite and investors stood to benefit if things went well, ultimately the risks of an economic collapse were borne by the government and hence by current and future generations of domestic taxpayers. Foreign borrowing was essentially a way for the country's private sector to socialize the risk of systemwide default.

A few governments contributed to the problem. For instance, the Vision 2020 plan set out by Malaysia's prime minister Mahathir Mohamad included the Bakun Dam (then Asia's largest hydropower dam), the Petronas Towers (one of the world's tallest buildings), a supermodern airport, and a new national administrative capital near Kuala Lumpur, appropriately called Putrajaya (City of Kings).[9] Mahathir's vision was certainly of pharaonic proportions: when I passed through Kuala Lumpur recently, the huge airport still looked impressive, well-maintained, and state-of-the-art—though it was largely bereft of planes and passengers. But generally, government excess was not the central problem (as it had been in previous developing-country crises, like that of Mexico in 1994). The fault lay with private excess funded by easy and hence dangerous foreign money.

The classic ingredients for a bust were in place: excessive investment financed with short-term debt, with the additional risk of a foreign-currency mismatch. All that was needed was the final trigger. This came from two related sources.

First, the overambitious investments themselves went sour. By early 1997, Alphatec had collapsed under its debts while its memory-chip plant was still under construction. Alphatec itself was only a small family-owned business with very limited experience in the semiconductor industry, and this lack of experience showed. Construction was plagued with delays: the plant was being built on land so marshy that concrete pilings had to be driven down to stabilize the buildings, at great cost. There was no clean water or power, both critical for chip manufacture, so Alphatec had to build the necessary facilities, adding further to costs. And even before high-tech plants like Alphatec's were completed, investors became concerned about their viability and started pulling out.

The second trigger was the depreciation of the Japanese yen against the dollar, starting in 1995. This made Japanese exports far more competitive than exports from East Asia, where currencies were linked more closely to the dollar. Rather than sourcing from Thailand, with its uncertain quality and small pool of scientists and engineers, importers around the world now preferred to return to tried and tested Japan. East Asian exports started faltering, corporate profitability plummeted, and investment projects started closing down.

Foreign investors started pulling out their money. Speculators joined the frenzy as they saw countries trying to defend exchange rates that were now distinctly overvalued. And as the countries used up their foreign exchange reserves in this defense, the likelihood of a devaluation became a certainty. The devaluation bankrupted first the many firms who had borrowed in foreign currencies and then the domestic banks that had lent to them. For even as these banks found that their borrowers could not repay, they had to repay their own foreign lenders. The East Asian miracle turned into a bust of gigantic proportions.

The East Asian banks turned to their governments, and the governments appealed to the IMF to give them the foreign currency that they needed to pay back foreign lenders and preserve their banks. Fund money came with conditions attached: actions that countries had to take—some before getting a loan, others after—to qualify as borrowers in good standing. Some conditions were relatively standard: after all, any lender, especially a lender who lends when no one else is willing, needs to put in place covenants to ensure that the borrower will repay. But others were onerous.

The East Asian governments believed the Fund overreached in two ways. First, it stipulated conditions that suggested it simply did not understand that it was dealing with a different client from its usual ones. By and large these were not governments, like Mexico's, that had overspent themselves into trouble. Rather, the domestic private sector had run amok with investment, with foreign lenders lacking discipline because of the implicit guarantees that they correctly surmised governments would honor. The immediate need was to restore financial stability, perhaps infuse some government stimulus to compensate for the sharp decline in economic activity, and then, with confidence restored, sort out the mess over time.

This was indeed what Western governments did in their own economies in 2008–2010, and what the IMF eventually turned to doing. But proud East Asian government officials were initially treated as derelicts who did not understand how to run clean governments. Overnight, managed capitalism was labeled crony capitalism, and there were certainly enough examples of cronyism to allow the Western financial press to go to town. Some of the initial policy advice from the Fund, the World Bank, and Western governments seemed to be focused on punishing the cronies, instead of recognizing that the system was so interconnected that many innocent people would suffer in the process. Empathy was missing, perhaps because managed capitalism seemed so alien to the outsiders who were now calling the shots.

The second way the Fund overreached was in setting conditions, often dictated by its major shareholders such as the United States, that attempted to reform the East Asian countries according to Western notions of governance. For instance, Indonesia was asked to undertake 140 or so actions in 1998, including disbanding the clove monopoly, strengthening reforestation programs, and introducing a microcredit scheme. To the cynic—and cynics were sometimes correct—these moves were really intended to open up large protected segments of the country to Western firms and advocacy groups. Although some of these measures may have benefited the country in the long run, these were decisions for the people themselves to take, not for foreign officials to require when the country was flat on its back. The unfortunate photo of the IMF managing director, Michel Camdessus, with his arms crossed and towering over a seemingly cowed President Suharto of Indonesia as he signed the IMF agreement suggested an image of the conqueror accepting the unconditional surrender of the defeated.[10] Although the true circumstances were more benign, the photo compounded the sense that this was a new form of financial colonialism.

### The Fault Line Deepens: The Divide between Developing Countries

In sum then, in a developed country, especially one with well-functioning capital markets and financial institutions, foreign investors typically have information and rights similar to those of domestic investors. They do not demand special rights and privileges; nor do they try to get implicit government backing (by lending via domestic banks) or explicit backing by lending to the government. Firms and households borrow directly, forcing foreign investors to make careful decisions. If they don't, they have only themselves to blame and have no recourse to the government.

In a developing country, by contrast, foreign borrowing is typically a last resort. Because foreign investors worry that they know far less than the well-connected domestic banks and are less able to enforce payment, they try to improve the security of their claims by requiring payment in foreign currency and by shortening the maturity of their loans. Paradoxically, the underdevelopment of the domestic financial system allows the late-arriving foreign investors to demand and receive privileges that typically eat into the value of the existing domestic investors' claims or, via the implicit guarantees offered by the government, into the taxpayers' wealth. Moreover, the protection they receive makes them less careful about what they finance. In turn, because borrowers, whether the current government or banks, do not face the full cost of foreign borrowing, they have a tendency to overborrow.

Parenthetically, readers will note that the U.S. subprime market, with its substantial quasi-government presence, was a departure from the developed-country norm and in many ways reflected the deficiencies present in developing countries. This is precisely the analogy that needs to be drawn. I return to these issues later in the book.

## Reforms

The crises of the 1990s had a differential impact on economies. Countries that were saving too little were forced into much-needed reforms. For countries like India, which experienced a crisis in 1991 as a result of large government and current-account deficits, and Latin American economies like Brazil, whose vulnerability stemmed from too little saving, the crises were a signal that the old model of managed but inward-looking capitalism was broken. Both India and Brazil liberalized their economies, reducing government control and ownership, removing price and interest-rate controls, bringing greater competition into the financial system, opening up to imports and foreign investment, and letting the exchange rate float. They also adopted more sensible macroeconomic policies, cutting government deficits (for a while at least) and improving monetary management.

During the long period of protected managed growth, they had built strong corporate organizations that were fully capable of prospering as competition increased. And enhanced competition brought out the best in these companies. Tata Steel (before it acquired the European steel giant Corus) had one of the lowest costs of steel production in the world, while Embraer, a privatized Brazilian aircraft manufacturer, developed a strong market in midsized planes around the world.

These late liberalizers had large enough domestic markets that they did not have to favor the export sector. Both Brazil and India "managed" their exchange rate, but they did not try to gain a serious competitive advantage by trying to hold it down. Moreover, with firms already strong, they did not have to repress the household sector—not that their now-vibrant democracies would have allowed them to! They liberalized deposit interest rates, cut taxes on households, and allowed the financial sector to expand household credit. As a result, both Brazil and India have healthy levels of private consumption and domestic-oriented production sectors that are almost as efficient as their export-oriented sectors. Although a boom in commodities has led to a rapid expansion in Brazil's exports, its economy is diversified and resilient enough to weather a temporary drop in commodities prices if it comes. For both these countries, the silver lining in the cloud of having missed the right moment to switch to exports is that they have not had to switch back. They now enjoy more balanced economies, less dependent on exports for growth.

The East Asian economies, with the exception of Indonesia, recovered quickly: their devalued currencies made them very competitive, and they expanded exports even while replacing imports with cheaper domestic production. They also slashed investment—on average, across Korea, Malaysia, and Thailand, investment came down from 41 percent of GDP in 1996 to 24 percent of GDP in 1998, and it stayed low. Domestic savings picked up a little initially, from 38 percent of GDP to 41 percent of GDP, but drifted down over time to below 1996 levels. This is important, for the reason for their rising trade surpluses is not that East Asian households cut back dramatically on consumption and increased their savings. Instead, governments and corporations cut back on investment. The net effect on the world's supply of savings was the same—from being net borrowers from the world economy, the East Asian economies started pumping their savings into it. But demand for investment goods—for hard assets such as plant and equipment—plummeted. These were typically goods that had been imported, so the reverberations were felt around the globe. The global supply glut again went looking for countries that would overspend.

## Summary and Conclusion

Countries that had focused on export-led growth learned an important lesson. It is a fool's game to succumb to the temptation of cheap goods and easy money: rapid debt-fueled spending invariably ends in tears. More specifically, because managed capitalism was hard for foreign investors to understand or navigate, they responded by retaining the right to exit at short notice, holding equity or short-term debt claims. And exit they did, sometimes without full regard to the country's fundamentals, so that financing with flighty foreign capital was akin to running a small bank without deposit insurance—a recipe for fragility. Although the exporters did understand the need for financial-sector reform, they did not believe that the crises indicated any problems in the broader strategy of export-led growth. Instead, the crises reinforced their beliefs that generating trade surpluses was even better than simply being export oriented, for it allowed the country to build foreign exchange reserves. The route to such surpluses was to cut back on investment, which also helped these countries avoid the boom-bust cycle in investments to which they had been prone.

The attempt by these exporters to achieve safety, though, has increased the rest of the world's vulnerability. The supercharged export-led growth strategy they have subsequently followed not only increases the burden on the rest of the world to create demand for their goods, but it also accentuates the domestic distortions the strategy previously created, which were highlighted in the previous chapter.

The new strategy also led to an enormous buildup of the exporters' foreign-exchange reserves. These reserves went looking for a home around the world. To attract them, a country had to be willing to spend much more than its own producers could supply, and it needed a strong financial system capable of attracting the inflows and reassuring the exporters that their savings would be safe, safer than the developing countries had been. The obvious candidate was the United States (along with, to a lesser extent, Spain and the United Kingdom).

The United States, with growing inequality making the political environment favorable to more debt-financed consumption (as I argue in Chapter 1), was a prime candidate to be the new demander of last resort. However, the policies in the early years of this century that pushed it firmly into the role of the world's new designated spender were driven by a new phenomenon: recoveries in the United States were increasingly "jobless," and the U.S. safety net was wholly inadequate to cope with them.

CHAPTER FOUR

# A Weak Safety Net

B ADRI ENTERED THE UNITED STATES as a student more than a quarter century ago.[1] After obtaining a handful of degrees, including a PhD in metallurgical engineering, he got a job in 1997 in a joint venture between a German firm and an American firm near Washington, DC, making state-of-the-art memory chips. Badri's first job was to help set up the fabrication line for a new set of chips and to reduce the fraction of defective chips produced. The task made full use of his considerable knowledge and skills because it required troubleshooting really complicated processes and machines. Seventy-hour weeks were common.

Over time, the American partner sold out. The German firm spun off the joint venture into a separate firm with its own traded shares, and later this firm split into two, with one part focusing on logic chips while the other part focused on the capital-intensive memory chip. So even as Badri spent years specializing in memory-chip fabrication, making smaller and smaller chips from larger and larger wafers, the company also shrunk—from being a joint venture between two large, deep-pocketed firms to being a diversified chip maker and eventually a stand-alone, narrowly focused, heavily indebted firm, in a capital-intensive industry with a history of feast-and-famine cycles.

The inevitable happened. After making a huge investment in the latest new technology, Badri's employer found itself in financial difficulties in early 2008. It had the choice of shutting down either its U.S. plant or its German plant. Knowing that it would face greater difficulties in shutting down the German plant and that it might be able to bargain for subsidies from the German government, it laid off all the workers at its U.S. plant.

Overnight, Badri found his six-figure income gone. Because the firm declared bankruptcy, it did not have to provide severance pay to compensate him for the 11 years he had worked at the firm. All he had now was a weekly unemployment check of $400, out of which he had to support his family of four as well as pay a mortgage. Even more worrisome was health insurance. He had been paying $50 a month for health insurance provided through his firm, which would no longer cover him and his family. As he turned to private insurance companies, he found that they refused to cover him because he had an elevated blood-sugar level and was at mild risk for diabetes. Even without this complication, private insurance would cost $1,100 per month for the family, which would eat up two-thirds of his unemployment insurance. Badri really needed a job, at the very least so that he did not have to play Russian roulette with his health and finances by remaining uninsured. He sent out hundreds of résumés, but no one was hiring. His unemployment insurance was running out, and he would have to eat into the savings set aside for his son's college education. In this respect, Badri was one of the lucky ones. Unlike many Americans in his situation, he had some savings!

In the meantime, his firm's U.S. assets were liquidated piecemeal, with other chip manufacturers buying some of the expensive machines for their own fabrication plants. These assets were quickly redeployed into new, profitable uses. Many months after closing the U.S. plant, the firm was forced to recognize the inevitable—that its business was uneconomic—and it closed the German plant also.

## The Willingness to Stimulate

We saw in the last chapter that in the late 1990s and early 2000s, the surpluses of the traditional exporters, augmented by the goods the developing countries were no longer buying, were looking for a market. With the world in recession after the dot-com bust, the United States pursued extremely expansionary fiscal and monetary policies over a sustained period, thus creating the excess demand to absorb the surpluses, financed with the savings that surplus countries were generating. In part, as I have argued, the United States had no option but to be the world's demander of last resort, because countries like Germany and Japan could not pull their weight. But the United States did not follow expansionary policies out of a sense of global citizenship. Instead, it was driven by its own domestic compulsions to stimulate to excess.

Badri's experience suggests an important reason why. Unlike workers in other rich industrial economies, workers in the United States are not automatically supported if a recession is deep and prolonged.[2] Americans have historically opposed substantial welfare: as a result, the country's safety net, including unemployment benefits, is weak. Since World War II, its economic system has been structured so that it reacts quickly and nimbly to adversity. Banks cut off poorly performing firms from new loans, while venture capitalists pull the plug on underperforming start-ups. Existing firms are shut down, and their assets are liquidated and sold to those who can use them better, as happened with Badri's firm. All this activity creates space for new firms to emerge. And because unemployment benefits do not last long, workers who lose jobs have strong incentives to find new ones, even if it involves a pay cut, changing careers, or moving across the continent.

Perhaps as a result of these circumstances, postwar recoveries prior to 1990 were rapid—on average, output recovered to prerecession levels within two quarters, and lost jobs were recovered eight months after the recession trough.[3] Government and central bank policy were meant to help in downturns, but only at the margin. Most of the brief pain was meant to be borne by banks, firms, and workers.

However, the 1990–91 recession broke this postwar mold. Output growth came back quickly, but jobs did not. Whereas production recovered within three quarters in 1991, it took 23 months from the trough of the recession to recover the lost jobs in 1991 recession. Those out of work or facing job losses are understandably anxious as they face potentially long periods of unemployment with few savings, a very limited period of unemployment benefits, and no health insurance. Politicians ignore the concerns of the anxious citizenry at their own peril. George H. W. Bush learned this the hard way: despite presiding over the end of the Cold War and a decisive victory in the first Gulf War, he lost his reelection campaign to Bill Clinton, largely as a result of voter dissatisfaction over job losses during the recession of 1990–91. One of Clinton's guiding principles, set forth by the campaign strategist James Carville, was "It's the economy, stupid." That lesson has been firmly absorbed. The view that the current unemployment rate is central to reelection prospects dominates thinking in Washington.

The weak safety net and the emergence of jobless recoveries imply that the American electorate has far less tolerance for downturns than voters in other industrial countries. The reason that stimulus was applied so long during the recovery from the 2001 recession was that even though output recovered in just one quarter in 2001, it took 38 months after the trough of the 2001 recession for all the lost jobs to be restored. Indeed, job losses continued well into the recovery. In an attempt to induce recalcitrant firms into creating jobs, both the government and the Federal Reserve, especially the latter, ended up aiding and abetting a house-price bubble and the financial crisis.

As the United States struggles with near-double-digit unemployment at the time of writing, there is panic in the corridors of power in Washington. Meanwhile, the capitals of continental Europe, where unemployment safety nets are stronger, seem to be taking similar levels of unemployment in their stride. Once again, there is extraordinary political pressure on Congress and the Federal Reserve to somehow produce jobs. Although there are some virtues to retaining the flexibility to tailor policy to the situation, policy made under the political gun and with political rather than economic objectives typically does not produce effective policy. It has two important effects: first, as I argue in this chapter, it tends to make the United States the reliable stimulator of first resort for the world, taking the burden off other countries and giving them less incentive to alter their growth strategies. Second, as I argue in the next chapter, the excessive political incentive to stimulate produces monetary policy that warps incentives in the financial sector and contributes to the kind of financial disaster we have just experienced.

## The Weak Safety Net

An important historical difference between the United States and most continental European countries has been the level of unemployment benefits. For example, a comprehensive study over the period 1989–94 shows that U.S. unemployment benefits were not only somewhat lower than in most continental European countries—the United States, on average, replaced 50 percent of lost wages, while France replaced 57 percent and Germany 63 percent—but these benefits ran out much more quickly. In the United States, on average, benefits ran out in six months, whereas in France benefits lasted for up to three years, and in Germany they lasted indefinitely. Since that study, German reforms have brought down the duration of benefits to one and a half years, but the maximum wage-replacement rates in both France and Germany have been increased somewhat, with little change in the United States.

There are holes even in the relatively scant unemployment benefits on offer in the United States. Although more than 90 percent of workers are covered by unemployment insurance, only about 40 percent of them receive benefits when they become unemployed. Some don't qualify for benefits because they have not worked long enough, others because they left voluntarily, yet others because they are involved in labor disputes, and still others because they do not make themselves available for work while unemployed.[4]

The worry for someone who loses a job in the United States is compounded by the absence of universal health care or affordable private medical insurance. Because America's tax code subsidizes health insurance provided through employers, the unemployed have to pay several times more to get the same benefits they obtained previously through their jobs. Moreover, even when individuals can afford it, private insurers can refuse them coverage if they have even a mild preexisting medical condition, as Badri did. Given that even the apparently healthy could have a preexisting condition they are unaware of, most Americans are understandably anxious about potential unemployment, and the desire of the unemployed to rejoin the ranks of the employed is immense. And when Americans are anxious, they are not shy about letting their representatives know. As unemployment mounts, so too does the pressure on politicians to do something.

## Jobless Recoveries

As we have seen, job growth in the United States from the trough of postwar recessions has typically been rapid. Thus even though the unemployment benefits are of short duration, in previous downturns they were enough to support most of the unemployed until they found a job. In contrast to the situation in continental European countries, long-term unemployment has been rare, perhaps because the short duration of benefits forced the unemployed to search harder and settle for less.

Economists are still arguing over why the 1990–91 and 2001 recessions in the United States were different. One theory is that unlike in past recessions, in which factories laid off workers temporarily when demand was low and rehired them when demand recovered, the economy at these times was undergoing deep structural change.[5] Resources were moving from mature old industries to new young ones—from steel to software, so to speak. As a result, laid-off workers had to search much harder and also retrain themselves for the available jobs—hence the jobless recovery. Although this argument is plausible, the evidence that there was much more mobility of workers between industries during these recessions is weak.

Another explanation has to do with the "cleansing" role of recessions. In the same way as regular small fires rid forests of undergrowth that could contribute to a greater and more devastating conflagration, recessions force firms to think hard about their resources and compel them to reallocate resources ruthlessly in a way that would not occur in more normal times. In the process they help the economy avoid deeper long-term damage. For example, supervisors accumulate all sorts of unproductive employees and positions over the course of expansions. Not only is it personally painful for a supervisor to fire an incompetent employee, it also damages morale among the rest of the staff, so the natural tendency is to avoid harsh actions. A recession offers supervisors an excuse to cut the dead wood: "We have to cut jobs in order to remain competitive." Furthermore, the anxiety of surviving employees is limited to the duration of the recession. Firms therefore use recessions to clean house effectively.[6]

What was different about the 1990–91 and 2001 recessions is that each came after nearly a decade of growth. According to this view, firms had acquired far more "undergrowth" during the long expansion: thus more cleansing was necessary and its effects more prolonged. Put differently, the longer the years of plenty, the longer the famine. But because we have not had many postwar recessions following long expansions, the evidence for this explanation is not overwhelming either.

Yet another hypothesis has to do with improvements in the hiring process. In earlier recoveries, firms would put out advertisements for positions, people would reply by mail, be screened, and then be called for interviews, all of which took time. Long lead times in hiring meant that firms had to worry that they might not have enough employees to meet the growing demand and could lose sales if they did not start hiring early enough. With the advent of the Internet, it is easier for firms with positions and candidates with the right qualifications to find a match. The Internet also makes it easier for firms to wait and watch their order books, hiring just in time to meet demand.[7] Of course, when every firm does this, it diminishes the incentive to hire: not only does unemployment persist, depressing demand, but the pool of available candidates is also likely to remain large, so there is no urgency to move quickly to hire the best candidates.

One piece of evidence in support of the "just-in-time" hiring theory is the greater dependence of firms on temporary workers in the two most recent recoveries, which suggests a reluctance on the part of firms to create permanent jobs. As temporary jobs grow in the current recovery also, William Dennis of the National Federation of Independent Business reaffirmed this view, saying: "When a job comes open now, our members fill it with a temp, or they extend a part-timer's hours, or they bring in a freelancer—and then they wait to see what will happen next."[8]

Regardless of which of the theories is right, if most or all future recoveries are likely to be jobless, the United States, with its weak safety net, is singularly unprepared for them.

## Why Is the Safety Net Weak?

Why are unemployment benefits so much more limited in the United States? Americans are not necessarily less caring or generous than the citizens of other rich countries. In fact, Americans typically give more to charity than people in many other industrial countries. According to one study in 2000, the average American gave $691 to charity, while the average for the United Kingdom was $141 and for Europe as a whole $57.⁹ If the explanation is not stinginess, what is it? There is no single answer to this question, but understanding the genesis of this policy is critical to figuring out why the United States has not been able to reform its system easily, and why so much of a burden has fallen on policy stimulus in recent times.

### *The Economic Answers*

Caricatures are useful because they can draw out the essential nature of the object being caricatured. If I had to caricature U.S. firms (or more broadly, Anglo-American firms, encompassing firms from Australia, Canada, New Zealand, the United Kingdom, and the United States), I would describe them broadly as *operating at arm's length* with their suppliers, lenders, customers, and employees, *innovative and radical* in thought and action, and *ruthless* in assigning both blame and rewards. Contrast these attributes with firms in continental Europe or Japan, which are better described as relying on *long-term relationships* with suppliers, banks, customers, and employees, *incremental* in thought and action, and more willing to share pain and gain among their associates. The spirit of the long-term relationship rather than the letter of the legal contract drives interactions.

These characteristics are neither static nor all-encompassing. Firms across the world are changing rapidly. In Japan, a country once famed for long-term employment, a career spent working for one company is no longer the norm, and a large number of young workers occupy temporary positions. Nor would it be difficult to find caring, sharing firms that have strong relationships with suppliers in the United States or ruthless ones in Europe. But I did say these were caricatures, correct in the broad sweep rather than in fine detail.

The point of drawing out these characteristics is to argue that they may belong together and may generate different forms of safety net. Specifically, mature firms in the arm's-length Anglo-American economies face a market-oriented financial system that depends on transparency and disclosure. Hard information like quarterly sales, earnings, and cash flow can be easily transmitted to investors in the market. But the more up-to-date information that management gets, such as incoming sales numbers or inventory buildup, as well as market rumors, is not easy to transmit widely to investors because it could be inaccurate as well as less concrete. Moreover, soft information such as management character, capabilities, and strength of purpose—which can often be gauged over time through personal meetings—simply cannot be transmitted to the market other than through assessments by investment analysts, whose own views may color their judgment. How, for instance, can investors gauge whether the CEO is in touch with everything that is going on in the firm or simply the talking head delivering the PowerPoint presentation at investor meetings—especially when he is politically astute at choosing which questions to answer?

By contrast, in the continental European and Japanese system, firms have stronger, longer-term, more relationship-based interactions with investors, who are typically institutions like banks and insurance companies. Firms can share tremendous amounts of inside as well as soft information with a banker whom they have interacted with for years. This relationship improves the banker's ability to make sound lending decisions and shape management actions, and the relationship gives her a greater incentive to help a troubled client firm because she knows the client will not abandon her lightly when good times come around.[10]

The arm's-length system applies pressure for hard measurable and communicable results, because this is how the market gauges top management. The pressure travels through the system, and managers who do not make their numbers are put on notice. In a downturn, the pressure is especially high because earnings become a key indicator of whether a firm is profitable and whether it should be cut off from funding. Firms have little incentive to nurse excess labor through a downturn, preferring instead to lay off redundant workers and hire them back, or hire new ones once the recovery sets in. Similarly, the market ruthlessly cuts off underperforming firms from finance, ensuring that they have to be restructured or liquidated—much as it forced Badri's employer to close its U.S. operations.

The relationship system allows top management a little more leeway. Because lenders know the management and can look beyond the numbers in a downturn, they can live with lower profitability for a while. The pressure to fire redundant workers is lower, especially if they are considered important and hard to replace in the longer term. Conversely, workers are more loyal and have the incentive to develop skills that make them especially valuable to the firm, even if those skills are not easily marketable elsewhere. Finally, governments tend to be willing to go the extra mile to preserve existing jobs.

A recent example of the differences may be useful.[11] In early 2009, as a result of the financial panic and the associated difficulty in securing financing, car demand plummeted around the world. In both North America and Europe, politicians approved billions of dollars of aid to car manufacturers because they felt the millions of jobs tied to the industry made it too big to fail. In the United States, General Motors and Chrysler secured government funding on condition that they take drastic action to restructure their firms, close unviable plants, and sell unprofitable brands. After an initial restructuring plan was rejected by government overseers as too timid, the firms did indeed take drastic action, emerging from bankruptcy significantly shrunken. By contrast, in France, Peugeot and Renault received substantial amounts of government funds on condition that they close no plants and fire no workers over the term of the government loan!

Does this mean the Anglo-American arm's-length system is all bad? Not necessarily. Resources are reallocated more quickly to profitable uses: perhaps the car industry does need to shrink substantially. Apart from the added efficiency, the willingness to be ruthless helps innovation. Past experience and relationships are of little value in driving radical innovation: indeed, because the natural human tendency is to do more of the same and to serve existing clients and needs well, past relationships can be positively detrimental.[12] The arm's-length approach has advantages here. For one, because new firms can be matched with new financiers, a wider range of matches is possible, and there is greater potential for new ideas to be financed. Also, because bad ideas are not permitted to continue sucking resources, this system can engage in riskier experimentation. The ruthlessness of venture capitalists in killing bad ideas once they are recognized to be unviable is far more important to their success than the ability to identify diamonds in the rough. The arm's-length system plants a thousand flowers, uproots hundreds when they do not thrive, and nurtures only a few to bloom. New opportunities abound, while old, tired ways of doing business are ruthlessly eliminated. The system's strength, then, is that it is not heavily biased toward preserving the privileges of incumbent firms and workers.

In the "relationship" system, incremental change comes easily because existing firms are able to develop variations on old themes, and financiers, having developed a deep understanding of the existing business, are willing to finance moderate innovation. But because few new firms can break in, and because the system is not geared toward generating dependable, hard information that would make new investors comfortable, dramatic innovation is harder. And because the system is not geared toward ruthlessly eliminating bad ideas, its willingness to experiment radically is also more limited. Badri's employer retained its German plant longer than its American plant in large part because of the nature of the system each plant operated in. And the more prolonged death throes of the German plant suggest that more resources were indeed wasted there while trying to maintain an unviable operation.

That U.S. research and development tends to be more innovative is suggested by the following data: in 2008, the United States and the European Union, which are roughly similar in the size of their GDP, accounted for about the same share of journal articles published worldwide in science and engineering (28.1 percent versus 33.1 percent). But the United States had a 51.6 percent share of the most highly cited (and thus typically pathbreaking) articles, while Europe had only a 29.6 percent share.[13]

The compatibility between the economic system and the nature of unemployment benefits is clear in the United States. The emphasis is on rapid restructuring in the face of distress, terminating dying enterprises, and financing new businesses. Recessions are a time of both destruction and new creation. Not only are jobs destroyed, but a whole set of new ones are created. Short-duration benefits give the laid-off worker the incentive to actively look for a suitable job. Mobility is easy across firms: because of the large number of workers being laid off, there is no stigma attached to unemployment. Entry into employment is also easy because jobs are not clogged up by incumbents; the constant churn frees positions. Badri, forced to find a job quickly, eventually moved to a start-up in the Midwest, earning a fraction of his earlier salary. But he is productively employed doing research on new materials and is acquiring an array of new skills.

The generous and long-duration unemployment benefits of the relationship system may appear less compatible with the relatively secure long-term jobs in that system. After all, greater job security would suggest a lower need for long-duration benefits. The reason that long-duration benefits make sense is the greater degree of specialization of jobs in the system and therefore the diminished mobility. The relationship system tends to be one of insiders and outsiders. Those on the inside—employed in firms or the government—have a fairly comfortable, secure existence. Those on the outside have a hard time breaking in, and the unfortunate few who lose their jobs and join the ranks of the outsiders are damned both because their past specialization may make it much harder to find appropriate jobs and because the system is not geared toward rapid and easy reentry. In such as system, unemployment benefits do little to expedite job searches; rather, they make a prolonged existence on the outside more tolerable and appease the anger of the unemployed.

Thus each system has developed unemployment benefits that are compatible with its underlying economic structure. This is not to say everything is perfect. Badri's job was clearly highly specialized, yet he was cast adrift overnight, without protection. Moreover, it is hard to say which came first: the benefits or the structure. Indeed, it is also possible that a common third factor, such as ideology or politics, drives both.

## The Politics of Benefits

The United States is parsimonious not just with unemployment benefits but with other forms of social welfare also. At the time of writing, it does not have universal health coverage, despite spending a greater fraction of GDP on health care than nearly any other advanced country. And it spends less on many other welfare programs. For instance, the United States spent 7 percent of GDP on old-age pensions and disability payments in 1998, whereas France spent 13.7 percent and Germany 12.8 percent.[14] Retirement benefits to people over age 65 were only 19.3 percent of the average worker's pretax income in the United States, compared to 58.6 percent in France and 37.2 percent in Germany. It is not that Americans have plenty of savings to compensate: the McKinsey Global Institute indicates that two-thirds of the early baby boomers—those born between 1945 and 1954, and among the wealthiest generations in history—do not have enough assets to retire comfortably.[15]

There may well be special aspects of the U.S. historical experience that drives its antipathy toward all forms of welfare benefits. Among these include the libertarian tradition in politics, the absence of strong nationwide workers' organizations, the concentration of poverty in segments of the population that are racially different, the large size and easy mobility within the economy, and the existence of competing economic jurisdictions that make centralized legislation difficult.

A number of historians have argued that there is something fundamentally liberal (in the classical or Lockean sense, that is, embracing the freedom of the individual and resisting significant government intervention in ordinary life) embedded in the cultural and political ethos of the United States. Having escaped the tyrannies and feudalism of the Old World, Americans did not have to combat a strong domestic aristocracy.[16] As a result, they did not develop a strong class consciousness or the need to use government to overpower oppressive domestic elites. The beliefs that are still expressed by many Americans in surveys—that the United States has virtually unlimited opportunities, that everyone has the capacity to become rich if they only work hard enough, and that anyone who remains poor probably has not tried hard enough—sit well with a desire for limited government and welfare. And although American opportunity and mobility may be a myth for the immobile and poor underclass and increasingly for much of the middle class, the reality of their experience has not yet altered the national ethos.[17]

A parallel set of arguments ascribes the American difference to the absence of strong workers' organizations in the United States. White American males did not have to fight domestic elites for the right to vote. As a result, a national workers' movement never really took hold in the United States—in contrast to the United Kingdom, for example, where workers' organizations developed during the fight for the vote in the nineteenth century.[18] The right to vote might have been an all-encompassing issue that united workers who were otherwise divided by local differences in work conditions and objectives. That it did not occur left labor unions fragmented.

Indeed, in the second half of the nineteenth century when strong labor unions were developing elsewhere, the fact that the United States was a large country with an uncultivated "frontier" meant that workers could simply pull up stakes and move if they found local conditions oppressive, and this flexibility in turn also limited the extent to which conditions could become oppressive for the mobile worker. The difficulty of organizing a nationwide workers' movement in a country where differences in circumstances were sizeable, and workers had individual options to exit tough conditions by moving on, should not be underestimated.

A related argument for why strong nationwide worker organizations did not develop is that (except in the South) the United States lacked a large oppressed peasantry who could make common cause with workers, and it did not experience the desperate deprivation and breakdown of authority that occurred in many countries in Europe after each of the world wars. Indeed, only 20 percent of the labor force in Western Europe had some form of pension insurance before World War I, only 22 percent had health insurance, and unemployment insurance was almost unheard of. Workers, many of whom had become politically aware while fighting in the trenches of World War I, organized after the war to demand some form of protection against economic adversity.[19] Their demands were voiced by socialist parties that gained strength in the postwar chaos, and many European countries did enact pro-worker legislation. By contrast, socialist parties have never commanded much voting power in the United States.

We should also not minimize the importance of population heterogeneity. "There but for the grace of God go I" offers a powerful rationale for social insurance. People are more willing to be taxed to benefit others if they believe that the benefits go largely to people like themselves, and not disproportionately to groups they do not identify with. This may also explain why Americans give generously to charities: they have more control over who the beneficiaries are.[20] Politicians who want to derail benefits legislation have often been quick to raise the specter of hard-earned taxpayer money going to the undeserving, irresponsible, and lazy, and such demagoguery is especially potent when the bogeymen look and behave differently from their constituents.

In much of the twentieth century, the targets for demagogues were African Americans, but over time Americans have learned to recognize the deeper purpose behind such language. More recently, illegal immigrants have emerged as the new target, and much angst is expended over the possibility that benefits may leak to them. Indeed, a battle has erupted in the most recent round of health care legislation over the access of illegal immigrants to any form of taxpayer-funded programs. In this debate, few legislators have asked how U.S. society can remain healthy and humane with a sick and unprotected immigrant population in its midst.

Finally, business interests and money power have always been an important force in the United States. Although these interests had the same difficulty in organizing as workers did in a large, diverse country—except when a specific piece of legislation collectively affected them and united them in opposition—they had two strengths workers lacked. First, firm owners aggregated the economic power of their firms and thus were individually much more powerful than any of their workers, even if owners as a group were not well organized. Second, if business conditions became oppressive in one state, owners could move investment to another state. The threat of the loss of business investment and the associated taxes gave states, especially industrial ones, strong incentives not to reduce business profitability.

Of course, not all benefits reduce long-term profitability. Firm owners are typically not hard-hearted Dickensian figures, squeezing every drop of blood out of their workers—indeed, such behavior rarely maximizes profits. Workers who feel safer (because of unemployment insurance and pension benefits) and are healthier (because of health insurance) might indeed be happier and work more enthusiastically for their employers, especially in skilled jobs where worker effort is essential but hard to monitor. It is likely, though, that in the early twentieth century, a significant proportion of U.S. employers were small and could not afford to pay benefits, and the nature of the work they offered did not require workers to be happy or enthusiastic. Fear of making these firms uncompetitive, and losing these kinds of businesses to other states, may well have prevented states from legislating benefits.[21]

Nevertheless, the safety net in the United States, albeit weak, does exist. Despite all the above-mentioned difficulties, legislation protecting workers was indeed passed during the Great Depression. The centerpiece of the legislation was the Social Security Act of 1935, which instituted not only old-age social security benefits but also unemployment insurance. Why did it happen when it did? The answers are interesting, for they suggest ways in which change may occur again in the United States.

First, the pain workers felt from Depression-era unemployment was immense and persistent. Unemployment quickly rose into double digits by mid-1930, peaking at 24.9 percent in 1933 but never coming down into single digits throughout the 1930s, despite a supposed recovery (and another subsequent plunge) during the Depression.[22] In 1939, at the onset of World War II, unemployment was around 18 percent. Moreover, it was nationwide. In John Steinbeck's haunting novel *The Grapes of Wrath,* the Joads, Oklahoma tenant farmers whose farm is no longer profitable, go looking for jobs in the promised land of California, only to find that there are none there either. This time, moving on was not the answer, and the effect was to unify worker demands across the country.

Second, Franklin Roosevelt obtained a strong political mandate, and broad nationwide legislation overcame the collective-action problem each state faced: the fear of frightening away business if it legislated worker protection alone.[23] Third, there were exceptions carved out in the legislation: for instance, in a nod to the powerful Southern Democrats who did not want to raise the cost of their black workers (or have the legislation derailed by politicians raising fears that benefits would go to blacks), agricultural workers were not covered. Finally, surprising as it may seem, strong business interests also supported the legislation.[24]

This last reason is interesting. Why would businesses want to increase their own costs? Having the state provide worker benefits had two tremendous advantages for some firms, especially large ones. First, firms that already paid their workers benefits like old-age pensions (because these made broader economic sense, as discussed earlier), could offload some of the costs on to the state. Moreover, all firms, especially pesky small competitors to big business, would be subject to the additional costs, whether or not they were able to increase profits by providing worker benefits. And for small firms employing unskilled workers, the imposition of worker benefits typically increased costs without any redeeming increase in profits. Thus the legislation reduced competition for powerful incumbents by eliminating one of the important advantages of entrants: their ability to pay low wages and benefits. Like much of the legislation during the New Deal era, the good parts came with bad, anticompetitive elements.

What are the lessons from all of this? Huge adverse economic shocks have powerful effects on concentrating the national mind because everyone is similarly affected. They thus offer opportunity for change. Even so, and despite large legislative majorities, compromise is inevitable because people also look beyond the calamity to their interests in the recovery. Finally, there is typically a trade-off between competition, innovation, flexibility, access, and efficiency on the one hand, and security on the other. Security implies a protection of privilege, a protection that has to be indiscriminate if it is to calm anxiety. But this invariably means that resources will be transferred to beneficiaries regardless of the efficiency with which they can use them. One person's safety comes at the expense of another's opportunity or efficiency, and good legislation has to tread carefully to achieve the right balance.

### The Problem with Discretionary Stimulus

I have argued that there are a number of reasons why the United States has a weak safety net. But why is that a problem? After all, the United States has a flourishing democracy that responds to the concerns of the people and can enact policies in a downturn to help those who are in difficulty. Unfortunately, policy made in the midst of a downturn is often hurried, opportunistic, and poorly thought out. Although deep crises offer an opportunity for serious rethinking and transformation, if new policies have to be devised in response to every downturn, the result is inappropriate, unpredictable, and excessive policy making.

John Maynard Keynes, perhaps the most influential economist after Karl Marx, argued that recessions were caused by a deficit of demand, and that governments could play a role in a recovery by increasing spending, financed by running budget deficits. His views enjoyed immense influence in the decades after World War II, but his policy recommendations were effectively institutionalized earlier, during the Depression, through structures such as unemployment insurance. If demand faltered, the government would automatically transfer purchasing power to people, for example through unemployment benefits. Also, because firms would pay lower taxes as a result of lower profits, taxes were effectively reduced. Most mainstream economists believed the case for increasing government spending beyond these "automatic stabilizers," except in truly severe recessions, was weak. Instead, much of the task of putting the economy back on the road to recovery was left to monetary policy.

In the United States, though, the absence of a strong safety net, coupled with slow job growth in recoveries, has made every one of the recent recessions "truly severe" from a political perspective. This has created tremendous pressure on governments to stimulate, both through fiscal means—tax cuts and spending increases—and through easy monetary policy. Some parts of the stimulus do go toward extending the safety net—for example, unemployment insurance benefits and subsidies for health insurance have been extended in the current recession for some laid-off workers. But stimulus packages invariably do a lot more. The key question therefore is this: If job recoveries continue to be slow, is there a problem with allowing stimulus to be discretionary instead of strengthening the safety net?

There is! First, workers themselves face tremendous anxiety when benefits are discretionary because they do not know if the recession will be deep and prolonged enough to provoke stimulus spending, and, even if it does, whether they will benefit. Second, both fiscal and monetary policies work with lags. The expenditure for roads that is voted on today will probably not be spent until many months from now. But voters want politicians to respond to their current needs. A politician's counsel of patience is taken as a reflection of impotence and is therefore not conducive to her reelection. If the current unemployment rate as well as current job growth drive policy actions, then it is possible that policy will remain far too stimulative for far too long. The roads that are budgeted for today will be built a year from now, when recovery is already well under way, potentially causing the economy to overheat and forcing costly policy reversals then.

Third, and perhaps most important, discretion leads to abuse. More problematic, when politicians exercise discretion at a time of great necessity, it leads to inventive abuse. Specifically, politicians bring out all their pet projects during a downturn, and then some more, all under the guise of stimulus to support recovery. Significant elements of spending are simply payback to powerful interest groups, or a fulfillment of election promises with little need to justify their short-term benefit. Over one-third of the stimulus package passed by the Obama administration in its early months consisted of one-time tax rebates, which are known to, and did, have little effect on spending: they were more a form of redistribution to fulfill election promises.[25]

As an example of more egregiously directed spending, $6.5 billion was approved for cancer research to appease a particular senator.[26] Cancer research is unlikely to create many jobs in the short term: indeed, it would be more appropriate if the money were spent slowly rather than wasted on harebrained proposals fished out from the bottom of researchers' drawers in response to an announcement of new grant funding. Yet it features as part of the stimulus simply because the need to pass a stimulus package gives every politician the right to a share of the pork.

Finally, even as I write, the real estate industry has ensured the renewal of a "temporary" tax break to first-time home buyers on the grounds that withdrawing it will seriously damage home prices. Such tax breaks amount to a subsidy to a few—first-time buyers, brokers, and construction firms—and typically have limited effects on growth because they simply substitute current sales for future sales. Their merit, if any, is that they are temporary, and thus bring forward purchases at a time when activity is lean. Renewal defeats their very purpose. But subsidies are an addictive drug. It is precisely because the benefits are enjoyed by the few (who lobby strongly for them) and the costs paid by the many (who don't care enough to lobby) that they endure.

Opportunism is bipartisan. When the 2001 recession hit, the U.S. Treasury did not stand idly by. In order to stimulate growth as well as fulfill campaign promises, the Bush administration cut taxes on earned income and on capital gains and dividends. This response, which differed from standard Keynesian prescriptions espoused by the Obama administration to boost government spending, reflected the more conservative, supply-side roots of the Bush administration: it was an attempt to improve the incentives for businesses to raise investment and production. But when coupled with rising expenditures on national security after the September 11 terrorist attacks on the World Trade Center, its effect on government finances was decidedly not conservative. More important, given that industry had been on an investment binge, the stimulus was unlikely to be effective in supporting investment and job growth in the short term, no matter what its long-term benefits.

The broader point is that discretionary fiscal stimulus tends to be based on ideology and on past obligations or interests rather than attuned to the needs of the moment. Clearly, if there is a strong case to be made that it will "work" in creating long-term jobs or averting a self-destructive downward spiral in the economy, few would dispute the need to spend. Typically, such action entails limited, targeted spending or tax measures. In practice, though, administrations use the shadow of the recession to do what they have always wanted to do. Rahm Emmanuel, President Obama's chief of staff, captured this mindset perfectly when he said, just before the Obama administration took office, "You never want a serious crisis to go to waste."[27]

The policies that tend to be legislated at such times are unlikely to be centrist. When the government of the day seizes the opportunity to ram through its longer-term policies, it naturally focuses on making down payments on policies that could likely be pruned by more prolonged, reasoned debate. The window afforded by the emergency therefore has led to more partisan legislation in the past and will likely do so in the future, especially because the increased polarization of Congress ensures that any legislative agenda that is not firmly centrist will have difficulty passing once the window of opportunity closes. Because partisan legislation tends to be reversed by future administrations from the other side, the lack of an effective safety net can lead not just to waste but also to more policy fluctuations and uncertainty.

There are three additional downsides to the absence of a strong U.S. safety net when recoveries are turning out to be jobless. First, even with the possibility of discretionary stimulus, workers themselves do not know if they will be supported and when: this uncertainty creates exactly the personal anxiety and political pressure that the safety net is meant to avert. Second, the United States' lack of a firm safety net and its willingness to stimulate until the jobs come home is well understood by the rest of the world. When a global downturn adds to the effects of the persistent structural demand shortfall created by export-led strategies, as it did in 2001, not only do many countries find it hard to stimulate their economies effectively, but they also know that in a global game of policy chicken, the United States will flinch first. Many countries hitch themselves to the U.S. engine and do commensurately less on their own. The weight the United States has to pull increases, and the likelihood that it will do it itself serious injury multiplies. Finally, and most important, the persistent and politically motivated monetary stimulus that accompanies discretionary fiscal stimulus is, if anything, even more dangerous for the long-term health of the U.S. economy, and indeed the world, for it affects the behavior of the financial sector. I turn to that fault line now.

# CHAPTER FIVE

# From Bubble to Bubble

NO CENTRAL BANKER HAS HAD to adapt his views more under the public eye than Ben Bernanke, the chairman of the Federal Reserve Board. In February 2004, in a speech to the Eastern Economic Association, Bernanke, then a governor of the Federal Reserve Board, spoke of the "Great Moderation," the observation that the fluctuations of output and inflation in industrial countries had come down steadily since the mid-1980s. Because the Holy Grail of economic management is strong, steady growth, without booms, busts, or high inflation, this trend suggested that something was working.

Bernanke considered three possible explanations: first, that we might have just been lucky, with the world economy experiencing fewer accidents such as war and oil-price increases over this period. Second, that economies had changed, for example as corporations developed systems to acquire sales information more quickly and to translate it more continuously into production and inventory decisions. Such improvements could explain how economies had been able to avoid the more dramatic inventory buildups and production cutbacks that had characterized previous recessions. Third, as a result of advances in our economic understanding, central bankers, many of them former academic economists, understood better how monetary policy affected economic output.

Because he is a careful economist, in addition to being a very good one, Bernanke suggested that there was merit in all three explanations. However, he stressed the view that monetary policy had become much better. Unlike the policy makers in the 1960s and 1970s, who operated with rudimentary and often incorrect beliefs about economic relationships, today's central bankers, he felt, understood far better how the economy works. Bernanke is, if anything, more cautious and nuanced than the typical policy maker, but the overall tone of his speech was triumphant: the policy levers for managing a modern economy were well understood, which was why we already had milder recessions. The implication, perhaps unintended, was that with steady progress, we could do away with recessions altogether.

By September 2008, however, Bernanke, now chairman of the Federal Reserve Board, having realized the limits of monetary policy, was pleading for help from Congress, arguing that "despite the efforts of the Federal Reserve, the Treasury, and other agencies, global financial markets remain under extraordinary stress. Action by Congress is urgently required to stabilize the situation and avert what otherwise could be very serious consequences for our financial markets and for our economy." In short, monetary policy was not working, and only a bailout of the financial system by Congress could stabilize the economy and avert a depression. Where had the Fed gone wrong?

With the benefit of hindsight, it appears that the Federal Reserve made two mistakes. First, the jobless recovery from the recession of 2001 induced the Fed to keep interest rates extremely low for a sustained period. A lot of excesses were building up, in the rest of the world as well as in the United States, but theory and politics conveniently came together to keep the Fed on hold. Second, the Fed actively encouraged the financial markets to believe it would follow an asymmetric policy: it would not lean against a potential unsustainable rise in asset prices, but it would remain ready to pick up the pieces if a bubble burst. Both these implied promises did considerable damage, because in attempting to stimulate sluggish job creation, they set off an orgy of financial risk taking.

Unfortunately, because the Fed's actions were consistent both with its mandate and with the prevailing academic orthodoxy, it has not been forced to rethink its policies. Moreover, in an environment of high and persistent unemployment, the political pressure on it to persist with such policies will make change very difficult.

## The Federal Reserve's Objectives

The Federal Reserve has a mandate from Congress to promote a healthy economy. This means maintaining maximum sustainable employment and stable prices. Also, it has been entrusted since its founding in 1913 (in the wake of the Banker's Panic of 1907) with helping to ensure the stability of the financial system.[2]

In the past, economists believed that the components of the healthy-economy mandate—the goals of maximum sustainable employment (high growth) and stable prices (low inflation)—were incompatible over the long run, because high growth might require high inflation. Implicit in this trade-off (known as the

Phillips curve after William Phillips, who found such a relationship in the U.K. economy between 1861 and 1957) was the belief that you could fool all of the people all of the time. Injecting more inflation would lead people to believe they were getting paid more for the goods they produced and to work harder—thus expanding output—not realizing that everything else was becoming costlier at the same time.

In the late 1960s and early 1970s, even as data suggested the Phillips-curve relationship between inflation and unemployment was breaking down, the "rational expectations" revolution started taking hold of monetary economics. It explained why the Phillips-curve relationship was theoretically untenable. The essential idea was that the public understood the objectives of policy makers and the frameworks they operated with, so they would not cooperate by being fooled. If the central bank had a policy of inducing high inflation, producers would rationally expect that all prices would go up and would not exert more effort when they saw the prices of their own products go up. Rather, they would understand that the additional dollar they earned was actually worth less in terms of its ability to purchase goods and services. The long-run level of employment of the economy would be determined by factors like the business climate, incentives to innovate, and the ability of firms to hire or lay off workers easily, not by inflation.

This view eliminated the incompatibility in the long run between the economic goals of low inflation and maximum sustainable employment. According to the new orthodoxy, by keeping inflation low and thus eliminating all the uncertainty and distortions associated with high and variable inflation, central bankers would give the economy its best chance of achieving its potential growth rate and thus maximum sustainable employment. However, there is still a short-run trade-off between growth and inflation, stemming from the notion that every economy has a potential growth rate—an inbuilt maximum safe speed. Make the economy go any faster, and wages and inflation start accelerating because demand exceeds productive capacity; slow it down, and wages and inflation start falling. When the potential growth rate is reached, the economy is effectively at maximum sustainable employment—all the unemployed are either fully occupied in searching for appropriate jobs or are unemployable—and any effort to further accelerate growth will only increase competition and wages for employed workers, and thus inflation. So the ideal central-bank policy is to keep the economy perpetually at its potential growth rate.

Unfortunately, no one really knows what the potential growth rate is, though they have reasonable guesses. And this rate can change if the structure of the economy changes—for example, if the industries that are dominant in the economy change. The best indicator for a central banker is inflation. A rise in the inflation rate indicates that the economy is exceeding the speed limit; if the inflation rate is falling, the economy can benefit from more stimulus. Of course, because monetary policy operates with lags—raise interest rates now, and the effects are felt in the economy only many months later—a central bank that waits until it stares inflation in the eye before withdrawing stimulus has waited too long. Therefore, central banks attempt to project what their policies will do (typically over a two- to three-year horizon) and adopt policies that will keep future inflation close to a target and thus maintain growth close to potential.

In the years before the crisis, central bankers and academia thus converged on variants of targeting inflation as their primary objective. Of course, they also had to consider the objective of financial stability. According to conventional wisdom, central bankers had only one instrument with which to carry out monetary policy—the short-term interest rate—and they could not target more than one objective with it. Concerns about financial stability would complicate and make less intellectually rigorous the process of setting monetary policy. Financial stability was left to be tackled through "prudential" measures like capital requirements and relegated to the less glamorous supervisory and regulatory arms of central banks.

### The Interest Rate and Its Effects

The Fed conducts monetary policy largely through the short-term interest rate (the overnight federal funds rate). It sets this rate by intervening in the interbank market for reserve money. Through this rate, the Fed hopes to influence the long-term interest rate. According to the most commonly held economic view, investors in the market see the long-term interest rate (say the ten-year Treasury bond rate) as being a function of the sequence of the short-term interest rates that are expected to prevail over time. So if the short-term interest rate is expected to remain low over the next ten years, the long-term interest rate will be low, whereas if the rate is expected to be low only for the next two months and then climb to a higher plateau, the long-term interest rate will be high. This reasoning is known as the *expectations hypothesis*. By holding down the short-term rate, especially if the market believes it will be held low for a sustained period, the Fed can influence expectations of the future short-term rate and hence the long-term interest rate.

Long-term interest rates are extremely important in the economy. A lower long-term interest rate increases the value of long-term assets such as equity, bonds, and houses because dividends, interest payments, and the services provided by the house are discounted at a lower rate. It thus increases household wealth and, consequently, spending. A low long-term interest rate also makes it less attractive for households to save and more attractive to consume, thus again contributing to demand. Finally, long-term interest rates determine the profitability of real investment: lower long-term interest rates make today's value of future profits higher, giving corporations more incentive to invest as well as greater ability to borrow.

The short-term interest rate may also have direct effects on economic activity. Many borrowing rates are tied to short-term interest rates: for example, the interest payment on an adjustable-rate mortgage falls if the Fed cuts interest rates, leaving more money for households to spend. Through a low policy rate, the Fed may also signal to the market that it intends to keep liquidity conditions—that is, the ability to borrow—easy over the foreseeable future. Banks and finance companies then have the incentive to make illiquid term loans, confident that they can refinance from the market.

What I have outlined is the conventional view of how monetary policy works. Let us now see how the Fed responded to the dot-com bust and the recession in 2001, and what the conventional view may have missed out.

## The Response to the Dot-Com Bust

After the crash in the NASDAQ index in 2000–2001 and the recession that followed, the Federal Reserve tried to offset the collapse in investment by cutting short-term interest rates steadily. From a level of 6½ percent in January 2001, interest rates were brought down to 1 percent by June 2003. Such a low level, unprecedented in the post-1971 era of floating exchange rates, sent a strong signal to the economy. House purchases picked up as more people found they could afford the lower mortgage payments. Increased housing demand encouraged more home construction, which was already being given a boost by the low interest rates at which developers could borrow.

Output growth, riding on productivity growth, was strong, but jobs were really what the public and politicians wanted. Growth by itself did not put food on the table, pay bills, or reduce anxiety for those who were unemployed and seeing their benefits running out, or for those who feared for their jobs.

Unfortunately, as we have seen, job growth simply did not pick up. Industrial and service companies continued pruning workers, and the new jobs in construction did not offset job losses elsewhere. Unemployment peaked only in June 2003, long after output growth had resumed and the recession was officially over.

With inflation low and unemployment high, the Fed's healthy-economy mandate suggested it should keep interest rates low. Indeed, given the level of unemployment and the consequent slack in the economy, Fed officials, including Ben Bernanke, openly worried about the possibility of deflation, even in mid-2003, when quarterly GDP growth was around 3 percent.[3] The Federal Reserve seemed to be influenced by the recent experience of Japan, which had faced prolonged price deflation and slow growth in the 1990s as a result of the collapse of its real estate bubble. But this concern was misplaced: unlike Japan, the United States in 2001 had not experienced a debt crisis, only a meltdown of the overvalued tech stocks. A debt crisis could have caused a downward spiral of bankruptcies, job losses, and fire sales that might have triggered a deflation. But the effects of a stock meltdown were, and historically have been, much milder.[4] Consumer price inflation in the United States never fell below 1 percent over this period, despite downward pressure from low-cost imports (we do not, of course, know what it would have been without the easy Fed policy); and more important, future expectations of inflation were firmly above 1 percent and nearer 2 percent, the Fed's unofficial target. Indeed, the disinflationary pressures at that time may well have arisen because foreign competition was forcing U.S. producers to become more productive as well as to keep wage increases limited, rather than because demand was excessively low.

By mid-2003, almost every measure of economic activity other than inflation and unemployment was picking up strongly. Demand in the United States was strong: the United States' trade deficit, a measure of the demand in the United States that was being satisfied from abroad, was widening rapidly. Indeed, one reason that the pace of U.S. job growth was especially slow in manufacturing may have been that countries outside the United States, like China and Japan, were resisting the appreciation of their currencies against the weakening dollar, thus ensuring that their exports continued to be competitive in the U.S. marketplace. The Fed was now effectively adding stimulus to a world economy that was growing strongly, with jobs being created elsewhere but not in the United States. Commodity prices around the world started a steady rise, suggesting that worldwide economic slack was decreasing. If the Federal Reserve, the world's central banker in all but name, had been focused on sustainable world growth, it should have been tightening monetary policy by raising interest rates. But its mandate covered only the United States.

John Taylor of Stanford University has pointed out that even measured against what is known as the Taylor rule (an empirical characterization of past Federal Reserve interest-rate policy, which sees the short-term policy rate as a function of the inflation rate and the gap between the output the economy is capable of and what it actually produces), the Fed should have started raising interest rates by early 2002.[5] But it continued to reduce rates until as late as June 2003. In a speech in 2010 at the American Economic Association's annual meetings, Ben Bernanke defended Fed policy, saying that if inflation was properly measured, the Fed had not departed from the Taylor rule during this period. In truth, the problem was that output growth had not resulted in job growth. And the Fed was focused not on output, as the Taylor rule would suggest, but on jobs.[6]

When the Fed finally started to raise rates in June 2004, it was extremely fearful of killing off a nascent jobs recovery. So it took pains to accompany its rate hikes with announcements that interest rates would be low for "a considerable period" and would rise slowly at a "measured pace"—namely, 25 basis points at every scheduled meeting of the board. This strategy clearly helped keep long-term interest rates low, but not because expectations of future short-term rates came down, as the expectations hypothesis would suggest. Instead, the risk premium on long-term government bonds—the additional spread that the market demands to take the risk of bond prices fluctuating—fell even as the Fed raised short-term interest rates, with the result that long-term interest rates fell and bond prices rose.[7] Indeed, a generally low premium for risk ensured that the prices of all risky or long-term assets, including housing, rose, even as the Fed raised rates slowly. The Fed's policy seemed to be working because it made risk more tolerable!

The Fed did worry about the deteriorating quality of lending and made some supervisory noises over time. But with its foot pressed firmly on the interest-rate accelerator, the supervisory measures were ineffective. Ultimately, it was probably also Fed actions that brought the party to an end. Higher short-term interest rates raised the payments on adjustable-rate mortgages as well as prospective payments on mortgages with rate resets. With demand for housing falling off (and Fannie and Freddie eventually tempering their purchases of mortgage-backed securities), house prices stopped rising. As a result, over-extended borrowers found it hard to refinance before the initially low "teaser" rates on their mortgages expired, and households began to default on payments. Foreclosures caused house-price declines, and the whole momentum of the boom was reversed. The Fed, as we now know, intervened too late. The bubble had inflated enormously, and the ensuing bust has been extremely painful.

### Did the Fed Make Mistakes?

With the benefit of hindsight, it easy to suggest that the Fed made mistakes even in the traditional conduct of monetary policy: for instance, it may well have overestimated the risk of deflation. In some ways, though, the threat of deflation seemed to be a low-probability red herring, put forth to explain why the Fed kept rates on hold. The true problem was unemployment, which made raising rates politically impossible. In the past, when economic growth and job recovery coincided, this was not an issue. With jobless recoveries though, growth and jobs became somewhat divorced. The Fed would have to be on hold for a long time if it wanted to see jobs reappear.

For those who believe the Federal Reserve is too independent, the notion that it is subject to political pressure may seem unthinkable. Yet, as Fed governors admit in private, pressure is applied all the time by Congress. Powerful politicians, in off-the-record conversations with Fed governors, frequently make veiled and not-so-veiled threats to scrutinize Federal Reserve activities and reduce its independence unless the Fed complies with their wishes. Although typically they stay off monetary policy, their desires are not hard to read when unemployment is high. Ironically, the Federal Reserve's desire to remain independent is the lever with which Congress makes it compliant.

At this time, however, the Fed needed little convincing to keep interest rates low. The prevailing orthodoxy suggested that Fed policy makers should worry only if inflation was getting out of hand. And it was not: inflation in the prices of goods (like cars and milk) and services (like haircuts and laundry) was quiescent, and indeed, if anything, the Fed feared deflation. So the Fed was free to focus on the second part of its mandate, full employment. Yet even while the Fed attempted to convince unwilling corporations to invest through ultralow interest rates, the prices of financial assets and housing were skyrocketing. But the orthodoxy suggested asset prices could be ignored.

### *Rising Asset Prices*

Rapidly rising asset prices should have sounded alarm bells. They were driven by a number of forces other than the traditional ones: increased risk taking, more foreign money looking for debt claims, and expanding credit.

Low short-term interest rates pushed investors to take more risk, for a number of reasons.[8] Some institutions, like insurance companies and pension funds, had contracted long-term liabilities. At the low interest rates available for safe assets, they had no hope of meeting those liabilities. Rather than falling short for sure, they preferred to move into longer-term riskier bonds, such as mortgage-backed securities, that paid higher interest rates. In addition, as long-term interest rates fell and the value of stocks, bonds, and housing rose, households felt wealthier and may have felt the confidence to take more risks. Some of these choices may have been irrational. As my colleague Richard Thaler has argued, when gamblers win money, they take more risks, because they treat their earlier winnings as "house" money—not their own—and therefore less important if lost. Whatever the reason, with investors more willing to take risks, the risk premium on all manner of assets came down.

One effect of the search for yield was that money moved out of the United States into other countries, especially into the high-yielding bonds, stocks, and government securities in developing countries. But many of these countries were fearful of losing out in the race to supply goods to the U.S. market. Their central banks intervened to hold down the value of their currency by buying the U.S. dollars that were flowing into their countries from the domestic private entities that had acquired them and reinvesting these dollars in short-term U.S. government bonds and agency bonds.[9] Thus, even as the Fed pushed dollars out, central banks in developing countries pushed them back in. In a number of industrial countries, private entities recycled the dollar inflows: German banks and Japanese insurance companies bought seemingly safe U.S. mortgage-backed securities with the dollars their customers deposited. The money leaving the United States looking for riskier assets around the world thus came back to the United States, looking for seemingly safe but higher-yielding debt-like securities. In some ways, Federal Reserve policy was turning the United States into a gigantic hedge fund, investing in risky assets around the world and financed by debt issued to the world.[10]

Credit also expanded. Rising asset prices themselves gave households and firms the collateral with which to borrow—a channel that Chairman Bernanke himself had pointed out when he was a professor at Princeton University.[11] Indeed, much of the financing of low-income borrowers was predicated on house prices rising and borrowers refinancing once the low teaser rates ran out. Thus a higher house price, rather than increased income, was the means through which borrowers would keep themselves current on payments.

In addition, the promise that liquidity would be plentiful over the foresee-able future meant that bankers were willing to make longer-term illiquid, and hence risky, loans.[12] But with firms unwilling to invest, banks went looking for deals that would create demand for loans.[13] One option was for private equity investors to acquire firms, relying on banks to finance the deals. Banks, in turn, packaged the loans they made—creating collateralized loan obligations (CLOs)—and sold debt securities against them, thus obtaining the funds to make yet more loans. The result was that larger and larger leveraged acquisitions were proposed to satisfy the seemingly insatiable investor hunger for debt claims. As the rush to lend increased, lending standards declined rapidly: the classic signs of the frenzy were "covenant-lite" loans, bereft of the traditional covenants banks put in to trigger repayment if the borrower's condition deteriorated, and pay-in-kind bonds, schemes by which borrowers who could not pay interest simply issued more bonds. As I argued earlier, the recent crisis was not caused only by lending to the poor!

## The Departure of Asset Prices from Fundamentals

Rising asset prices would not be a problem if markets were well behaved and kept asset prices tied to fundamentals. In the case of housing, prices should be a function of interest rates, local demographics, household incomes, and local zoning regulations constraining the supply of housing.

Unfortunately, asset price growth can be self-reinforcing. For instance, higher house prices give existing homeowners home equity that they can borrow against to make the down payment for better houses, leading to a rise in prices for those houses as well. And a history of house price growth can lead naive new home buyers to swallow their real estate agent's sales pitch and put their money down expecting the price appreciation to continue. Indeed, for a while such ex-pectations may be logical, because there are many more existing homeowners with enough home equity to move up.

In most markets, savvy investors can take a contrarian position when prices depart too much from fundamental value. In the housing market (as well as in the market to take firms private), few opportunities exist for investors to take a short position—that is, sell houses they do not have so as to make a killing when prices fall. This typically means that the optimistic, who buy housing, tend to have undue influence.[14] So house prices, and more generally, asset prices, can rise excessively, and their reacquaintance with reality can be brutal indeed.

Central bankers argue that they really should not be in the business of figuring out when asset prices are too high: after all, do they really know that much more than market participants? This not a silly argument. Many markets work well by themselves, and introducing the whims and fancies of the central bank governor into the way prices are determined could create more problems than it solves. But history warns that markets such as housing, which are driven by bank lending, are different: not only are they very thin (relatively few house sales determine the value of housing for the whole country), but they also do not allow for investors to take short positions. Prices in these markets can run away from fundamentals. And the adverse spirals associated with house-price busts can be very damaging indeed : as prices fall, lending vanishes, and people cannot repay their mortgages; thus foreclosures increase, and prices drop further.

The key warning signal of unsustainable growth in asset prices is an accompanying growth in credit.[15] Before the crash of 1929, the warning signal was the growth in margin loans against shares even as stock prices increased. Before the most recent recession, alarm bells should have sounded in every central bank meeting as a boom in real estate lending accompanied house price growth, and lending to private equity grew with ever-higher transaction prices. Indeed, credit growth has historically been one of the factors determining how central bankers set policy interest rates; but in recent years, academics have persuaded many of them that such behavior is archaic. To their credit (no pun intended), the European Central Bank and some developing-country central banks, like the Reserve Bank of India, have continued to pay attention to credit growth in determining their monetary policy.

Rapid credit growth was deemed of importance in the past partly because it was thought to presage inflation and partly because it reflected a possible deterioration in the quality of credit. Academics argued that the links between credit growth and inflation were tenuous (here they were right) and that credit problems were a historic curiosity in industrial countries because of improvements in bank management and supervision (here they were obviously wrong).

A second argument central bankers offer is that in the midst of a frenzy, when investors expect double-digit rates of price growth, raising rates by a fraction of a percent is ineffective.[16] There are two difficulties with this argument. First, the key issue is expectations. If the central bank can convince investors that it is serious about fighting asset-price inflation—in the same way as it convinces them it will fight goods-price inflation—expectations about price growth can deflate fast, especially in the early stages of a bubble. Put differently, small changes in the central bank interest rate can affect expectations about price growth considerably. The fact that asset prices are growing at double-digit rates does not mean that policy rates have to be raised commensurately. Second, bubbles develop based on a kind of "greater fool" theory—that even if an asset is already trading at an inflated price, someone will be willing to buy it at an even more inflated price. By signaling that it will tighten liquidity conditions, and thus constrain financing and trading, the central bank can signal to investors that there will be fewer fools out there with the capacity to buy, making it more difficult for the bubble to grow.

Indeed, instead of discouraging the development of bubbles, the Fed encouraged it through an implicit commitment, which might have done far more damage than any other Fed action. This commitment, the so-called "Greenspan put," essentially said that the Fed could not really tell when asset prices were building up into a bubble, and so instead the Fed would ignore asset prices but stand ready to pick up the pieces when the bubble burst. To understand why this commitment was made, we need to go back to 1996.

### The Greenspan Put    115,149

In late 1996, the Fed chairman, Alan Greenspan, an astute and experienced (though somewhat ideological) economist, became concerned about the high level of the stock market. In a famously brave speech at the American Enterprise Institute, he wondered whether the central bank should also worry when the prices of real estate, equities, and other earning assets were rising rapidly. And in the opaque language that he had perfected, he came as close as a central banker can to saying he thought stocks were overvalued:

> But how do we know when irrational exuberance has unduly escalated asset values, which then become subject to unexpected and prolonged contractions as they have in Japan over the past decade? . . . We as central bankers need not be concerned if a collapsing financial asset bubble does not threaten to impair the real economy, its production, jobs, and price stability. . . . But we should not underestimate or become complacent about the complexity of the interactions of asset markets and the economy. Thus, evaluating shifts in balance sheets generally, and in asset prices particularly, must be an integral part of the development of monetary policy.[17]

In his autobiography, Greenspan admits wondering whether the market would understand what he was getting at.[18] It did—and ignored him! The stock market opened substantially lower the next day but regained its losses in a day. And it was right to ignore him, because the Fed did not follow up Greenspan's concern with an increase in interest rates, even though he had hinted at such action in his speech. Greenspan never explained why he did not act: quite possibly his hand was stayed by the furious reaction he engendered when market participants realized he was trying to talk the market down.

Instead, the Fed watched while stock prices continued rising in the dot-com boom, as companies without earnings or even revenues sold shares at astronomical prices based on the number of "eyeballs" they attracted to their websites. The Fed even cut rates following the Russian debt default in 1998 and the collapse of the hedge fund Long-Term Capital Management, and raised interest rates mildly starting only in 1999.

When the stock market eventually crashed in 2000, the dramatic initial response by the Fed ensured that the recession was mild even if job growth was tepid. In a 2002 speech at Jackson Hole, Alan Greenspan now argued that although the Federal Reserve could not recognize or prevent an asset-price boom, it could "mitigate the fallout when it occurs and, hopefully, ease the transition to the next expansion."[19] This speech seemed to be a post facto rationalization of why Greenspan had not acted more forcefully on his prescient 1996 intuition: he was now saying the Fed should not intervene when it thought asset prices were too high but that it could recognize a bust when it happened and would pick up the pieces.

The logic was not only strangely asymmetrical—why is the bottom easier to recognize than the top?—but also positively dangerous. It fueled the flames of asset-price inflation by telling Wall Street and banks across the country that the Fed would not raise interest rates to curb asset prices, and that if matters went terribly wrong, it would step in to prop prices up. The commitment to put a floor under asset prices was dubbed the "Greenspan put." It told traders and bankers that if they gambled, the Fed would not limit their gains, but if their bets turned sour, the Fed would limit the consequences. All they had to ensure was that they bet on the same thing, for if they bet alone, they would not pose a systemic threat.

Equally important, the willingness to flood the market with liquidity in the event of a severe downturn sent a clear message to bankers: "Don't bother storing cash or marketable assets for a rainy day; we will be there to help you." Not only did the Fed reduce the profitability of taking precautions, but it implicitly encouraged bankers to borrow short-term while making long-term loans, confident the Fed would be there if funding dried up. Leverage built up throughout the system.

For a long time, central banks justified not focusing on asset prices by arguing that if Alan Greenspan had acted on his intuition in 1996, he would have snuffed out a boom that, despite the slump in 2000, took the stock market and U.S. household wealth to unprecedented heights. On March 2, 2009, though, the S&P 500 closed at 700, below its level of 744.38 on the day in 1996 when Alan Greenspan made his fateful speech. Of course, to date it has regained substantial ground, but perhaps Greenspan could have averted thirteen years of lost returns if indeed he had backed his words with action on interest rates. Whether the political system would have allowed him to do so is, of course, another matter.

## Monetary Policy and Financial Stability

The recent recession has started some rethinking on the objectives of monetary policy, though even as I write, the Fed is keeping interest rates at rock-bottom levels because unemployment is high, even while all manner of asset prices are rising. The saving grace today is that credit growth is still tepid, and it is unlikely that we will have another housing boom while memories of the last one are still fresh. But the financial sector is, if anything, innovative, even in the ways it gets into trouble!

I said earlier that academics and central bankers had converged on the view that there is no incompatibility between the objectives of seeking maximum growth and keeping inflation low in the long run. But there does seem to be some incompatibility between the monetary policies that encourage real investment and growth—maintaining predictably low interest rates over a sustained period and expressing a willingness to flood the market with liquidity when it is tight—and the monetary policies that discourage the coordinated one-way bets by financial market participants that have proved so damaging—pursuing unpredictable policies with no assurance of liquidity support.

The argument that monetary policy has no role in leaning against asset-price bubbles is both timid and self-serving, and it takes the Fed out of a key role it can play in assuring financial stability. Of course the Fed should proceed cautiously and lean against an incipient bubble only when there is substantial evidence that it exists, tempered by the knowledge the fears of a bubble could be baseless. To resign the role of party pooper, however, is to buy political accept-ability at great risk to the economy.

More controversial is whether the Fed should cut policy interest rates to rock bottom in order to revive the economy. Although such an action seems costless, it imposes an enormous cost on savers and offers an enormous windfall to debtors, especially banks. Because it is a relatively hidden transfer, it elicits lit-tle comment or protest, especially as well-off savers tend to keep their heads down at times of crisis. But it is a transfer nevertheless, amounting to hundreds of billions of dollars a year. Moreover, it offers a one-way bet to bankers: plunge the system into trouble, and they will get a great deal on interest rates. Finally, it is not clear that ultralow nominal interest rates (around 0 percent) offer a significantly greater incentive for firms to invest than merely low interest rates (2 to 3 percent), but the difference in risk taking between ultralow and low in-terest rates could be enormous.

More damaging still is the Fed's ongoing attempt to prop up housing prices, both indirectly through low interest rates and directly by lending into the hous-ing market. Although such support is justified as a way to allow the bubble to deflate slowly, it contributes to prolonged delays in adjustment in the housing market. Instead of homeowners and lenders biting the bullet on losses and mov-ing on, they have the incentive to wait and see. But so long as there is a prospect for further adjustment, buyers, too, stay out of the market. And unless the over-supply in the housing market is cleared out, builders have little incentive to re-sume construction. The Fed could be not only delaying the recovery of the housing market but also reinforcing the sense that it will not get in the way of price increases but will prevent price falls. The Greenspan put is quickly becom-ing the Bernanke put.

In sum, the Fed's conduct of monetary policy between 2002 and 2005, while roundly criticized by all but central bankers and monetary economists (with no-table exceptions), had two important limitations. First, it was fixated on the high and persistent unemployment rate and did its best to bring it down by trying to encourage investment. It signaled that it would keep rates low for a sustained period and offered the Greenspan put if firms were still not convinced. Critics should recognize that this fixation was in full accord with its mandate and, more important, that there would have been political hell to pay if it had raised interest rates much earlier than it did. This policy, however, may have had a greater effect on credit growth and asset prices than on job creation outside the real estate in-dustry: corporations were still working away the excesses of the dot-com boom.

Second, the dominant academic orthodoxy indicated that so long as inflation was quiescent, central bankers had nothing to worry about. Indeed, to
worry was to destroy the purity of the theoretical system that had been built, for
that would admit of multiple objectives and lead to market confusion. Instead,
central bankers should keep their eyes fixed on inflation (or the lack thereof)
and let bank supervisors worry about risk taking. Unfortunately, the supervisors had been muzzled, this time on the ideological grounds that they would
do more harm than good by restraining the private sector.

The bottom line is that the debate over monetary policy, which was once
thought settled, will have to be reopened again. Among the most pressing issues
are the trade-offs between policies intended to generate investment and employment and policies intended to ensure financial stability. Asset-price inflation will have to enter the policy debate. Moreover, the Fed will have to consider
whether it is setting policy only for the United States, or, in reality, for a much
larger global economy. Much needs to be done.

## Academia's Failings

This is as good a point as any to try to understand the failings of academic
economists in the macroeconomic sphere. Many commentators have gone overboard in poking fun at economists' models, deriding them as oversimplified.
Others wonder about the excessive mathematical complexity of some modeling,
and yet others combine the criticisms by arguing that human behavior is too
complex to be captured by mathematical models.

The most realistic model would be one that details all individuals and their
whimsical behavior, and all institutions, but it would be hopelessly complex and
of little value in analysis. The whole point of economic modeling is to create useful simplifications of the economy that allow us to analyze what might happen
under varying policies and conditions. The test then is whether the model is a
useful simplification or an oversimplification.

Many past macroeconomic models had a single representative agent making
all decisions. The representative-agent models were easy to work with and did
offer useful predictions about policy, but they took for granted the plumbing
underlying the industrial economy—the financial claims, the transactions, the
incentive structures, the firms, the banks, the markets, the regulations, and so
on. So long as these mechanisms worked well, the models were a useful simplification. And during much of the "Great Moderation" that Bernanke referred to,
the plumbing worked well and served as a good basis for abstract reasoning.

But as soon as the plumbing broke down, the models were an oversimplification. Indeed, the models themselves may have hastened the plumbing's breakdown: with the Fed focused on what interest rates would do to output rather than to financial risk taking (few models had a financial sector embedded in them, let alone banks), financial risk taking went unchecked.

In a haunting parallel to Robert Lucas's famous critique of Keynesian models, in which he argued that those models would break down because modelers did not account for how the economy would react to policies that attempted to exploit past correlations in the data, modeling that took the plumbing for granted ensured the breakdown of the plumbing. In coming years, macroeconomic modeling must incorporate more of the plumbing, which has been studied elsewhere in economics.

The danger is that monetary economists will try to wish away the links between monetary policy, risk taking, and asset-price bubbles. Bernanke came close to doing so in his 2010 speech to the American Economic Association, where he argued that it was not the Fed's defective monetary policy—which he considered entirely appropriate, given the Fed's views on inflation—but its inadequate supervision that helped trigger the crisis. He concluded: "Although the most rapid price increases occurred when short-term interest rates were at their lowest levels, the magnitude of house price gains seems too large to be readily explained by the stance of monetary policy alone. Moreover, cross-country evidence shows no significant relationship between monetary policy and the pace of house price increases."[20]

Of course, no one claims that the Fed alone was responsible for the housing debacle. Government policies favoring low-income housing, as well as private-sector mistakes, contributed significantly. But to suggest that it had no role is disingenuous. Indeed, a detailed study published in the *Federal Reserve Bank of St. Louis Review* in 2008 presents evidence that "monetary policy has significant effects on housing investment and house prices and that easy monetary policy designed to stave off the perceived risks of deflation in 2002–2004 has contributed to a boom in the housing market in 2004 and 2005."[21]

Moreover, there is no reason why there should be a strict relationship across countries between monetary policy and the rate of house-price growth over any common period of time: the rate of price growth might depend on a variety of factors that are specific to each country, including how high house prices already are.[22] The broader point is that monetary economists need to take note (as they are now doing) of the other channels through which monetary policy might have effects.

## Summary and Conclusion

As developing countries cut back on demand following their crises in the 1990s, and as industrial-country corporations worked off their excess investment following the dot-com bust, the world's exporters searched once again for countries that would reliably spend more than they produced. The United States, which was already pushing to encourage household consumption to appease those left behind by growth, had added reasons to infuse substantial fiscal and monetary stimulus in response to the downturn: the jobless nature of the recovery and the weak U.S. safety net. In addition to a substantial fiscal stimulus that pushed a government budget that was temporarily in surplus into large fiscal deficits, the Fed kept its foot pressed on the monetary accelerator, even while giving all sorts of assurances to the markets on its willingness to maintain easy monetary conditions and to step in to provide liquidity in case the financial markets had problems. These assurances had the desired effect of leading to an explosion of lending, which unfortunately continued expanding and deteriorating in quality even after the Fed started tightening. For an unsustainable while, though, the United States provided the demand the rest of the world needed.

The U.S. political system is acutely sensitive to job growth because of the economy's weak safety nets. The short duration of unemployment benefits in the United States, as well as the substantially higher costs of health care for those who do not have jobs, were not excessively painful when recessions were short: they gave laid-off workers strong incentives to find new jobs even while U.S. businesses created them. But if recessions are likely to be more prolonged than in the past, the system has to change, if only because the old social contract—short-duration benefits in return for short recessions—is breaking down.

One reason is simply moral. No modern economy should force workers who lose their jobs to make such painful decisions as choosing which of their children to protect with medical insurance. Not only is this situation barbaric, it is also unsustainable, for those who lose out economically have every incentive to use political means to regain what they have lost. While a democratic system eventually responds, the response can be unpredictable, adding to worker uncertainty. There is a strong case for strengthening the U.S. safety net in ways that will not hamper the flexibility of the economy greatly.

Another problem with a weak safety net is that the United States tends to overreact, and other nations underreact, to downturns. Because every country knows that the politically vulnerable United States has to respond with expansionary policies and that some U.S. demand will spill over to the rest of the world, their incentive to change the structure of their economy, or their policies in downturns, is commensurately less.

But perhaps the most important problem is that the ad hoc policies the United States is forced into do enormous damage to the long-term health of the economy, both directly and through their effects on the financial sector. One could argue that discretionary fiscal and monetary policy in the midst of a downturn gives the United States the ability to calibrate its response to the sever-ity of the downturn. But fiscal policy undertaken at the point of a gun is rarely as dispassionate or as well thought out as one might like. Yes, Congress could simply extend unemployment benefits, as it has done in the current recession. But politicians often want to do more. And the public's anxiety gives them the license to bring out all their pet projects, all the favors to special interests, and all the schemes their ideological leanings and political connections predispose them to.

Similarly, as we have seen, the Federal Reserve, though ostensibly indepen-dent, has a very difficult task. It is extremely hard to ensure rapid job growth in an integrated, innovative economy where firms use recessions to refocus on be-coming more productive or to strengthen their global supply chains, shifting jobs elsewhere. Moreover, the new technologies employed in hiring allow firms the luxury of waiting to fill positions. The sustained easy monetary policy that is maintained while jobs are still scarce has the effect of increasing risk taking and inflating asset-price bubbles, which again weaken the fabric of the economy over the longer term. If the United States cannot tolerate longer bouts of unemploy-ment, but those bouts are here to stay, we risk going from bubble to bubble as the Federal Reserve is pressured to do the impossible and create jobs where none are forthcoming.

It is now time to turn to vulnerabilities in the financial sector to see why the fault lines came together to make banks take the risks they did. I focus on two issues. First, why did mortgage lending go berserk (which is the subject of the next chapter)? Second, why did the banks take on so much default and liquid-ity risk (which is the subject of Chapter 7)?

# CHAPTER SIX

# When Money Is the Measure of All Worth

**W**HEN THE FRENCH MONARCHY was strapped for money in the eighteenth century, it found more and more creative ways to raise funds.[1] One of these was to sell annuities—government bonds that paid out a fixed amount until the death of the person on whom the annuity was written. Annuities were very popular with the public, for they offered beneficiaries a guaranteed income for life in a time before there were old-age pensions. The monarchy liked them because it received payment up front.

The monarchy targeted these annuities at wealthy men—typically in their early fifties—who had the means to buy an annuity and who, given low life expectancies at that time, typically did not have very long to live. Annuities were priced so that they were a fair deal for such men. However, it was possible for the buyer of the annuity to make the payments dependent not on his own life span, but on that of someone else. Perhaps this loophole was not inadvertent, for it increased demand for the annuities: for example, it might have made annuities attractive to a wealthy merchant who wanted to settle his daughters for life. But it did mean that the clever investor could make money off the government. He could pick as beneficiaries healthy young girls (then as now, women lived longer than men) whose family history suggested a genetic predisposition to long life, and who had survived early childhood (infant mortality was very high in those times) as well as the dreaded smallpox. He could then buy annuities on their lives from the French government. A carefully selected, healthy ten-year-old girl would have much higher odds of surviving for a long time than the typical beneficiary of the annuity, and the payments received during her lifetime would far exceed the cost of the annuity.

This is indeed what a group of Geneva bankers did. They selected groups of thirty suitable girls in Geneva and purchased a life annuity on each from the French government. They then pooled the annuities so as to diversify the risk of accidental early mortality among the girls and sold claims on the resulting cash inflows to fellow citizens of Geneva. This early form of securitization thus allowed the bankers to create a virtual money machine, buying policies cheaply from the French government and reselling them for a higher price to investors. The investments were popular—especially because the bankers were reputable and the underlying annuities were claims on the government—and sold well.

However, buyers had not reckoned with the risk of government default. When the French Revolution broke out in 1789, the monarchy was overthrown, and the revolutionary government soon fell behind in its annuity payments. It eventually made payments in worthless currency. The Geneva bankers, who owed investors in harder Swiss currency, did not have the wherewithal to pay, and they defaulted, as in turn did many of the investors who had borrowed to invest in the "sure" thing.

There are four important and enduring lessons from this historical mini-crisis. First, few have a better nose for a good moneymaking opportunity than bankers. It is not that bankers are excessively greedy. Even though Adam Smith did put self-interest at the heart of capitalism when he wrote, "It is not from the benevolence of the butcher, the brewer, or the baker that we expect our dinner, but from their regard to their own interest," few businesspeople are entirely without concern for the impact of their activities on their societies.[2] Rather, their willingness to exploit any advantage that will help them make money, however dodgy (albeit legal) it may be, stems partly from the nature of competitive banking, where there are few easy opportunities to make money, and partly from the way banker performance is measured—almost exclusively by how much money the banker makes rather than by her impact on real activity. The disconnect between banking and real lives and livelihoods is most apparent in the arm's-length financial systems that are found in countries like the United States and the United Kingdom.

A second lesson is that bankers invariably find the biggest edge in taking advantage of unsophisticated players or players who do not have the same incentive to make money. Clearly, individuals who are unschooled in finance are a potential target, but often these individuals realize their ignorance and give their custom only to trusted intermediaries. Moreover, they typically have too little money to be of interest to the smartest bankers. More attractive targets are the moderately schooled managers of large pools of funds, such as pension funds or foreign state-owned funds, who know not that they know not and are thus easily taken advantage of. But perhaps the most attractive target of all is the government itself. The government has nonmarket, noneconomic objectives, and however astute its representatives may be, these make it easy prey for clever bankers. Moreover, whereas a naive individual is soon relieved of all his money, the government has deep pockets, and exploiting them can sustain many a banker's luxurious lifestyle for a long time.

Third, banker behavior tends to be self-reinforcing, at least for a while. In the example of the annuities, as the profits from the first insurance scheme become apparent, they not only attract more bankers to the activity but also push up the prices of the securities issued by the first scheme, sending a still stronger signal to bankers. Similarly, as initial housing loans start to look profitable, more banks extend loans, thereby pushing up house prices and making the initial loan look even more solid. This behavior can exaggerate investment trends and move prices far away from fundamentals. Early movers may convince themselves they are geniuses, even though they are only the leaders of a herd that is rapidly headed toward a cliff. But the growth of the herd itself can make what would have been a minor loss by some adventurous bankers and their investors into a much more serious loss for the community.

Finally, there is safety in numbers, because the responsible government cannot let all its bankers fail, given the likely collateral damage to the citizenry. So even the revolutionary government in France continued paying the hated monarchy's debts for as long as it was able. This is not necessarily to imply that bankers start out with the expectation that they will fail and be bailed out: bankers understand that failure is never pleasant, however forgiving the government. It may well be that the thought of a bailout really does not cross their minds. Rather, the problem created by the anticipation of government intervention is that the bankers, caught up in the herd's competitive frenzy to cash in on the seemingly lucrative opportunity, are not slowed by more dispassionate market forces—what I have referred to as the *unintentional guidance* of the key actors' actions by markets or voters. In such a situation, lenders to banks do not demand proper compensation for the risks the banker takes, because they know the blow will be softened by the government—and in behaving thus, lenders facilitate risk taking and herd behavior. The normal disciplinary role of markets (which themselves may sometimes be caught up in the frenzy) is dulled by repeated government intervention.

I draw modern parallels in this chapter and the next. The sophisticated U.S. financial sector responded to the government's desire to promote low-income housing, as well as to foreign demand for highly rated debt securities. The edge the financial sector exploited was the unthinking, almost bureaucratic, way both the mortgage agencies and foreign investors evaluated the issued securities. Market discipline broke down as mortgage brokers found they could peddle all sorts of junk, especially because the deterioration in credit quality was masked by the immense amount of money pouring into the sector. When the crash eventually came, the government and the Federal Reserve, unable to stand by and see homeowners suffer, stepped in to prop up the price of homes and of mortgage-backed securities, validating much of the extraordinary insouciance of the market.

In this chapter, I explain why the fault lines we have examined earlier, acting on an amoral financial sector with a finely honed eye for opportunity, combined to cause a steady deterioration in the quality of mortgage lending. In the next, I explain why banks held on to so many of the risky asset-backed securities on their own balance sheets.

## Pecunia Non Olet

Most of us do not work for money alone. Some want to change the world, others to create objects of art and culture that will endure. Some strive to gain fame, while others are content to do good anonymously. For many people, though, the visible effects of one's work are its greatest reward. For the teacher, witnessing the eureka moment when understanding finally dawns on a student; for the doctor, the incredible joy of saving a patient's life; for the farmer, the sight of acres and acres of golden wheat swaying gently with the breeze—for all these people, their primary motivation is the knowledge that their work makes the world a better place.

A simple experiment done by researchers at MIT and the University of Chicago verifies the importance of larger meaning to motivation and work. Harvard students, the subjects in the experiment, were asked to put together Lego Bionicle models (small snap-together models) from kits they were given (the MIT researchers probably thought this would be a real challenge for Harvard students!). Subjects were paid at a declining rate for each additional model built, so that eventually they would stop because the effort involved in building an additional model was not worth the pay. In one version of the experiment, each completed model was placed in front of the subject, and the subject was given another identical box from which to build another. In the second version of the experiment, the subject was handed a second box, but even while he or she was putting the model together, the researcher dismantled the just-completed model and put it back in the first box, so that this box could be handed to the subject when the model built from the second box was complete.

The simple difference of whether the subject's work was allowed to endure (at least for the duration of the subject's participation) or whether it was undone immediately, leaving not a trace, made an enormous difference in the willingness to work, even though the monetary benefits were identical. Subjects completed an average of 10.6 Bionicles when the completed models were left standing in front of them and only 7.2 when the completed ones were dismantled in front of their eyes. Thus they continued to make Bionicles for lower wages when the experiment was structured to give the work more meaning. Seeing the fruits of your labor, even in something as trivial as model building, seems important for motivation![3]

In some jobs, it is very hard to see the effects of one's work. On an assembly line, a worker is just one cog in a huge production machine, and her role in the final product may be small. No wonder modern management techniques try to make each worker feel important both individually and as part of a team: the Japanese *kaizen* system of continuous improvement, for example, involves all workers in making changes to enhance productivity, no matter how small the changes might be.

Many jobs in a competitive, arm's-length financial system are problematic for two reasons: First, like the worker on an assembly line, the broker who sells bonds issued by an electric power project rarely sees the electricity that is produced: she has little sense of any material result of her labors. She is merely a cog in a gigantic machine. Second, the most direct measure of a financial sector worker's contribution is the money—the profits or returns—she makes for the firm. Money here is the measure of both the work and her worth, and this is where both the merits of the arm's-length financial system and its costs arise.

Take, for instance, a trader who sells short the stock of a company he feels is being mismanaged (that is, he borrows and sells stock he does not have, anticipating the price will go down and that he will be able to buy the stock back later at a lower price to close out his position at a tidy profit). Few people are more vilified than short sellers, who are seen as vultures feasting on the misfortune of others. But they perform a valuable social function by depriving poorly managed companies of resources. A company whose stock price tanks will not be able to raise equity or debt finance easily and could be forced to close down. The trader who shorts the stock does not see the workers who lose their jobs or the hardship that unemployment causes their families; all he sees are the profits he will make if he turns out to be right in his judgment. But it is his very oblivion to the larger consequences of his trades that makes him such an effective and dispassionate tool of change.

Despite the protestations of the management of targeted firms and their political backers, the trader does not cause the firm to go out of business. If the trader is wrong and the firm is well managed, other traders will take the opposite side, buy shares, push up the share price, and make the short seller lose money. It is typically only when the short seller's opinions are widely shared, and firm management is awful, that the share price tanks. Mismanagement is the source of the firm's troubles; the trader merely holds up a mirror to reflect it. Indeed, the more disconnected the trader is from the people in the firm, the more reliable a mirror he is able to provide. But herein lies the rub. Because the trader is at a distance from the real consequences of his actions, the best measure of the trader's value to society is whether he made money from the trade: a profit indicates that he was right to short the firm short and that society will benefit from his actions.

Although market opinion is not always right, more often than not, it is. Management at the energy giant Enron lashed out at short sellers, but the short sellers, like James Chanos at Kynikos Associates, understood there was something deeply wrong with its accounting. Essentially, Enron had set up off–balance sheet entities to which it "sold" its failing projects at a hefty profit, thus creating the appearance of both profitability and growth, even though the reality was just the opposite. It was the short sellers who made Enron's stock price plummet and forced the company to shut down even while the firm's traditional bankers supported its creative accounting with yet more creative loans. As Chanos later wrote, defending the short seller's role as professional skeptic: "We spoke with a number of analysts at various Wall Street firms to discuss Enron and its valuation. We were struck by how many of them conceded that there was no way to analyze Enron, but that investing in Enron was instead a 'trust me' story. One analyst, while admitting that Enron was a 'black box' regarding profits, said that, as long as Enron delivered, who was he to argue?"[4]

Chanos made millions and acquired fame from his analysis and his willingness to challenge the herd on the question of Enron's value, but it is this very strength of the arm's-length system—that money is the measure of all things— which also is its weakness. An old Latin saying, *Pecunia non olet*, translates as "Money has no odor." The very anonymity of money, the fact that it is fungible and its provenance hard to trace, also makes it a poor mechanism for guiding employees' activities toward socially desirable ends. Did the trader make her returns by being more astute than others like her, or did she make it by front-running her clients (trading ahead of a large client order so as to make money when that client's order moved prices)? Did the mortgage broker make his fees through offering a variety of sensible options to the professional couple who were looking to upgrade their house, or by urging an elderly couple to refinance into a mortgage they could not afford? Although the former course is preferable in each case, the latter is easier for the trader or broker; and because the wrong choice also makes money, has few immediate consequences, and sets off few alarm bells, it is the one that is most tempting.

In sum, bankers are not the horned, greedy villains the public now sees them to be. In the classes I have taught over the years, the future bankers were as eager, friendly, and ready to share as the other students in class, although perhaps a little smarter (remember, this was a time when the financial sector paid far more than other professions and attracted the best talent). I have no doubt they continue to be decent, caring human beings. But because their business typically offers few pillars to which they can anchor their morality, their primary compass becomes how much money they make. The picture of bankers slavering after bonuses soon after they had been rescued by government bailouts was not only outrageous but also pitiable—pitiable because they were clamoring for their primary measure of self-worth and status to be restored.

Usually, competitive market mechanisms keep the search for profits on a track that also ensures it enhances value to society. This is the fundamental reason why free-market capitalism works and why bankers usually do good even as they do very well for themselves. However, the fault lines we have identified can warp the tracks. The finely incentivized financial system can then derail rapidly. By putting all the blame on the financial system, we fail to recognize the role played by the fault lines. Excoriating the immorality of bankers has made for good rhetoric and politics throughout history, but it is unlikely to address the fundamental reason why they can cause so much harm. Let us see how these effects were at work in the origination of dubious subprime mortgages.

## Brokers and What Went Wrong

There were plenty of examples of horrendous mortgage loans made in the run-up to this most recent crisis. Many were made by New Century Financial, which was founded in 1995 with about $3 million of venture capital, as government support to the subprime market increased. Because subprime lending was an innovation with enormous potential opportunities, it attracted ample venture-capital funding. New Century went public in 1997. After surviving a scare the next year, when Russian loan defaults caused investors to flee risky businesses and some subprime lenders went out of business, it grew rapidly.

Companies like New Century reached customers mainly through small, independent mortgage brokerages. Mortgage brokers found customers, advised them on available loans, and collected fees for handling the initial processing. With New Century and its rivals competing fiercely for business, brokers often favored lenders who were able to make loans quickly. As one broker put it, he liked working with New Century because it was "very easy."[5] New Century rarely demanded reviews of the appraisals on which loans were based. Because it outsourced business to brokers, it could ramp up its business quickly, without having to hire a lot of employees or find office space. Brokers worked out of their own homes and cars and were often willing to go to customers' homes in the evening or on the weekend. As a result of such rapid expansion, New Century was the second largest subprime mortgage lender in the country at one time, originating nearly $60 billion in mortgages in 2006.

It does not take a genius to push loans to those who have credit problems, and New Century did not penalize brokers for the quality of loans they originated until in early 2007, when it was too late.[6] The *Wall Street Journal* highlighted an example of the kind of loans being made.[7] Ruthie Hillery was struggling to make the $952 monthly mortgage payment for her three-bedroom home in California. In 2006, a mortgage broker persuaded the 70-year-old Hillery to refinance into a "senior citizen's" loan from New Century that she thought would eliminate the need to make any payments for several years. Instead, the $336,000 adjustable-rate loan started out with payments of $2,200 a month, more than double her income. By the end of the year, when she could not keep up payments, Ms. Hillery received notice that New Century intended to foreclose on the property. As her lawyer put it: "You have a loan application where the income section is blank. How does it even get past the first person who looks at it?" According to Ohio's assistant attorney general, Robert M. Hart, New Century's underwriting standards were so low "that they would have sold a loan to a dog."[8]

New Century was immensely successful for a while in spite of its appalling credit standards. And despite the prominence given in the media to such cases, it grew not primarily because it preyed on vulnerable retirees but because of rising house prices and securitization. With house prices rising, New Century's brokers could make loans with affordable initial teaser rates, anticipating that by the time borrowers had to make higher payments, their house prices would have risen, and they could refinance once again into a low rate. Indeed, this scheme was a virtual money machine, because the cost of refinancing could repeatedly be swept into the new, larger, mortgage—until house prices stopped rising. At that point, all those mortgages with resets to higher rates would turn into real debt—the kind that actually has to be repaid—and the high required repayments would resemble the balloon repayments that proved so burdensome to homeowners during the Depression.

New Century's management must have known that house prices would not rise indefinitely. So why did they continue making risky mortgage loans almost until the day they filed for bankruptcy? One answer is that the company did not hold on to the mortgages it made but sold them to investment banks who packaged them together and sold securities (which were vastly overrated by the rating agencies) against the package to Fannie and Freddie, pension funds, insurance companies, and banks around the world.

So did no one care about credit quality? The investment banks (and their rating agencies) did care, after a fashion. To sell the mortgages on, they had to satisfy themselves that the underlying credit quality was sound. In the past, when a bank made a mortgage loan that it intended to hold on its books, it called the prospective borrower in. The loan officer interviewed him, sought documents verifying employment and income, and assessed whether the borrower was able and willing to carry the debt. These assessments were not just based on hard facts; they also included judgment calls such as whether the borrower seemed well mannered, cleanly attired, trustworthy, and capable of holding a job. Cultural cues such as whether the applicant had a firm handshake or looked the loan officer in the eye when answering questions no doubt played a role—as, unfortunately, did race. But many of these judgment calls did seem to add value to credit evaluations. So did the loan officer's knowledge that his client would be back to haunt his conscience if he put him in an unaffordable house.

But as investment banks put together gigantic packages of mortgages, the judgment calls became less and less important in credit assessments: after all, there was no way to code the borrower's capacity to hold a job in an objective, machine-readable way.[9] Indeed, recording judgment calls in a way that could not be supported by hard facts might have opened the mortgage lender to lawsuits alleging discrimination. All that seemed to matter to the investment banks and the rating agencies were the numerical credit score of the borrower and the amount of the loan relative to house value. These were hard pieces of information that could be processed easily and that ostensibly summarized credit quality. Accordingly, the brokers who originated loans focused on nothing else. Indeed, as the market became red-hot, they no longer even bothered to verify employment or income. Part-time gardeners became tree surgeons purportedly earning in the middle six figures annually.

The judgment calls historically made by loan officers were, in fact, extremely important to the overall credit assessment. As they were dispensed with, the quality of mortgage-origination decisions deteriorated, even though the hard numbers continued to look good till the very end. It really does matter if the borrower is rude, shifty, and slovenly in the loan interview, for it says something about his capacity to hold a job, no matter what his credit score indicates. Moreover, brokers and New Century had an immense incentive to keep the volume of originations up so that they could collect fees—and they now knew which numbers to emphasize. So brokers felt little compunction in helping willing borrowers massage their credit scores, and they recruited pliant appraisers who would keep the loan-to-value ratio down by offering outrageously high appraisals for the house.[10] Because they seemed willing to do virtually anything to close the deal, New Century's loan department became known as "Close More University."[11]

Eventually, though, New Century's weak standards caught up with it. Increasingly, its borrowers could not even make their first few payments and defaulted. These defaults were problematic because the banks buying the mortgages for packaging could return mortgages that defaulted early to New Century. With more and more mortgages returning onto its books, and lenders withdrawing their lines of credit, New Century eventually filed for bankruptcy. One has to marvel at the sheer chutzpah of New Century's founder, Brad Morrice, who said in a news release announcing the company's bankruptcy on April 2, 2007, that it had "helped millions of Americans, many who might not otherwise have been able to access credit or to realize the benefits of homeownership."[12] He neglected to mention that for millions of these homeowners, their houses were like millstones around their necks, drowning them in a sea of debt.

### Assigning Blame

The private financial sector bears an enormous responsibility for what happened. But did the brokers act immorally? Clearly, misleading retirees about their payments was wrong and bordered on the illegal. But although these are the cases that still make the headlines, it is not obvious that predatory lending of that sort was the norm. Brokers and firms like New Century provided many a homeowner with what they were asking for: refinancing at low rates, with little thought for the future. Should the broker have counseled the debt-ridden homeowners they were working with to cut back on consumption, pay off credit card debts, and move to a smaller, more affordable house? Perhaps some would have done so had they thought they would see their clients again. Knowing, however, that the mortgages they originated would be packaged and sold, they had little stake in the relationship, other than the fees—fees that indicated to them they were doing God's work. Arm's-length transactions do not foster empathy or a long-term focus.

There is, however, another check on arm's-length transactions—a well-functioning competitive market. If New Century had been forced to sell its originations for fair value, it would never have originated the risky mortgages it did or put so many borrowers into unaffordable houses. The competitive market would have provided the mechanisms to keep First Century on track. Somehow, and unfortunately, the market was willing to pay much higher values for these mortgages than they were worth and did not exercise its customary discipline.

One reason might be that the market was irrationally exuberant and believed the poppycock that house prices would never go down. There is, however, mounting evidence that much of the boom and bust was concentrated in low-income housing, suggesting that this was not generalized irrationality and that other factors may have been at play.[13]

A more plausible argument is that the strong government push for home ownership by lower-income households led to an enormous increase in the volume of money poured into this sector. The brokers, lenders, packagers, and rating agencies simply did not have the personnel or capacity to manage the enormous workloads effectively. Although they may have worried about potential damage to their reputation from the slipshod work they were doing, the enormous fees they generated apparently allayed those worries.[14] For example, many of New Century's senior managers were industry veterans who knew they had the license to print money only for a limited time: even as New Century's liquid assets fell in the period 2005–2007, as it was forced to absorb losses on loans it had to take back on its books, its dividends per share increased.[15]

This is not a complete argument, for it only kicks the conundrum one step down the road. It explains why the investment banks (and rating agencies) acted as boosters for New Century's faulty mortgages, but not why they could sell them to others at a hefty premium. Either the final buyers were fooled by ratings or there was strong demand for these originations, without much thought to underlying price or quality.

Certainly some of the bureaucratic pension funds and foreign banks did not care what they bought so long as it promised a high yield and was rated AAA, though they should have wondered why they seemed to be getting return without risk. Hindsight suggests they should have trusted less and verified more, even if they believed in the institutions of arm's-length markets, such as rating agencies. But the damage was also done by agencies like Fannie and Freddie, which had to buy an enormous fraction of subprime mortgage-backed securities to meet a government-imposed quota, and by government organizations like the Federal Housing Administration, which contributed to the unsustainable demand in this segment of the housing market. As Peter Wallison of the American Enterprise Institute points out: "As of the end of 2008, the Federal Housing Administration held 4.5 million subprime and Alt-A loans. Ten million were on the books of Fannie Mae and Freddie Mac when they were taken over, and 2.7 million are currently held by banks that purchased them under the requirements of the Community Reinvestment Act (CRA). These government-mandated loans amount to almost two-thirds of all the junk mortgages in the system, and their delinquency rates are nine to fifteen times greater than equivalent rates on prime mortgages."[16]

As problematic as the mandates was the rapidity of the ramp-up. Given the volumes that the agencies and government organizations were pushed to buy quickly, they could not have exercised a lot of quality control, beyond focusing on the obvious hard parameters such as credit scores, which, as we have seen, proved problematic. Perhaps if politicians had been in less of a hurry to extend home ownership to the poor, the mortgage originations could have been more careful, the oversight by rating agencies more thorough, and buyers more circumspect about what they were buying.

Where did the buck stop? Not with New Century's founders, who sold their stock holdings as the firm's fortunes deteriorated. Not with the brokers, who made fat commissions while the gravy train chugged along. Not with the rating agencies, who did not notice, or chose to ignore, the deterioration in the underlying quality of mortgages. Not with some of the homeowners, who spent to excess while treating homes they should never have owned as virtual ATMs. It stopped with the retiree who was fooled into taking out an expensive mortgage and, at an age when she should be without worries, is now facing eviction. It stopped with the pension funds and insurance companies who are now sitting on sizeable losses that will depress the investment returns of every household that relies on them. And above all, it stopped with the taxpayer, whose dollars bailed out Fannie and Freddie, and who stands behind the Federal Housing Administration.

## Summary and Conclusion

Financial sector performance, especially in an arm's-length system where the financier does one-off transactions and rarely has a long-term relationship with the final customer, can often only be measured by how much money the financier makes. The personal checks and balances that most of us bring to bear when we are employed in other activities—we ask ourselves if we are producing a socially useful product—operate less well in finance because, with few exceptions, making money is the raison d'être for the financier. In this competitive environment, small distortions to prices can make the financial sector go significantly off track.

Many have attributed the excesses to greed. But greed, or more prosaically, self-interest, is the driving force in any type of arm's-length transaction. It is a constant, and it cannot explain boom and bust. The private sector did what it always does: look for the edge. Unquestioning foreign money and domestic money partly driven by government mandates may have given it the impetus to take subprime lending to its disastrous conclusion. This is not meant to hold the private sector blameless but simply to argue that there are enormous risks in bringing together deep-pocketed investors who are not adequately conscious of prices and risks, and the highly motivated private financial sector.

The role of foreign investors is particularly interesting. Foreign central banks were confronted with vast dollar inflows as exports to the United States expanded, and as U.S. investors looked abroad to escape from low U.S. interest rates. As the central banks bought dollar assets in an attempt to keep the domestic exchange rate from appreciating, they looked for a little extra return. Being conservative, they had to invest their dollars in debt, and the implicit protection that Fannie and Freddie's debt enjoyed led them to gravitate toward it. Thus the money pushed out to developing countries by the Fed's low-interest policy came back to help expand the agencies' purchase of subprime mortgage-backed securities. Knowing that the agencies enjoyed the implicit guarantee of the government, the foreign central banks really did not care about the risks the agencies took. Somewhat ironically, the developing country central banks did to the United States what foreign investors had done to them in their own crises.

Equally problematic were private foreign investors like the German Landesbanks, which trusted the ratings on mortgage-backed securities and, together with Fannie and Freddie, bid up the prices for these securities, making them far more attractive to create than they should have been. The emerging market crises that I described in Chapter 3 indicated the difficulties that arise when a relationship-based system is financed with arm's-length money. To some extent, what we see in the recent crisis are the problems created when the arm's-length system is financed with foreign and domestic quasi-government money that is less sensitive to price and risk.

The story of the current crisis does not end here. Somehow the private financial sector contrived to convert its edge into an instrument of self-destruction, for the commercial and investment banks that packaged the mortgages together and sold mortgage-backed securities ended up holding large quantities of them. More than anything else, this phenomenon is what transformed what would otherwise have been a contained U.S. housing bust into a devastating global financial crisis. To understand why this happened, we have to delve deeper into the motivation of the modern banker, going beyond returns to the nature of risk. I investigate that question in the next chapter.

# CHAPTER SEVEN

# Betting the Bank

ROUGHLY 60 PERCENT of all asset-backed securities were rated AAA during the lending boom, whereas typically less than 1 percent of all corporate bonds are rated AAA. How could this be, especially when the underlying assets against which the securities were issued were subprime mortgage-backed securities? Was this a sham perpetrated by the rating agencies?

Theory suggests it did not have to be a sham. In certain circumstances, a significant percentage of the securities issued against a package of low-quality loans can be highly rated.[1] An example and some simple probability analysis can make the point. Suppose two mortgages, each with a face value of $1 and a 10 percent chance of total default, are packaged together. Suppose further that the investment bank structuring the deal issues two securities against the package—a junior security with face value of $1 that bears the brunt of losses until they exceed $1, and a senior security that bears losses after that.

The senior security suffers losses only if both mortgages default. If mortgage defaults occur independently (that is, they are uncorrelated), then the senior security defaults only 1 percent of the time. This is the magic of combining diversification with tranching the liabilities—that is, creating securities of different seniority. Put a sufficient number of subprime mortgages together from different parts of the country and from different originators, issue different tranches of securities against them, and it is indeed possible to convert a substantial quantity of the subprime frogs into AAA-rated princes, provided the correlation between mortgage defaults is low.

In normal times, the correlation between residential mortgage defaults *is* low, because people default only because of personal circumstances such as ill health or because they lose their jobs (for cause, rather than as part of a general layoff). No one really knew what that correlation would be in bad times, when many people might lose jobs because of the poor economy and house prices might fall across the country, making refinancing hard. If the correlation was still low, then the ratings were appropriate. If the correlation was high, then all bets were off—if, for example, the correlation was 1, then the senior securities would default as often as the junior securities, that is 10 percent of the time.

The AAA-rated tranches of mortgage-backed securities looked very attractive because they offered a higher return than similarly rated corporate securities. But some should have paid a far higher return because they were in fact very risky. Default correlations were much higher than the rating agencies or investors anticipated. First, the quality of the originated mortgages was low, and many borrowers relied on refinancing as house prices rose to make their payments, so a fall in house prices and the drying up of refinancing almost ensured default for many. Second, far too many packages were poorly diversified across areas: too many mortgages came from the same suspect, aggressive broker from the same subdivision in California.

Indeed, the fact that so many banks were exposed to the same diversified pools increased the likely default correlations, for banks across the country would simultaneously cut back on mortgage lending and refinancing if there was a problem in the market. This collective response would ensure that the problem spread across the country. Of course, the good times gave no inkling of the size of the problem, because in an atmosphere of rising prices and easy refinancing, no one defaulted. Much like a financial Venus flytrap, though, AAA mortgage-backed securities masked their risk with their ratings, and their attractive returns drew in many an investor innocent about finance and many more who should have known better.

Among the firms that should have understood the risk better was the American International Group (AIG). Its now-infamous financial products unit (AIGFP) sold insurance through credit-default swaps on billions of dollars of asset-backed securities, including senior (AAA-rated) tranches of the mortgage-backed securities described above. It promised buyers of the swaps that if the insured securities defaulted, AIGFP would make good on them. The unit was thus betting that defaults would be far rarer even than the market anticipated. Privately, AIGFP executives said the swaps contracts were like selling insurance for catastrophic events that would never happen: they brought in money for nothing! As was widely reported in the media, AIG recognized billions of dollars of profits over this period, and AIGFP's head, Joseph Cassano, pocketed over $200 million in compensation.[2]

However, in 2007 and 2008, the asset-backed bonds that AIGFP insured plummeted in value as the economy slid into recession, mortgage-default correlations proved larger than anticipated, and defaults became more likely. Even though few bonds actually defaulted, AIGFP's liability on the swaps it had written increased steadily as it became more likely that AIGFP would have to pay out. As late as 2007, Cassano maintained confidently that "it is hard for us, without being flippant, to even see a scenario within any kind of realm of reason that would see us losing $1 in any of those transactions," even while AIGFP was losing billions of dollars as it had to mark its portfolio down.[3] Eventually, the losses became too heavy to ignore, and Cassano was let go. But he wasn't fired: he "retired," with a contract paying him $1 million a month for nine months and protecting his right to further bonus payments. AIG's counterparties started demanding collateral to ensure that AIG would make good on its swap liabilities. In September 2008 AIG started the process of becoming the recipient of the largest monetary bailout in U.S. history, receiving more than $150 billion from the U.S. government.

## Tail Risk

Although it is not surprising that risky mortgage-backed securities were created, it is surprising that seemingly sophisticated financial institutions, including those who originated these securities, held on to significant portions of them. These were typically AAA-rated securities, which had some default risk associated with them. Financial firms also took on other kinds of default risk, such as the securities issued by the collateral loan obligations where they had parked the loans made to finance acquisitions and buyouts. To top it all, many of these investments were financed with extremely short-term debt, ensuring that if problems emerged with the asset-backed securities, the financial firms would have immense problems rolling over their debt.

Why did financial firms take on both the default risk associated with highly rated asset-backed securities and the liquidity risk associated with funding long-term assets with short-term borrowing? As I explain in this chapter, the particular way these risks were constructed made them especially worth taking for large banks—indeed, perverse as it may seem, it made sense for banks to combine both risks.

There was something special about the nature of these risks. Clearly, banks felt that default was unlikely. Not only were the securities issued against a diversified pool of mortgages or loans, but also the securities the banks held (or that AIG guaranteed) were senior, highly rated ones, so that defaults on the mortgages or loans had to be numerous to trigger off default on the securities. Similarly, the chances that financing would dry up were also deemed small.

These risks were, then, what are known as *tail risks,* because they occur in the tail of the probability distribution—that is, very rarely.

A second feature of these risks, though, was that systemwide adverse events would be necessary to trigger them: to cause the senior securities to default, mortgages across the country would have to default, suggesting widespread household distress. Similarly, funding would dry up for well-diversified, large banks only if there was a systemwide scare. A third feature, perhaps the most important one from society's perspective, is that these risks are very costly when they are realized, so they should not be ignored despite their low probability.

Unfortunately, these very features of systemic tail risks ensure that they are ignored by both financial firms and markets. Ironically, this also increases the probability that they will occur. When bankers attribute their problems to an unlikely event akin to a one-in-ten-thousand-year flood (thereby implicitly absolving themselves, for who could anticipate such a rare event?), they neglect to mention that their actions have increased the probability of such an event—to something like one in every ten years, approximately the periodicity with which Citibank has gotten itself into trouble in the past three decades.

I describe here how the structure of incentives in the modern financial system leads financiers to take this kind of risk. I next discuss why the corporate governance system did not stop such risk taking, and why various markets, especially markets for bank debt, were also unperturbed.

### Why Did Bankers Take on Tail Risk? Searching for Alpha

To understand the structure of incentives in the financial sector, we have to understand the relationship between risk and return. The central tenet in modern finance is that investors are naturally risk averse, so in exchange for taking on more risk, especially risk that may hit them when they are already in dire straits, they demand a higher return. Therefore, riskier assets tend to have lower prices (per dollar of future expected dividend or interest that they pay) and thus produce higher expected returns: stocks typically return more than Treasury bills. There is therefore an easy way for a banker or fund manager to make higher average returns for his investors; all he has to do is take on more risk by buying stocks instead of Treasury bills. This means the relative performance of a fund manager cannot be judged by returns alone: they must be adjusted downward in proportion to the risk being taken.

The bread-and-butter work of financial economists is to build careful econometric models describing the "appropriate" or market-determined level of return for taking on a certain level of risk. Financial managers are deemed to out-perform the market only if they beat this benchmark return. The lay investor's version of such benchmarking is to compare the manager's return with a return on a benchmark portfolio consisting of similar securities: for example, the re-turns generated by a fund manager investing in large U.S. firms will be compared with the return on the S&P 500 index of large U.S. stocks. Such benchmarking is logical, because the investor can easily achieve the returns on the S&P 500 in-dex by buying a low-cost index fund, and a manager should not earn anything for merely matching this return. Instead, investors will reward a manager hand-somely only if the manager consistently generates excess returns, that is, returns exceeding those of the risk-appropriate benchmark. In the jargon, such excess returns are known as "alpha."

Why should a manager care about generating alpha? If she wants to attract substantial new inflows of money, which is the key to being paid large amounts, she has to give the appearance of superior performance. The most direct way is to fudge returns. In recent times, some fund managers, like Bernard Madoff, simply made up their numbers, while others who held complex, rarely traded securities attributed excessively high prices to them based on models that had only a nodding acquaintance with reality. But it is easy to track and audit the re-turns most financial managers generate, so fudging is usually not an option, even for those with consciences untroubled by committing fraud. What, then is a financial manager to do if she is an ordinary mortal—neither an extraordinary investor nor a great financial entrepreneur—and has no bright ideas on new se-curities or schemes to sell?

The answer for many is to take on tail risk. An example should make the point clear. Suppose a financial manager decides to write earthquake insurance poli-cies but does not tell her investors. As she writes policies and collects premiums, she will increase her firm's earnings. Moreover, because earthquakes occur rarely, no claims will be made for a long while. If the manager does not set aside reserves for the eventual payouts that will be needed (for earthquakes, though rare, eventually do occur), she will be feted as the new Warren Buffett: all the premiums she collects will be seen as pure returns, given that there is no ap-parent risk. The money can all be paid out as bonuses or dividends.

Of course, one day the earthquake will occur, and she will have to pay in-surance claims. Because she has set aside no reserves, she will likely default on the claims, and her strategy will be revealed for the sham it is. But before that, she will have enjoyed the adulation of the investing masses and may have salted away enough in bonuses to retire comfortably to a beach house in the

Bahamas. With luck, if the earthquake occurs in the midst of a larger cata-
clysm, she can attribute her disastrous performance to a one-in-ten-thousand-
year event and be back in another job soon. Failing in a herd rarely has adverse
consequences.

More generally, at times when financing is plentiful, so that there is immense
competition among bankers and fund managers, the need to create alpha pushes
many of them inexorably toward taking on tail risk. For tail risk occurs so rarely
that it can be well hidden for a long time: a manager may not even be aware he
is taking it. But the returns are high, because people are willing to pay a lot to
avoid being hit by cataclysmic losses in bad times. So if the manager produces
the returns but his investors do not (at least for a while) account for the additional risk the manager is taking with their money, the manager will look like a
genius and be rewarded handsomely. He may well come to believe that he is one.
In other words, it is the very willingness of the modern financial market to offer
powerful rewards for the rare producer of alpha that also generates strong incentives to deceive investors.

Because these incentives are present throughout the financial firm, there is
little reason to expect that top management will curb the practice. Indeed, the
checks and balances at each level of the corporate hierarchy broke down. What
is particularly pernicious about tail risk is that when taken in large doses, it generates an incentive to take yet more of it. A seemingly irrational frenzy may be
a product of all-too-rational calculations by financial firms.

### Risk Taking on the Front Lines

A well-managed financial firm takes calculated and limited risks, risks that will
make money for the firm if they pay off but will not destroy the firm if they do
not. Firms like AIG, Bear Stearns, Citigroup, and Lehman Brothers took risks
that were virtually unbounded, albeit low in probability. The most obvious factor driving this behavior seems to be the compensation system, which typically
paid hefty bonuses when employees made profits but did not penalize them significantly when they incurred losses. The profitable one-sided bet this offered
employees was known variously as the Acapulco Play, IBG (I'll be gone if it
doesn't work), and, in Chicago, the O'Hare Option (buy a ticket departing from
O'Hare International Airport: if the strategy fails, use it; if the strategy succeeds,
tear up the ticket and return to the office). That such strategies were common
enough in the industry as to have names suggests that not all traders were obliv-
ious to the risks they were taking.

The Swiss banking giant UBS ran into trouble because its investment banking unit became entranced by the profit it was making from borrowing at the
AA-rated bank's low cost of funding and investing the funds in higher-return,
high-rated asset-backed securities.[4] The regulatory requirements for bank capital to be set aside to back such a strategy were minimal because the underlying investments were highly rated. The resulting interest spread was small, but
multiplied by the $50 billion the unit invested in the strategy, it made a tidy
profit for the bank while the going was good and resulted in large bonuses for
the unit. Needless to say, this practice of picking up pennies in front of a steam-
roller was successful only until the subprime catastrophe rolled all over UBS's
profits.

Some smart traders in a number of banks understood and grew increasingly
concerned by the risks that were being taken by the units creating and holding
asset-backed securities. At Lehman, for example, fixed-income traders started
selling these securities short, even while the real estate and mortgage unit loaded
up on them.[5] Clearly, any unit that is focused on creating and holding a certain
kind of asset is naturally reluctant to declare an end to the boom it has ridden. The
unit's size, power, and reputation become too closely related to the asset class, and
its head becomes an interested booster. For Lehman's mortgage unit to declare an
end to the mortgage boom would have been to sign its own death warrant. But
knowing that those close to the action may become unreliable in assessing the associated risks, a firm's risk managers should step in to curtail further investment.
In many firms they did not, and it is important to understand why.

Risk managers should adjust every unit's returns down for the risk it takes,
reducing perverse incentives to take risk. The kinds of risks that were taken in
the recent crisis—default or credit risk and liquidity risk—were not difficult for
a trained risk manager to recognize, so long as she could see the unit's books.
For risk managers to become concerned, however, and for top management to
share their worry can be two very different things.

In many of the aggressive firms that got into trouble, risk management was
used primarily for regulatory compliance rather than as an instrument of management control. At Citigroup, for example, risk managers sometimes reported
to operational heads who were responsible for revenue, putting the fox in charge
of the chicken coop.[6] Reflecting the typical firm's view of their importance, risk-
management positions were paid significantly less than positions in operational
units, thereby ensuring that they attracted less talented people who commanded
less respect: not surprisingly, studies show that firms where risk managers were
not independent of the operational units and were underpaid relative to other

managers performed poorly in the crisis.[7] Their weakness was compounded as the boom continued. When a CEO adjudicated a dispute between his star trader, who had produced $50 million in profits every quarter for the past ten quarters, and his risk manager, who had opposed the trader's risk taking all along, the natural impulse would be to side with the trader. The risk manager was often portrayed as the old has-been who did not understand the new paradigm—and the risk takers had the track record to prove it.

I remember a meeting between risk managers of major banks and academics in the spring of 2007 at which we academics were surprised that the managers were not more worried about the risks stemming from the plunging housing market. After our questions elicited few satisfactory replies, one astute veteran risk manager took me aside during a break and said: "You must understand, anyone who was worried was fired long ago and is not in this room." Top management had removed all those who could have restrained the risk taking precisely at the point of maximum danger. But if that were the case, then the blame for encouraging the bet-the-firm tail risk taking that was going on must lie with top management.

## Risk Taking at the Top

What was management thinking? An obvious answer is that they, like their traders, were taking one-way bets. However, an intriguing study suggests that bank CEOs in some of the worst-hit banks did not lack for incentives to manage their banks well.[8] Richard Fuld at Lehman owned about $1 billion worth of Lehman stock at the end of fiscal year 2006, and James Cayne of Bear Stearns owned $953 million. These CEOs lost tremendous amounts when their firms were brought down by what were effectively modern-day bank runs. Indeed, the study shows that banks in which CEOs owned the most stock typically performed the worst during the crisis. These CEOs had substantial amounts to lose if their bets did not play out well (no matter how rich they otherwise were). Unlike those of some of their traders, their bets were not one-way.

One explanation is the CEOs were out of touch. An unflattering portrayal of Fuld has him holed up in his office on the 31st floor of Lehman's headquarters with little knowledge of what was going on in the rest of the building.[9] Indeed, in a tongue-in-cheek op-ed piece in the *New York Times*, Calvin Trillin argued that Wall Street's problem was that it had undergone a revolutionary change in the quality of personnel over generations.[10] In Trillin's time in college, only those in the bottom third of their university class used to go on to Wall Street careers, which were boring and only moderately remunerative. But even while the dullards ascended to the top positions at the banks, Wall Street became a more exciting and challenging place, paying people beyond their wildest dreams. It started attracting and recruiting the smartest students in class, people who thought they could price CDO squared and CDO cubed (particularly egregious forms of securitization involving collateralized debt obligations) and manage their risks. As Trillin writes: "When the smart guys started this business of securitizing things that didn't even exist in the first place, who was running the firms they worked for? Our guys! The lower third of the class! Guys who didn't have the foggiest notion of what a credit default swap was. All our guys knew was that they were getting disgustingly rich, and they had gotten to like that."[11]

The suggestion that bosses, recruited in a staid and regulated era, were of lower caliber than the employees they had recruited from the top of the class in a deregulated and high-paying era is not completely without foundation. An intriguing study of the U.S. financial sector indicates that the earnings of corporate employees in the financial sector relative to employees in other sectors started climbing around 1980, as the sector was deregulated.[12] Moreover, jobs became more complex in the financial sector, requiring significantly more mathematical aptitude. Indeed, although there is little divergence between the wages of financiers and engineers at the college level, there is significant divergence among postgraduates (with postgraduate financiers increasingly earning more than postgraduate engineers). MBAs and PhDs began to fill the ranks of analysts and managers in financial firms. Therefore, not only was the financial sector demanding more highly educated people, but it was also paying them more and therefore probably attracting better talent than it had in the past— consistent with my observations that many of the smarter students in my MBA classes gravitated to finance. Clearly, deregulation and the subsequent surge in competition and innovation increased the demand for, and hence returns on, skills in the financial sector.

Although it is tempting to conclude that some of the CEOs were both untalented and clueless relative to their subordinates, the corporate hierarchy is inherently a tough climb and weeds out a lot of incompetents, especially in the unforgiving and fiercely competitive financial sector. It is hard to imagine that the majority of top management in the early 2000s, most of whom had probably joined in the already exciting 1980s and survived a number of ups and downs, were not highly capable and intelligent individuals. Sheer incompetence among the top management does not explain the crisis.

A better explanation is that CEOs were vying among themselves for prestige by making more profits in the short term or by heading league tables for underwriting or lending, regardless of the longer-term risk involved. I wrote a paper describing such incentives following bank troubles in the early 1990s, and I think the phenomenon is more widespread.[13] Stan O'Neal, the CEO of Merrill Lynch, pushed his firm into the seemingly highly profitable asset-backed securities business in an attempt to keep up with rivals like Goldman Sachs. He monitored Goldman's quarterly numbers closely and often questioned colleagues on the companies' relative performance.[14] Merrill's lack of experience in the area eventually resulted in enormous losses and a shotgun marriage with Bank of America.

The pressures on the CEO may have come not just from shareholders or personal egos but also from aggressive subordinates. Citigroup CEO Chuck Prince's comment in July 2007, only a month before markets started freezing up, has become emblematic of CEOs' role in the current crisis. Replying to a journalist who asked why his bank continued to make loans on easy terms to fund takeovers, he said: "When the music stops, in terms of liquidity, things will be complicated. But as long as the music is playing, you've got to get up and dance. We're still dancing."[15]

This comment was commonly interpreted as reflecting the cavalier attitude of bankers toward risk and the mad chase for immediate profits. Months later, I met Prince at a conference where we were on a panel together, and I asked him what he had meant. He explained that even though he knew there were risks, as the first sentence of the quote suggests, he simply could not shut down lending, which was critical to securing investment banking deals: the moment he did so, he would have lost many key employees to other rivals who were still "dancing." So the decision to continue lending was not so much an attempt to make short-run profits as an attempt to preserve Citigroup's franchise in investment banking and its capabilities for the future. Of course, in making the kind of loans they did, his employees jeopardized not only their unit's franchise but the entire bank. Hindsight suggests that Prince and Citigroup would have been better off if they had sat out a few dances.

A few CEOs appear to have stood up to their employees. The CEO of JP Morgan, Jamie Dimon, played a key role in preventing his bank from taking a bigger position in highly rated mortgage-backed securities, and in unwinding its existing positions, beginning in 2006.[16] As he often emphasized to his staff, "We have got to have a fortress balance sheet! . . . No one has the right to not assume that the business cycle will turn! Every five years or so, you have got to assume that something bad will happen."[17] He also beefed up pay for risk managers, so that these positions attracted knowledgeable traders. He tried to ensure that they had clout. And although he had a much deeper understanding of derivatives than many of his fellow CEOs, he also had a rule: if he did not understand how a business made money, he would not participate in it. Not taking risks one doesn't understand is often the best form of risk management. Firms with less confident or respected CEOs simply followed the herd over the cliff, pushed by the ambitions of their employees.

But before we attribute too much or too little foresight to CEOs, let us consider the findings of another sobering recent study, which looks at total top-management pay across financial institutions before the crisis and its relationship with subsequent performance.[18] The study finds that some firms tended to pay their top management a lot more aggressively in the period 1998–2000, correcting for obvious factors like the size of the bank (big banks pay more because they tend to attract, and need, better talent). Aggressive payers included the usual suspects like Bear Stearns, Lehman, Citigroup, and AIG, whereas more conservative paymasters included firms like JP Morgan. The study finds that those who paid the most aggressively before the crisis were also those who had the worst stock-return performance during the period 2001–2008, the highest stock-return volatility, the highest exposure to subprime mortgages, and, by some counts, the highest leverage. Aggressive pay practices seem to have gone together with aggressive risk taking and subsequent poor performance during the crisis, much as my earlier discussion suggests.

Interestingly, though, the researchers repeated the exercise over a different time frame, looking at how those who compensated aggressively during the 1992–94 period fared between 1995 and 2000. Over this period, the same firms were aggressive payers, but they did phenomenally better than the conservative payers. Their stock returns were much higher, though measures of risk, such as stock-return volatility, were also high. The authors conclude that performance did not depend on the astuteness or incompetence of particular CEOs: rather, some banks had a culture of risk taking and of compensating very heavily over the short term, which attracted like-minded traders, investors (aggressive banks had more short-term institutional investors holding their shares), and even CEOs. When these banks did well during boom times, their CEOs were lionized as heroes; but when they did extremely poorly during the credit crisis, their (usually former) CEOs became villains. The CEOs were probably neither. They were just loading up on risk, including tail risk; but this time it just did not pay off.

Past experience may even have led CEOs to overestimate their ability to deal with tail risk. A passage from a *New York* magazine article about Lehman is revealing:

> By the end of 2006, some at Lehman had begun to think that real estate was nearing the end of its run. Mike Gelband, who was responsible for commercial and residential real estate, had by then turned decidedly bearish. "The world is changing," Gelband told [Richard] Fuld during his 2006 bonus review, according to a person familiar with Gelband's thinking. "We have to rethink our business model."
>
> But given the importance of real estate to Lehman's bottom line, that wasn't what Fuld wanted to hear. Fuld had seen his share of cyclical downturns. "We've been through this before and always come out stronger," was his attitude. "You're too conservative," Fuld told Gelband.
>
> "We've been lifted by the rising tide," Gelband insisted.
>
> Fuld, though, wondered if the problem was with Gelband, not the market. "You don't want to take risk," he said—a deep insult in the trader's vernacular.[19]

Soon Gelband was fired, and Lehman continued piling up risk. In its last days, it brought back Gelband to try to save the bank, but it was too late, and Lehman was bankrupted by the panic of 2008. More generally, aggressive banks' risk taking had paid off in the past, which is why their richly compensated CEOs were sitting on enormous amounts of equity. They did not seem to realize that it was risk, not capabilities, that had brought them their past returns. And this time when they rolled the dice, what turned up was very different.

Although it would be too strong to say that CEOs had little influence—Stan O'Neal converted staid Merrill into an aggressive risk taker—perhaps the most important thing any CEO did was to arrive in the right CEO suite. Somewhat tellingly, Jamie Dimon parted ways with Citigroup and, by way of Bank One, joined the conservative JP Morgan. He tightened processes considerably at JP Morgan, perhaps partly because his admonitions fell on receptive ears. It is unclear whether he would have had the same influence at Citigroup. A *New York Times* columnist, Andrew Ross Sorkin, reports a conversation between Bob Willumstad, the CEO of AIG, and Robert Gender, its treasurer, as AIG was running out of money: "It was then that Willumstad accepted the fact that JP Morgan might not be willing to provide any further funds. AIG's treasurer, Robert Gender, had already warned him that that might be the case, but Willumstad hadn't fully believed him. 'JP Morgan's always tough,' he reminded Gender. 'Citi will do anything you ask them to do; they just say yes.' But the prudent Gender only acidly replied, 'Quite frankly, we can use some of the discipline that JP Morgan is pushing on us.' "[20]

In sum, the pattern of tail risk taking in some aggressive banks paid off for a considerable time. The management of these banks does not appear to have realized how much their performance depended on luck, or how their own collective actions precipitated the events they should have feared.

### Shareholders

One question arises immediately: If indeed the aggressive banks were clearly identifiable, why did the market not punish them before the crisis? Banks that ranked in the worst quartile of performance during the crisis had much higher stock returns in the year before the crisis, 2006, than banks that ranked in the best quartile.[21] So the market seemed to support the behavior of the risk takers by boosting their stock price before the crisis.

Those who believe that markets are grossly inefficient would quickly construe this outcome as evidence that the stock market typically gets it wrong, and that theories that markets efficiently aggregate all public information into prices —versions of the "efficient markets hypothesis"—are hopelessly misguided. Yet nothing in the theory says the market should be spot on all the time. The market may not have full information—after all, even regulators were later surprised by the quantities of asset-backed securities the banks carried both on and off their balance sheets. Moreover, even if it assigns appropriate probabilities to all possible events, only one of those events will be realized. Viewed with the benefit of hindsight, especially if an extreme event occurs, the market will seem as if it got matters wrong, and indeed it will have done so. But this is not to say that anyone could have consistently done better. In the jargon of economists, that the market is believed to have rational expectations about events does not mean that it has perfect foresight.

More generally, there is a danger in judging risk taking while looking back from the depths of a crisis, especially one as severe as the recent one. From that perspective, any risk taking beforehand seems irresponsible, redolent of mismanagement. Conservatism seems prescient and astute—indeed, it seems so much in tune with the times that it becomes the strategy of choice after the crisis, when in fact more risk taking would be appropriate. However, the right way to judge actions taken before the crisis is whether the risk taking was expected to be profitable.

And it may well have been that shareholders, protected by limited liability from bearing the extreme losses induced by tail risk (because shareholders can simply abandon their shares when their value hits zero, whereas partners in an unlimited-liability partnership must repay the money owed to debt holders or forfeit their wealth), deemed the expected profits from taking on tail risk worthwhile—they took the gains while the debt holders and the taxpayer absorbed the tremendous losses. Put differently, Jimmy Cayne (of Bear Stearns), Dick Fuld (of Lehman), and Chuck Prince (of Citigroup) might still be feted as giants of the financial industry had events followed the most probable course. This is not to say that the risks they took on were good for society, only that they may have been reasonable bets for shareholders to take.

The actions of corporate boards, which are the representatives of shareholders, might give us a sense of where shareholder interests lay. Not all boards were equally competent, but Citigroup's board, with stalwarts like Robert Rubin, the former treasury secretary and CEO of Goldman Sachs, might give us an inkling as to what knowledgeable shareholders might have opted for. There is evidence that this board pushed Citigroup into taking more of the risk that brought it to its knees.[22] Although we cannot tell whether the board was independent or in management's pocket, it apparently did not restrain the bank's risk taking.

Finally, equity markets were not entirely unaware of the risks. From the second quarter of 2005 to the second quarter of 2007, the two-year implied volatility of S&P 500 options prices—the market's expectations of the volatility of share prices two years ahead—was 30 to 40 percent higher than the short-term one-month volatility.[23] This figure suggests that the market expected the seeming calm would end, even though the high level of the market indicated it did not place a high probability on events turning out badly for shareholders. But this is precisely how we would expect the market to behave if it believed the banks were taking on subsidized tail risk.

Thus far, as we have moved through the corporate hierarchy, from trader to risk manager to CEO to corporate board to shareholder, we have found little concern anywhere about the tail risks that were building up, especially in the aggressive banks. Many of the actors—traders, management, and shareholders—typically focused on the advantages of taking the tail risk. In insurance parlance, they would get a share of the premiums that flowed in while the going was good, and they would be protected by limited liability from having to make massive payouts if the extreme risk hit. Who then would absorb the losses?

Typically, the answer ought to be the bank's debt holders. In the case of commercial banks, some were FDIC-insured deposit holders, who would not bear losses in any case, while others protected themselves by lending short term and demanding security to back their lending. If defaults on asset-backed securities mounted, the short-term lenders thought they would be able to withdraw ahead of the collapse. But not all of them could hope to escape without taking a hit. Why were they not more worried?

Similarly, why were holders of long-term, unsecured debt not extremely fearful, especially given the higher future expected volatility reflected in share options? Bank debt holders typically hate volatility, as they get none of the upside gains and bear all the downside risk. Bank debt spreads, a measure of a bank's anticipated risk of default, remained very moderate until just before the crisis.

## How the Helping Hand of the Government Hurts

It is hard to argue that debt holders were ignorant of the risks, especially when equity options markets seemed to be signaling possible trouble. The obvious explanation for their continued exposure to risk is that debt holders did not think they would need to bear losses because the government would step in. There were two possible reasons for this complacency—reasons that were in fact borne out by events. First, unsecured bondholders worried less than they should have because of the prospect of direct government intervention in housing and credit markets if matters took a turn for the worse. Second, the institutions that took the most risk were those that were thought to be too systemic to be allowed by the government to fail. The bank's debt holders would not have had to face any risk of default if the government bailed the firm out. Not only would confidence in a bailout have kept debt costs from rising in proportion to bank risk taking, but also, with little concern expressed by debt holders, management had an even broader license to take on leverage to boost returns for equity.

Consider the nature of the tail risks. Unlike ordinary loans or individual mortgages, where defaults occur in isolation, highly rated, diversified mortgage-backed securities were likely to risk default only if mortgages across the country defaulted. If such an improbable eventuality were to occur, the government would likely be drawn in to supporting the market for housing and for housing finance: it could not possibly sit idly by as millions of homeowners defaulted. Similarly, when such a systemic event occurred, not only would large banks find refinancing difficult, but corporations ranging from the large to the tiny would also face significantly greater financial constraints. Again, it was unlikely the Fed would stand by idly if liquidity vanished, especially given the promises Chairman Greenspan had made. So the systemic nature of tail risks ensured that banks would be collectively in trouble if a crisis occurred, and that government support would be forthcoming. This mitigated the costs of those risks.

And that support has indeed been forthcoming. Specifically, in order to support the housing market, the federal government has introduced tax measures that encourage home ownership, including the first-time home buyer's tax credit. Since September 2008, Fannie Mae, Freddie Mac, and the Federal Housing Authority have lent hundreds of billions of dollars to low-income borrowers in an attempt to keep house prices from collapsing. The financial website Bloomberg.com estimates that in 2009, the Fed and the Treasury together purchased $1.3 trillion worth of agency-issued mortgage-backed securities, 76 percent of the gross issuance (including refinancings), and more than three times the net increase in the size of the market. Estimates suggest that these purchases lowered mortgage rates by about 75 basis points.[24] The special inspector general's report to Congress on the Troubled Asset Relief Program (TARP) in January 2010 states: "The government has done more than simply support the mortgage market. In many ways it has become the mortgage market with the taxpayer shouldering the risk that had once been borne by the private investor."[25] The *Financial Times* reports Neil Barofsky, the special inspector general, as saying: "All of the things that were broken in the housing market and the different roles that different private players have played, some of which we recognize now . . . actually contributed to the bubble and to the ensuing crisis, are really being replicated by government actors."[26]

Even outside the housing market, the Fed pulled out all stops, especially after the collapse of Lehman. The Fed cut interest rates to rock bottom and created a variety of innovative programs to lend to the private sector, while the Treasury recapitalized firms through TARP. The Federal Deposit Insurance Corporation (FDIC) also chipped in by temporarily insuring all bank debt in 2008 and upping the quantum of deposit insurance. Banks that remembered the Fed riding to the rescue in 2001 with rock-bottom interest rates, and Alan Greenspan's subsequent dictum that the Fed would "mitigate the fallout when it occurs and, hopefully, ease the transition to the next expansion," were not wrong in anticipating that they would be helped out of a tight corner yet again. The banks that had taken on liquidity risk and survived were rewarded with substantial profits—but some did not live to see happy days return.

Perhaps an equally important driver of bank bond-holder complacency was the knowledge that the large banks they had lent to were likely to be deemed too systemic to fail by the authorities. Herd behavior put the issue largely beyond doubt: if many large banks took the same tail risks, they would all be weak at the same time, and the chances that the government would risk a panic by letting any one of them go would be proportionately diminished. Henry Paulson, secretary of the treasury and thus the leader of the rescue in the Bush administration, writes about the FDIC-led resolution of Washington Mutual in September 2008:

> Unfortunately, the WaMu solution was not perfect, although it was handled smoothly using the normal FDIC process. JP Morgan's purchase cost taxpayers nothing, and no depositors lost money, but the deal gave senior WaMu debt holders about 55 cents on the dollar, roughly equal to what the securities had been trading for. In retrospect, I see that in the middle of a panic, this was a mistake. WaMu, the sixth-biggest bank in the country, was systemically important. Crushing the owners of preferred and subordinated debt and clipping senior debt holders only unsettled the debt holders in other institutions, adding to the market's uncertainty about government action.[27]

Thus even though shortly before WaMu's resolution the market fully expected debt holders would not be paid in full, and even though the FDIC had the full legal authority to impose losses on the bondholders, the secretary of the treasury expressed remorse over the action. Given that the only time a large, well-diversified bank can get into trouble is in the midst of a nationwide downturn and possible panic, the secretary's logic would protect bank bondholders from ever suffering losses and remove an important source of market discipline on banker actions.

In sum, if bank management had fully understood the risks they were taking, their decisions could have evolved as follows. In the early stages of taking on a tail risk, such as the default risk in mortgage-backed securities or the liquidity risk in borrowing short term to fund long-term assets, they would have proceeded cautiously and even surreptitiously. After all, the profits from such activities would look a lot healthier if no one knew the risks they were taking. Accordingly, Citibank's off–balance sheet conduits, holding an enormous quantity of asset-backed securities funded with short-term debt, were hidden from all but the most careful analysts.

But as enough banks imitated the innovators and took on similar risks, and as it became common wisdom among market participants that the market would be supported in the event of a crisis, there would have been strong incentives to load up on the tail risks, even if such activity became visible. The market would have focused on the profit potential of such risk taking, knowing that most of the losses, in the remote eventuality that they occurred, would be passed on to the government and the taxpayer. Indeed, an entity financed with short-term borrowing, knowing that it would be unable to repay its debts if liquidity dried up, had a powerful incentive to double up on its bet that liquidity would always be available —by buying assets that would fall in value if liquidity dried up and by leveraging even more. The simple reason is that limited liability protected its shareholders against losing more if its bets went wrong and liquidity did dry up; and if it guessed right, it would make a ton of money.[28] No wonder exposures to both mortgage-backed securities and short-term leverage increased steadily before the crisis.

Anticipation of government interventions would have made it even harder for any bank to justify a conservative stance during the run-up to the crisis. For instance, one of the rewards of maintaining a very liquid balance sheet is that when liquidity dries up in markets, the bank can purchase assets at bargain-basement prices from those who have been too aggressive. But if the Fed intervenes to lend freely at such times, the discount on assets is far less than it would otherwise be. Many troubled banks held assets through the crisis that they should have been forced to sell, reducing the punishment they suffered for maintaining illiquid balance sheets and reducing the potential gain to bottom-feeding conservative banks.

Finally, all this behavior increased the likelihood of the tail risk's materializing substantially. When few banks maintain liquid reserves even while leveraging their balance sheets to the hilt, the slightest adverse shock can tip the system over into a full-fledged panic. Similarly, as purchases of mortgage-backed securities increase without much attention being paid to default risk, mortgage lending expands and the quality of lending deteriorates, making widespread default more likely if house prices start dropping.

In all this, one cannot ignore the actions of the regulator. One of the factors propelling banks into mortgage-backed securities was their low capital requirements relative to direct lending. The market, however, priced these securities as if they were riskier than the regulators believed them to be (as indeed they were). Banks thus collected the higher return on these securities while maintaining little capital, thereby obtaining a seemingly healthy return on capital. In a sense, therefore, regulators inadvertently pointed banks toward these securities. In some ways practices like this are an unavoidable consequence of regulation. If banks have an incentive to take risk, they will always look for opportunities to get the greatest bang for the regulatory buck. But the regulatory mistake of requiring too little capital for certain activities is then compounded because in taking advantage of regulatory mistakes, banks build up exposure to the same risks. The dynamic associated with systemic risk exposures then kicks in: if everyone is exposed to the same risk in a big way, the authorities have no option but to intervene to support banks and the market if the risk materializes—in which case a bank maximizes profits by increasing exposure to the risk.

## Summary and Conclusion

The problem of tail risk taking is particularly acute in the modern financial system, where bankers are under tremendous pressure to produce risk-adjusted performance. Few can deliver superior performance on a regular basis, but precisely for this reason, the rewards for those who can are enormous. The pressure on the second-rate to take tail risk, thus allowing them to masquerade as superstars for a while, is intense.

The market should theoretically encourage good risk management and penalize excessive risk taking. But tail risks are difficult to control for two reasons. First, they are hard to recognize before the fact, even for those who are taking them. But second, once enough risk is taken, the incentive for the authorities to intervene to mitigate the fallout is strong. By intervening, the authorities reduce market discipline, indeed inducing markets to support such behavior. Bankers may in fact have been guided into taking tail risks as markets anticipated government intervention in the housing market and liquidity and lending support from the Fed and the FDIC.

This argument is not meant to absolve bankers. Some understood the risk they were taking and ignored it; many did not recognize it but should have. What is particularly alarming is that the risk taking may well have been in the best ex ante interests of their shareholders. One should judge the Citigroup's board's competence not only by the fact that its share price sank below $1 in the midst of the crisis but also by the fact that the price reached the mid-$50s just before the crisis in the spring of 2007. The stock market is not an anonymous, distant entity: it is us, and collectively we feted activities that eventually proved highly detrimental to society. Indeed, bank CEOs who remained conservative were doing the right thing by society but quite possibly not by their shareholders. Certainly, this seems to have been the market's view before the crisis hit.

Put differently, solutions are fairly easy if we think the bankers violated traffic signals: we should hand them stiff tickets or put them in jail. But what if we built an elaborate set of traffic signals that pointed them in the wrong direction? We could argue that they should have used their moral compass, and some did; but, as I indicated in the previous chapter, the industry's entire system of values uses money as the measure of all things. Solutions are much more difficult if it turns out that the signals are broken, at least from the perspective of our collective societal interests.

Moreover, I do not mean to suggest, by attributing some of the crisis to bankers' and market confidence in a government bailout, that the authorities should sit back and watch the economy collapse. Rather, I want to emphasize that the combination of incentives for high-powered performance that are inherent in the modern financial system and the unwillingness of a civilized government to let failure in the financial sector drag down ordinary citizens generates the potential for tail risk taking and periodic, costly meltdowns. Even as I write, the enormous amounts of taxpayer money being directed at the housing market and the banks are creating new expectations about government and Fed behavior in the next crisis. Our central focus in any reforms should be on dispelling such expectations, and that is the topic I turn to now.

CHAPTER EIGHT

# Reforming Finance

W E HAVE MADE A FULL TOUR DE TABLE in searching for the underlying causes of this crisis. As I write, financial sectors around the world have been brought back from the brink through a combination of government guarantees, injections of capital, and central bank lending. Rock-bottom interest rates continue to bail out banks at the expense of savers: if banks can borrow at almost no interest and lend at a hefty spread, it is hard for them not to make money. Government spending across the world seems to have helped maintain activity, though it is still uncertain whether heavily indebted households, especially in the United States, will take up the task of spending when the government stimulus runs out. The most likely prognosis is for a period of relatively slow growth and mounting government debt obligations in industrial countries. Fortunately, though, we have stopped following the path of the Great Depression. Costly as this crisis will prove, it could have been worse.

The fault lines and fragilities I have identified will not, however, simply go away with the passage of time. Some of them, indeed, are deepening. They will need to be addressed directly. But even while politicians sense the need for reforms, public distrust is growing for anything that has to do with the status quo. Radical proposals traverse the blogosphere—though with all the upheaval, the public tolerance of the additional uncertainty associated with change is also low.

The public has lost faith in a system where the rules of the game seem tilted in favor of a few. Some of the bailout proposals, put together over sleepless weekends, seem poorly thought through at best and tainted by corruption at worst. *Rolling Stone*'s Matt Taibbi has called Goldman Sachs—a bank with alumni in every corner of the government, and, despite its protestations to the contrary, a significant beneficiary of the rescue—a "blood-sucking vampire squid."[1] The epithet seems to have stuck, epitomizing the public mood. Tin-eared bankers have not helped, paying themselves huge bonuses soon after being rescued by an ongoing public bailout, and, perhaps more infuriatingly, expressing surprised hurt at the public reaction.

The private sector, however, is not alone in deserving blame. There is substantial evidence that government intervention and regulatory failure had as much of a role to play in this crisis as private-sector failure: indeed, it was the coming together of the two that had the most severe consequences. The temptation for politicians, however, will be to blame, and reverse, every precrisis trend on the grounds that it is somehow associated with, and hence responsible, for the crisis—and the trend was toward a greater role for the private sector. The targets for the forces of reaction are obvious. The public has expressed widespread revulsion against the liberalization that led to more vibrant financial markets and freer financial institutions. The forces against globalization— the greater integration of countries through trade, multinational firms, capital flows, and migration—are also regrouping, gaining succor from the natural willingness to look abroad for the roots of one's problems. Diehard socialists are celebrating the grand crises that they see as harbingers of the collapse of capitalism.

Finance, markets, globalization, and free-enterprise capitalism will endure beyond this crisis. But recent events do ask us to make hard choices, not about capitalism itself, but about the form of free-enterprise capitalism we desire. If we do not mend the fault lines, we could well have another crisis, albeit different in its details from the current one. Another crisis will tax already stretched public and household finances, as well as the fraying political consensus behind the system, perhaps to breaking point. Reform will then be much harder. Instead of testing providence, we should take this crisis as a wake-up call for reform.

We have hard choices to make, as the good and the bad are typically closely intertwined. Radical positions that see the system as fundamentally broken are popular. They fit in with the public mood, and they are easy to tout in these times, their greatest merit being their distance from the current system.

In defending the basic structure of a system that has failed, I face the risk of being dismissed as a conservative, an unregenerate apologist, or worse, a toady of banking interests that favor the status quo. But although systemic failure does imply the need for serious reform, it does not mean that a radically different system would be better. I believe we have to work to fix the system, but there is a lot worth keeping. So the choices I propose are not necessarily meant to shock: they are meant to fix the problems I have identified, which are serious indeed. I start with the financial sector, where so many fault lines meet.

To begin, we have to take a stand on whether the financial sector actually helps the process of economic growth and well-being or whether it is just a sideshow, an irrelevance that makes its presence felt only by imploding period-ically. If the latter is the case, then reform is easy: prohibit many of the current activities of the financial sector, create a few stable monopolies, regulate all re-maining activities very closely, and forget about the sector for the next few decades. Serious economists and policy makers have called for such reforms, broadly under the rubric of "making finance boring." If the financial sector *is* central to economic growth, though, reform becomes more challenging, be-cause we have to limit finance's ability to do damage while harnessing its cre-ative energies. This is the challenge I address in this chapter.

To make the debate more concrete, I outline polar-opposite positions on a specific issue: expanding access to credit. I argue that it is both democratic and efficient to continue to expand the range of choices people have. Regulatory re-form that attempts to do otherwise will not survive in the long run, especially in a democracy. The real issue confronting us, therefore, is how to harness the benefits from financial development while limiting its instability. I outline some of the principles that reforms will need to respect and then take on the concrete issue of how we can reduce the incentive to take on tail risk that was so perva-sive during the current crisis. I end with thoughts on how to make the system resilient to unforeseen dangers.

## Democratization versus Debt

The financial sector is, in many ways, the brain of a modern economy. When it functions well, it allocates resources and risk effectively and thereby boosts eco-nomic growth while also making lives easier, safer, and more fulfilling. It broad-ens opportunity and attacks privilege. It works for all of us. Of course, when it works poorly, as it has done recently, it can do enormous damage while bene-fiting a very few.

A narrower concern, but one that touches every household, is whether ac-cess to finance is so dangerous that some people should be kept from it, or their access severely regulated. Diametrically differing views exist on whether broadening access to borrowing through developments such as credit cards, home equity loans, and payday lending is good or bad. One view is that the democra-tization of credit is an eminently desirable development.[2] It allows households to borrow against future income and smooth their consumption and expendi-ture over time, while also affording small entrepreneurs the ability to start their ventures: many a small venture has been started through borrowing on credit cards.

Proponents of this view make the fundamental assumption that most households are rational and responsible: they will borrow only as much as they need, with full awareness of the consequences. Any attempt to constrain their choices is paternalistic and unwarranted. Indeed, proponents of this view use the term *credit* to denote borrowing. *Credit*, according to the *Random House Dictionary*, is defined as "confidence in a purchaser's ability and intention to pay," and the term accords well with traditional American optimism about the future. If the best is yet to come, why not borrow against it and make today better still?

The opposite view is that borrowing is immoral, a giving in to temptation. Those who are indebted have no self-control and no sense of personal responsibility. Some of the blame goes to financiers (cast as loan sharks), who hold out easy access to lending, and some goes to marketers and advertisers who instill in the unsuspecting public desires for goods they do not need. Nevertheless, the overall consequence of broadening access to financing is, according to this view, overconsumption and overindebtedness, a temporary, illusory prosperity that leads eventually to poverty and remorse. Proponents of this view prefer the term *debt*, denoting *obligation*. There is a long tradition reflecting this view in the United States, epitomized by Benjamin Franklin in *Poor Richard's Almanac*: "But, ah, think what you do when you run in debt; *you give to another power over your liberty*. If you cannot pay at the time, you will be ashamed to see your creditor; you will be in fear when you speak to him, you will make poor pitiful sneaking excuses, and by degrees come to lose your veracity, and sink into base downright lying; for, as Poor Richard says, *the second vice is lying, the first is running in debt* ."[3]

Credit as a key to opportunity and as a means to the consumption you deserve, or debt as sin and as a mortgaging of a future you will never have—these two opposing views run through American history, with the former gaining ascendancy during boom times and times of rising inequality, and the latter gaining ground in downturns, when sobriety or rank pessimism returns. They represent a way of rephrasing the question I started with earlier: do we want to harness finance's creative energies, or do we think finance is so dangerous that most people should not have access to it and it should be stuffed back in the box it came from? Society's attitude toward financial reform hinges on whether it believes people and firms, by and large, can be trusted to make sensible financial decisions when given the means to do so.

The academic debate on this question is not conclusive. Even as research in behavioral economics tells us that some people make consistent mistakes in their financial decisions, it also tells us that a lot of behavior is rational and sensible. Indeed, as I argue throughout this book, it is typically not the rationality of the decision makers that is a problem. Rather, it is whether the apparent payoffs from decisions fully reflect the costs and benefits to society. Our goal should be to make decision makers internalize the full consequences of their decisions, rather than prevent them from making decisions altogether.

More generally, even if we conclude that some people took on too much debt during the boom, shutting off their access to some markets or limiting their financial choices (typically through legislation restricting the products, prices, or institutions they have access to) is paternalistic, undemocratic, and the surest way to ensure that the protected never have the opportunity to learn or improve themselves. Of course, we need to ensure they are given every opportunity to understand why certain choices are poor choices and to recognize the mistakes people traditionally make so that they can change their behavior. We should also ensure that they are protected from rank predators. But limiting choice is not the answer.

Free societies do revert to more paternalism and more constraints on choice following a crisis. It is natural to blame the crisis on the greater freedom to choose: if only choice had been more restricted (and, of course, with hindsight, it is crystal clear what the restrictions should have been), we would not have made the bad choices that were made, or so goes the thinking. The overall trend in civilized democratic societies, however, is to expand choice for all, not constrain it, let alone constrain it for only some. From a practical standpoint, regulations that limit choice may be popular in the aftermath of a crisis but will inevitably be whittled away as the memories of the crisis fade. And enacting regulations that will soon be outmoded and voted down carries an inherent cost: it creates a momentum for deregulation among the public that could go too far. It is better to get regulation right than to err in either direction.

In sum, if we reject the view that finance is a largely useless activity, or that we can keep its benefits only for a select and knowledgeable few, then the purpose of reform should be to draw out what is best in finance for the largest number of people while minimizing the risk of instability.

## Broad Principles of Reform

What guiding principles must reforms adhere to? Let me outline the key ones and then go on to a concrete example.

## *Should We Limit Competition?*

A healthy financial system that benefits citizens requires competition and in-novation. Oligopoly implies easy profits for the incumbents, profits they are loath to jeopardize by taking on risk. By contrast, the goal of broadening access, to reach new and underserved customers as well as future innovators, requires a financial system that is willing to take reasonable risks, and thus it requires competition. This is not a popular view at a time of crisis in a free-market econ-omy, for the natural tendency is to blame the market and factors like competi-tion that make it free.

One of the main concerns during the Great Depression was that prices were too low, and the mistaken diagnosis was excessive competition. The New Deal solution was to prop up prices by forming cartels. To smooth the political path for the needed legislation, words like "economic cannibalism" and "cut-throat price slashing" were used to describe competition.[4] Formerly "rugged individ-ualists" became "industrial pirates." Regulations meant to create cartels and sup-press competition became "codes of fair competition," while various forms of officially sanctioned collusion were described as "cooperative behavior." Of course, incumbent firms were fully complicit in the regulation and cartelization of the economy, for it made things easier for them.

The concerns during the recent crisis centered primarily on the underpric-ing of risk. Once again, it would be tempting but wrong to blame competition between banks. The right approach would be to reduce the various distortions to the pricing of risk that stem from actual and potential government interven-tion, as well as from herd behavior. We should not worry so much about rugged individualism as about undifferentiated groupthink, for that is the primary source of systemic problems.

A competitive system is also likely to produce the financial innovation nec-essary to broaden access and spread risk. Financial innovation nowadays seems to be synonymous with credit-default swaps and collateralized debt obligations, derivative securities that few outside Wall Street now think should have been in-vented. But innovation also gave us the money-market account, the credit card, interest-rate swaps, indexed funds, and exchange-traded funds, all of which have proved very useful. So, as with many things, financial innovations span the range from the good to the positively dangerous. Some have proposed a total ban on offering a financial product unless it has been vetted, much as the Food and Drug Administration vets new drugs. This proposal probably goes too far, as many products are minor tweaks on previous ones, are not life threatening, and cannot really be understood until tried out. Modest and free experimentation should be allowed but proliferation limited until regulators are satisfied they understand the innovation well, and the systemic risks it poses have been dealt with.

More generally, in an ever-changing global economy, stasis is often the greatest source of instability, for it means the system does not adapt to change. Competition and innovation, by contrast, help the system adapt, and if properly channeled, are key to ensuring variety, resilience, and therefore dynamic stability. Critics will be quick to point out that competition and innovation lead to greater instability during the run-up to a crisis: after all, securities like the CDO squared and the CDO cubed were so devilishly difficult to price that they had no market once mortgages started defaulting. However, it is not competition per se, but rather the distorted banker incentives and the distorted price of risk that led to the creation of these instruments.

### Reduce Incentive and Price Distortions: Manage Expectations of Government Intervention

As I argue in Chapter 7, some of the incentives to take excessive risks may have resulted from a breakdown of internal governance within banks, and some from a breakdown of external governance. These mechanisms need to be fixed, and I discuss some options below. But the primary reason for a systemic breakdown is invariably the underpricing of risk. One reason for underpricing is irrational exuberance: initial, moderate underestimates of risk feed on each other until they become a frenzy. Usually, though, such bubbles rarely occur out of the blue. The underpricing of risk in the period leading up to the recent crisis stemmed, in part, from anticipated government or central bank intervention in markets. And certainly, since the crisis hit, the Treasury and the Fed have intervened massively in markets, thus verifying the expectations. We need to find a way to dispel the notion that the government or its agencies will prop up a market, whether the market for housing or the market for liquidity.

### End Government Subsidies and Privileges to Financial Institutions

As damaging as government intervention to help specific markets is government intervention to prop up specific financial institutions. The essence of free-enterprise capitalism is the freedom to fail as well as to succeed. The market tends to favor institutions that are protected by the government from failing, asks too few questions of them, and gives them too many resources for their own good. Moreover, such protection distorts the competitive landscape. We have to aim for a system in which no private institution has implicit or explicit protections from the government, one in which every private institution that makes serious mistakes knows it will have to bear the full costs of those mistakes.

### Enact Cycle-Proof Regulation

As we emerge from the panic, righteous politicians feel the need to do something. Regulators, with their backbones stiffened by public disapproval of past laxity, will enforce almost any restrictions, while bankers, whose frail balance sheets and vivid memories make them eschew any risk, will be more accepting of such restrictions. But we tend to reform under the delusion that the regulated institutions and the markets they operate in are static and passive, and that the regulatory environment will not vary with the cycle. Ironically, faith in draconian regulation is strongest at the bottom of the cycle, when there is little need for participants to be regulated. By contrast, the misconception that markets will govern themselves is most widespread at the top of the cycle, at the point of maximum danger to the system. We need to acknowledge these differences and enact cycle-proof regulation, for a regulation set against the cycle will not stand. To have a better chance of creating stability throughout the cycle—of being cycle-proof—new regulations should be *comprehensive, nondiscretionary, contingent,* and *cost-effective.*

Regulations that apply comprehensively to all levered financial institutions are less likely to encourage the drift of activities from heavily regulated to lightly regulated institutions over the boom. Such a drift has been a source of instability, because its damaging consequences come back to hit the heavily regulated institutions in the bust, through channels that no one foresees. For example, the asset-backed securities that Citigroup had placed in thinly capitalized off-balance sheet vehicles came back onto its balance sheet when the commercial paper market dried up, contributing immensely to Citigroup's troubles. We have to recognize that because all areas of the financial sector are intimately interconnected, it is extremely hard to create absolutely safe areas and imprudent to ignore what happens outside supposedly safe areas.

Regulations that are nondiscretionary and transparently enforced have a greater chance of being adhered to, even in times of great optimism. Compliance can be more easily monitored by interested members of the media and the public, thus offering some check on the regulator. The regulated also have a good sense of how regulations will be implemented. One example of such regulation is the FDIC Improvement Act of 1991, which mandates that regulators take a series of ever more stringent actions against a bank as its regulatory capital drops below specified levels. The weakness in the act is that regulatory capital is hard for the public and the press to measure in real time, so it is difficult to gauge whether regulators are following through on the requirements of the law. Nevertheless, the act suggests a possible direction for new regulation.

Wherever possible, regulations should come into force only when strictly necessary: they should be triggered by adverse events rather than be required all the time. Such contingent regulations have two effects. First, because they kick in only some of the time, they are less cumbersome than regulation that is not contingent, and banks will not invest as much ingenuity in trying to evade them. Second, the level of the regulatory requirement—such as the required level of capital—can then be increased if necessary, so that it has the desired effect when really needed.

Finally, regulations that are not particularly costly for the regulated to implement or for the regulator to enforce are less likely to be evaded or ignored. Moreover, they are likely to have more staying power as memories of past problems fade.

### Reducing the Search for Tail Risk

Let us apply all these principles to a concrete question: how do we prevent the systematic tail risk taking that nearly destroyed the financial system? I have focused on two related examples of tail risks—the risk of default embedded in senior asset-backed securities and the liquidity risk inherent in financing potentially illiquid assets with very short-term debt. I examine detailed proposals for reducing such risk, because measures that seem reasonable at first glance often raise more concerns on closer examination.[5]

As I argue in Chapter 7, there are huge incentives at every level in the financial system to take on these tail risks if they can be concealed from those assessing performance. Those giving up the tail risk are willing to pay a premium to do so, while those taking it on and downplaying the eventual risk of payout can treat the premium as pure profit, the product of their natural brilliance rather than merely a compensation for risk. The premium paid by those selling the risk increases in proportion to the anticipated loss if the risk actually hits (they pay more if they think earthquakes will do more damage); and the higher the premium, the more of the risk the sellers are willing to take on (because they do not anticipate being around when their firms have to make good the loss). Too many firms will be eager to take on risks that have extremely costly consequences, and they will compete to take the risk at too low a price. The net result is that too much of the risk will be created.

Matters grow worse if, because of the extent of risk taking, everyone anticipates that when the risk actually materializes, the government or the Federal Reserve will be drawn in to support the markets underlying the tail risk, or the institutions taking it on. In that case, those taking on the tail risk will find it worthwhile even if it is common knowledge that they are doing so, because the government backstop will make it profitable. Few financial institutions will want to be left out of the orgy of risk taking. So what starts off as an attempt to take on hidden risk and fool the market will, if enough firms get in on the act and induce an anticipation of government intervention, become an overt and profitable play that is rewarded by the market.

If tail risk is knowingly taken, or knowingly encouraged by securities markets, the way to deal with it is to alter incentives throughout the corporate hierarchy, the financial firm's liability structure, and its regulatory structure. One seemingly obvious way to reduce the perverse incentive to take tail risk before risk taking becomes systemic is to do away with all pay tied to performance: to pay bankers like bureaucrats. Of course, firms can offer other rewards for performance, such as status and promotions, that are harder to eliminate. And even if it were possible to prevent evasion of the rules, there would be another obvious downside; bankers would have no incentive to work hard or take calculated risks. In today's competitive, fast-moving economy, bureaucratic bankers would not be an improvement over the status quo. What we need from bankers is competent risk management, not complete risk avoidance. So we have to find ways to reduce the incentive to take tail risk even while rewarding bankers for performance so that they continue to offer innovative products that meet customer needs and lend to the risky but potentially very successful start-up.

This means that wherever possible, the risk taker should suffer targeted penalties if the risk materializes, so that society does not feel the need to absolve them because the innocent, the connected, or the politically vocal will suffer alongside. Of course, extremely high penalties will deter even ordinary risk taking, so the penalties will have to be appropriately calibrated. It may also well be that no one, including markets, can anticipate some risks. To deal with such possibilities, it is necessary to build some private-sector buffers to absorb shocks, as well as make the system resilient to them. I will now be more specific.

### Altering Incentives Generated by Compensation

The most obvious form of tail risk taking is conducted by individual traders or company units, as was the case at AIG's Financial Products Division, whose staff benefited from the extraordinary profits and associated huge bonuses on the way up and were retained with high bonuses to clear up the mess they created on the way down. One way to make units internalize small-probability tail risks that senior management or risk managers may not see or understand is to hold a significant part of a unit's bonuses in any year in escrow, subject to clawbacks based on the unit's performance in subsequent years—a suggestion I made before banker bonuses became a political football.[6] Simply put, if a trader makes a hefty bonus this year, only a fraction should be paid out to her this year, with the remaining amount held back by the bank to be paid out over time on condition that her positions do not lose all the money earned this year in subsequent years. This will give the trader a longer horizon, creating some uncertainty about whether any tail risk she takes could actually hit before her bonus is paid, thus giving her greater incentive to avoid it.

Of course, such a compensation structure will be effective only if a trader knowingly takes tail risks, not if she is unintentionally guided into taking them. Crude limits on the positions individual traders or units are allowed to take, and mandatory diversification requirements, may also be necessary, not so much to prevent tail risk taking but to minimize the loss if it does occur.

### Incentives at the Top

The proposals above to manage tail risks presume that top management wants to curb such risk taking. I have discussed a number of reasons why CEOs might not want to do so, such as their desire to match the profits shown by other risk-taking managements and their insouciance about the downside because they believe that the government will intervene. Some old-time bankers reminisce fondly about the time when investment banks were partnerships, and partners had their entire wealth at stake. Given the size of banks today and their international sprawl, it would be difficult to convert them back into closely held partnerships in which mutual monitoring by partners inhibits excessive risk taking. And forcing banks to shrink might not make them safer. We have also seen that simply giving management an equity stake may not be enough—they realize enormous gains if the risk taking pays off but have limited liability if it does not.

Instead it may be useful to consider ways to place some of the burden of risk on top management, without necessarily having entire classes of claims being subject to that risk. For instance, the Squam Lake Working Group (a non-partisan group convened by Professor Ken French of Dartmouth College after the recent crisis to propose reforms) has suggested not only holding back some portion of top management bonuses and reducing them if there are future losses—much like the clawbacks I discussed earlier—but also writing these "holdbacks" down if the firm has to be bailed out in any way. Thus the holdbacks would serve as junior equity and give strong incentives to management to take precautions to avoid a bailout.

The financial firm's board is meant to be another check on mismanagement. But even when tail risk taking is not in the shareholders' interests, the bank's board of directors may not be an effective source of deterrence. Board members are generally poorly informed when they are truly independent, and excessively cozy with management when they are not. Lehman's board, for instance, consisted of very respectable independent directors. But at the time it filed for bankruptcy in 2008, of the ten-member board, nine were retired, with four over the age of 75.[7] One was a theater producer, another a former Navy admiral. Only two had direct experience in the financial services industry. Although advanced age is no disqualification, it typically suggests some remove from the cut-and-thrust of modern finance. Such a board, whose risk committee met only twice a year, had only limited ability to monitor Lehman's risk taking.

Boards can be strengthened by requiring more financial services expertise of directors, as well as by drawing them from outside Wall Street. Furthermore, a board can obtain better information if the risk managers in the firm are required to report directly to it on a regular basis. The board's risk committee should also have regular meetings to discuss firmwide risk with unit heads across the firm, without top management present, so that they have a sense of what is going on from those who are closest to the action. Of course, if competent boards are propelled by the same risk-taking incentives as top management, we will have to look elsewhere for ways to discipline risk taking.

Could bank supervisors play a role in monitoring risk taking by top management, as a second line of defense beyond the board, so to speak? Some commentators, including, famously, Alan Greenspan, were skeptical that supervisors would be able to do so. Supervisors are typically less well paid than private-sector executives, though they have more job security. Except for those really motivated by public service, supervisors tend to be either less talented or extremely risk averse, neither of which is a particularly helpful attribute in modulating private sector risk taking. Nevertheless, supervisors have two strengths that can make them useful checks on private risk taking. First, they have different incentives: they focus more on the small-probability risks of disaster than does the private sector. Second, they can demand data from firms across the industry and obtain a very good picture of where risk concentrations are building up. Because the tail risks that matter most are those that the whole system is exposed to, well-informed supervisors can monitor aggregate financial-sector exposures and warn firms that are taking too much risk to cease and desist.[8] The key is to be neither so intrusive that supervisors constantly substitute their judgment for that of the private sector nor to be so laissez-faire that they ignore systemic risk buildup.

For such a system to work, we need better information. Currently, far too few financial institutions know on a daily basis what their risk exposures are: what might happen if interest rates move up by 25 basis points, if Italian government bonds are downgraded, or if a bank in Ohio is seized by regulators. As a consequence, the regulators and supervisors do not know, either. That AIG was in deep trouble seemed to be news to the regulators who were attempting to deal with Lehman's impending failure—in part because AIG had found itself a weak regulator by buying a small savings and loan and ensuring its banking activities were regulated by the Office of Thrift Supervision.[9] In this day and age, for a regulator to be uninformed is unconscionable. Much of the process of acquiring and analyzing information can be automated. Regulators can require that this information be shared with them on a continuous basis, offering standard procedures and models with which to calculate the exposures. Standardization would be especially useful in the case of illiquid securities, assets, or positions, for which each institution currently calculates values and exposures in its own way, so that their reports are not comparable.

Of course, supervisors rarely find the right balance between intrusion and laissez-faire, and political pressures tend to make them excessively lax in booms and conservative in downturns, just the opposite of what their behavior ought to be. If the gathered information were made public, however, it could offer a measure of public oversight over supervision. For instance, once the information about aggregate exposures and individual financial-firm exposures was put together, much of it could be shared with the markets, after some delay, in a way that could be easily digested. Supervisors would be forced to explain their actions (or inaction) if exposures were seen to be excessive.

Regulatory authorities are often unwilling to reveal too much detail about exposures for fear that this may trigger the very panic they seek to avoid. Clearly, the wrong time to start revealing exposures is when the public is anxious about bank health. The right moment to start is in normal times, when no one is likely to panic. After that, if data on exposures are made public on a regular basis, the public can exert steady and healthy pressure on the financial firms.

Public exposure can reduce tail risk taking in its early stages, for tail risk is of significant value to management at that stage only if the public is unaware of the extent of the company's exposure to risk. Bond holders will typically not be happy to learn that the hundreds of millions in dollars of profits made in the past quarter came from taking on trillions of dollars' worth of exposure to particular rare events.

## The Repricing of Financial Claims and Incentives

Public exposure can work by making the financial claimants on a financial firm check excess risk taking. Of course, equity holders, who get much of the benefit, may actually favor tail risk taking if the financial firm's equity cushion is thin relative to the size of the firm: they have little to lose. So a larger capital cushion is necessary to deter risk taking. Below, I suggest ways that such capital can be raised. Also, as I argue above, many debt holders—not just insured depositors but even holders of long-term unsecured debt—thought they would be bailed out by the government, so the interest rate they demanded did not adjust upward as the financial firm took more risk. But debt holders could be an effective constraint on risky behavior if they bore the downside risk, for their future anticipated losses would be reflected in the higher interest rate they demanded from the financial firm. If interest rates move up substantially on a large portion of the financial firm's debt when it takes more risk, thereby reducing profits, both management and the board may be deterred from risky behavior. At the very least, such an increase in rates paid will be a strong signal to the public and to regulators that the financial firm is taking substantially more risk. Therefore, regulatory reform should focus on ensuring that an important segment of a financial firm's debt holders know they should expect painful losses if the financial firm takes too much risk.

But neither equity holders nor debt holders will worry much once risk taking becomes so systemic that the market comes to rely on government intervention to prop up markets when the risk hits. In that situation, management and stockholders or bondholders unite to see risk taking as a value-maximizing activity. And if the firm is deemed too systemically important to be allowed by the authorities to fail, the financial firm's investors are unlikely to ever bear the full cost of big losses. This is a situation tailor-made for encouraging tail risk taking, because the firm makes a lot of profits in good times—everyone purchases tail risk insurance from firms like AIG that will be propped up by the government—and AIG runs to the government for a bailout if the costly tail risk ever hits. Let us take these situations in turn.

### Government Intervention in Markets

With the government so heavily involved in mortgage lending, both directly through the FHA and Ginnie Mae and indirectly through Fannie Mae and Freddie Mac, there was little chance that the market for housing finance, especially subprime housing finance, would be left unsupported even if a big shock hit. Similarly, the Fed and Treasury have supported virtually all the big banks that chose to take liquidity risk.

Clearly, the way to reduce tail risk taking under these circumstances is to back off from government intervention, to the extent possible. There is no inherent reason why the government should have such a large presence in the market for housing finance, other than the fact that the middle class has grown used to implicit housing subsidies. Government conservatorship of Fannie and Freddie gives it an opportunity to create true private-sector housing finance by breaking up these monoliths and creating a handful of private entities, none of which have an implicit government guarantee. At the same time, both the FHA and Ginnie Mae should be shrunk steadily. Although some think the fickleness of the private sector—as evidenced by the current drying up of private subprime housing finance—is a reason for the government to maintain its presence, it is the unsustainable levels to which house prices have been pushed, in part because of that very government presence, that has caused private finance to dry up.

Similarly, there really is no reason other than political pressure for the Fed to take us from bubble to bubble by cutting interest rates to near zero and flooding the market with liquidity. Ironically, the lesson from the Great Depression—that letting the banks go under is not a good idea—has been so well absorbed by the Fed that it is played for a patsy by the banks. One reform I discuss in Chapter 9 is to create a stronger social safety net. That would take some pressure off the Fed to keep injecting stimulus so long as jobs are not growing.

In addition, the exercise of monetary policy should be rethought to take into account its effects on risk taking by the private sector. Financial stability should become a more explicit part of the Fed's mandate, given as much weight as employment and low inflation. The Fed ought to ask itself whether it is possible that nominal interest rates could be too low, even when the economy is in trouble. The nineteenth-century editor of the *Economist,* Walter Bagehot, was fond of saying, "John Bull can stand many things but he can't stand 2 percent." Similarly, John Doe cannot stand interest rates near zero, and when the Fed pushes short rates very low, especially when deflation is not a clear and present danger but just a possibility, savers move to holding riskier assets, pushing all manner of risk premiums down and prices up. A rock-bottom nominal short-term interest rate prompts risk taking and makes price bubbles more likely; it is unclear, however, that it is much more helpful in prompting corporate capital investment and job growth than a somewhat higher but still low nominal short-term interest rate.

Moreover, if the Fed on occasion has to cut interest rates sharply, it should be prepared to raise interest rates higher than strictly warranted by economic activity once the emergency is over. Such interest-rate policies will reward those who maintain liquid balance sheets and prevent others from becoming overly illiquid in their activities.[10] It will also offset the one-sided discriminatory intervention by the Fed that favors debtors at the expense of savers.

Neither set of recommendations—disengaging from housing or following a more evenhanded monetary policy—will be easy to adopt. Powerful groups, including real estate developers and financiers, have an interest in seeing continued government involvement in real estate. Should we wait for the next deep crisis for the government to distance itself? Similarly, monetary economists and central bankers (often cut from the same cloth) will think it crazy that interest rates should be related to anything other than real activity—a point made abundantly clear by Ben Bernanke in his speech to the American Economic Association in Atlanta on January 3, 2010. As we have seen though, the financial sector can affect real activity with a vengeance. We have made the mistake of not paying attention to risk taking before; we should not make it again.

### Eliminating "Too Systemic to Fail"

One reason why markets did not penalize financial firms that took on large amounts of tail risk was that they thought the firms were too systemically important to be allowed to fail by the government. Here again the government has substantiated these beliefs by bailing out nearly every large or interconnected bank, including, most controversially, large banks that had bought insurance from AIG. The government simply cannot afford to be seen as a soft touch by financial firms or the market. Hence one of the most important items on the reform agenda is to ensure that no private financial firm is deemed to have the protection of the government.

Entities that are widely known to be too systemic to fail not only have warped incentives, but they also have a competitive advantage over entities that do not enjoy such implicit protection: they can take on costly tail risks secure in the knowledge that they can appropriate the resulting revenues in good times while passing on the risk to the government in bad times. Equally problematic, market investors, also knowing that they will be kept whole by the government, have no incentive to discourage them. Indeed, because the strategy offers tremendous potential profits and limited losses (to the equity holders, that is), equity investors will applaud it: the most risk-loving banks had the highest stock prices before the onset of the crisis. Because bond holders will not demand a higher premium for bearing the risk of losses, banks can double up their bets with leverage. Finally, because these banks enjoy a lower cost of financing, they can grow even larger and more complex; and they have an incentive to do so to make themselves even more systemic.

When a downturn hits, the problems associated with entities deemed too systemic to fail multiply. Resources are trapped in corporate structures that have repeatedly proved their incompetence, and further resources are sucked from the taxpayer as these institutions destroy value. Confident in the knowledge that the government will come to their rescue, these institutions can play a game of chicken with the authorities by refusing to take adequate precautions against failure, such as raising equity.

Perhaps just as important are the political consequences of such rescues. It is hard for the authorities to refute allegations of crony capitalism. Aside from the stated intent of saving the economy, there is no discernible difference between a bailout motivated by the sense that institutions are systemically important and one motivated by the desire of those in authority to rescue their friends or their once and future employers. Even as conspiracy theorists have a field day, painting everyone remotely associated with the financial system into a web of corruption, the damage to the public's faith in the system of private enterprise is enormous: it senses two sets of rules, one for the systemically important and another for the rest of us. And the conspiracy theorists do have a point: the leeway afforded to the authorities in choosing who is too systemic to fail allows tremendous scope for discretion, and hence corruption.

I have avoided referring to institutions as too *big* to fail. This is because there are entities that are very large but have transparent, simple structures that allow them to be closed down easily—for example, a firm running a family of regulated mutual funds. By contrast, some relatively small entities—examples include the monoline bond insurers who guaranteed municipal bonds, and Bear Stearns —caused substantial stress to build up through the system. A number of factors other than size may cause an institution to be systemically important, including its centrality to a market, the extent to which other systemically important institutions are exposed to it, the extent to which inflicting losses on the liability holders will also inflict disproportionate losses on the assets, and the complexity of the institution's interactions with the financial system, which may render the authorities uncertain about the systemic consequences of its failure and reluctant to take the risk of finding out.

There are three main ways of dealing with these problems. First, try to prevent institutions from becoming systemically important. If they do become important, force them to have additional private-sector buffers to minimize the need for the government intervention. If, despite these buffers, they do become truly distressed, make it easier for the authorities to allow them to fail. I discuss each of these measures in turn.

### Keeping Institutions from Becoming Systemically Important

A number of suggestions are circulating on how to keep institutions from becoming systemically important. The most common is to stop them from expanding beyond a certain size, an idea most closely associated with the former Fed chairman, Paul Volcker. While prima facie attractive, this proposal has weaknesses.

Although large institutions are more likely to be systemic, size is neither a necessary nor a sufficient condition. Bear Stearns was not considered large by most calculations, though it was considered connected enough to need saving. On the other hand, the mutual-fund group Vanguard manages more than a trillion dollars in assets but would probably not qualify as systemic. Not all aspects of size are equally troubling.

Moreover, even if we could be specific about the aspects of size that are troubling, banks would try to evade any restrictions on size by economizing on whatever measure served as a criterion, whether assets, capital, or profits. Crude size limits would likely lead banks to conceal a lot of financial activity from the regulator, only to have it come back to light (and to balance sheets) at the worst of times. There are many legal ways to mask asset size. Instead of holding assets on their balance sheet, banks can offer guarantees to assets placed in off-balance sheet vehicles, much like the conduits of the recent crisis. If, instead, capital were the measure, then we would be pushing banks to economize on it as much as possible; this is hardly a recipe for safety. And if it were profits, we would be inviting healthy banks to park profits elsewhere while rewarding sickly ones by allowing them to expand indefinitely.

Also, being big has some virtues. Larger banks may be better at diversifying and attracting managerial talent (including risk managers). Although a poorly managed $2 trillion bank creates immense problems for the system, the problems could be even greater with one hundred banks of $20 billion in size, each of which has taken similar risks. What is important is not size per se but the concentration and correlation of risk in the system, as well as the extent of exposure relative to capital. Indeed, in the past regulators have intervened to bail out a system because entities were too numerous to fail—the forbearance displayed to the U.S. savings and loan industry in the early 1980s being one example.

Instead of imposing a blanket size limit on institutions, regulators should use more subtle mechanisms, such as prohibiting mergers of large banks or encouraging the breakup of large banks that seem to have a propensity for getting into trouble. Entities such as the Federal Trade Commission already have such authority. Although there are always concerns about whether regulators will use these sorts of powers arbitrarily, they are no more difficult for legislators and courts to oversee than are powers based on anticompetitive considerations.

Turning to proposals to limit activities by insured banks through some modern version of the Glass-Steagall Act of 1933, these again seem less attractive on further reflection. Obviously, some activities of a large bank add considerably to risk and opacity. To the extent possible, these should be clearly separated in legal entities that are not affected by the bank's failure. For instance, banks should not attempt to use client assets that are pledged to them in their prime brokerage units (units that lend securities, offer loans, and undertake asset-management functions for clients, typically hedge funds) in further transactions.[11] The commingling of client assets with the bank's own funding activities reduces transparency, increases risk, and was an important reason why many investment banks experienced runs in the current crisis, as clients tried to withdraw their assets before they got entangled in the bank's bankruptcy. Of course, such a separation would increase a bank's cost of borrowing, but the benefits here might outweigh the costs.

Proprietary trading—in which the bank uses its balance sheet, partly funded by government-insured deposits, to take speculative positions—is another activity that has come in for censure. The reason critics want to ban it is, in my view, wrong, but there is another reason to consider limiting it. Critics argue that proprietary trading is risky. It is hard to see this as an important cause of the crisis: banks did not get into trouble because of large losses made on trading positions. They failed because they held mortgage-backed securities to maturity, not because they traded them. Regional banks have failed by the dozen because of loans they made for commercial real estate, an activity that no one is talking of prohibiting. It is a fallacy to think that just because certain activities are prima facie riskier than others, keeping banks from those activities will make banks safer overall. In truth, if banks want to take risk, they can simply go further down the spectrum of risk in any of the activities permitted to them. For example, so long as they can lend, they can freely make unsecured, long-term, "covenant-lite" loans to heavily indebted firms. The focus should be on limiting their overall incentive to take risks and their propensity to join with other banks to take risks as a herd, rather than to ban a specific activity, unless the activity has no redeeming financial purpose.

Nevertheless, there is another reason for considering ways to limit proprietary trading. Banks that are involved in many businesses obtain an enormous amount of private information from them. This information should be used to help clients, not to trade against them.[12] Banks effectively have an unfair informational advantage over the rest of us in trading: they can use inside information, despite the presence of firewalls within a bank that are meant to prevent sensitive client or market information from being shared with traders. This advantage should be reduced by limiting proprietary trading. I say *limiting* because some legitimate activities, including hedging and market making, could be hard to distinguish from proprietary trading. A crude overall limit on a bank's trading for its own account, no matter what the purpose, is one possibility, but it suffers from the same problems as any crude limit has. Perhaps an initial crude limit, refined over time with experience, as was the case with capital requirements, may be the way to go.

The best way to keep institutions from becoming systemically important might not be through crude prohibitions on size or activity but through the collecting and monitoring by regulators of information about interinstitution exposures as well as risk concentrations in the system. The regulator could ensure, through command and control, that the system is not overexposed to any single source of risk, institution, or class of institutions. Regulators themselves would need to be monitored; hence, as I suggested earlier, information on exposures should be released periodically and publicly, after the passage of an appropriate amount of time. Such measures would be less dramatic and punitive than size or activity limits but more easily enforced and probably more effective.

### Building Better Buffers

Despite the best efforts of the authorities in discouraging financial institutions from becoming systemic, some institutions will become so. Perhaps some will have special capabilities that enable them to dominate certain product markets or customer clienteles; others may just be highly efficient and thus big. Whatever the reason, once a systemically important institution becomes seen as such, it will automatically enjoy some advantages in funding and in selling its products. To offset these advantages, regulators can require these institutions to hold more capital. Equity capital is costly.[13] The implicit tax on the institutions (because equity capital is a more expensive form of financing for financial institutions than debt) would serve to offset their financing advantage, and, by creating additional buffers, make it less likely that they will become a drain on the taxpayer.

Precisely because equity capital is costly, regulators need to think of ways to achieve the necessary size of capital buffers without imposing huge costs that banks will try to evade. Regulators could put less emphasis on additional permanent-equity capital and more on contingent capital, which is infused when the institution or the system is in trouble. In one version of contingent capital, systemically important banks could issue debt that would automatically convert to equity when the bank's capital ratio falls below a certain value.[14] In another, systemically important levered financial institutions would be required to buy fully collateralized insurance policies (from unlevered institutions, foreigners, or the government) that would infuse capital into these institutions when they are in trouble.[15]

Both convertible contingent debt and capital insurance are exposed to significant downside risk and, if properly priced by the market, will be the proverbial canary in the coal mine: they will reflect the market's perception of the extent of risk taking by the firm. Of course, for the risk to be properly priced, everyone should know that the authorities will not bail out this class of claims, no matter how they treat the rest of the firm. One reason the authorities bail out financial-firm claim holders is that they do not know whether these claims are held by other financial firms: by letting the claims bear losses, they could be precipitating a cascade of failures. It is therefore important that regulators prohibit any levered financial firms from holding contingent convertibles or writing capital insurance (or, for that matter, holding unsecured long-term debt issued by other leveraged financial firms). Instead mutual funds, pension funds, and sovereign wealth funds should be the holders of choice.

By requiring systemically important entities to have stronger buffers against failure, regulators would reduce the likelihood that they would take advantage of their status. If a firm is made near fail-safe by its equity cushion, the prospect of government protection against failure confers little advantage.

### Making Financial Firms Easier to Resolve

In dire crises, some systemically important firms may eat through their capital and be close to failure no matter how good the prior supervision or how ample the equity buffers. If some of their activities are essential to overall economic health, we need to figure out how to "resolve" them—to keep the core businesses running while imposing appropriate costs on investors. One of the key objectives of a resolution mechanism is to impose appropriate losses on debt holders so that debt holders do not merrily acquiesce in equity holders' tail risk taking without demanding an additional risk premium, confident they will be bailed out by the government if necessary.

Regulators currently do not have resolution authority over nonbank financial firms or bank holding companies, and proceedings in ordinary bankruptcy court would take too long: the financial business would evaporate in the meantime. It is therefore essential for regulators to obtain resolution authority, which would effectively allow them to function as a bankruptcy court. One reason that bankruptcy proceedings are slow is that the court needs to determine all the assets and liabilities of a firm before it decides what can be preserved and who should bear the losses. With simple bank structures, all this information is readily available. But systemically important institutions generally have far from simple structures. Some of the complexity simply builds over time, as firms are put together through mergers or start businesses across borders; some comes from attempts to avoid taxes or hide activities from regulatory authorities; and some comes simply from untidy management. Lehman had more than six hundred subsidiaries when it filed for bankruptcy.

Because it is a nightmare to resolve such an institution today, let alone do it quickly, bailouts may seem like the only practical option. One way out, however, is to put the onus of the task back on the financial institutions themselves. Every systemically important institution should meet with regulators periodically to review its "living will," a plan that would enable it to be resolved quickly—ideally, over a weekend—in the event of imminent failure. Such a plan would require institutions to track and document their exposures much more carefully and in a timely manner, probably through a much better use of technology. To prevent this from becoming merely a cursory formality, much of the detail in a living will could be released to the public and markets in a form that is easy to digest.

Because it might well be impossible to anticipate all contingencies, the living will might be of limited use in guiding the actual resolution of an institution. Nevertheless, it could be immensely useful in simplifying bank structures. Not only would the need to develop a plan give such institutions the incentive to work with regulators to minimize organizational complexity and improve the ease of resolution, but it might indeed force management to think the unthinkable during booms, thus helping it avoid the costly busts. Most important, it would convey to the market the message that the authorities are serious about allowing the systemically important to fail. As we leave the crisis behind, this will be the most important message to convey.

## Resilience

Having discussed how we can reduce tail risk seeking, as well as the related problem of having entities that are considered too systemic to fail, let me turn to the possibility of unknown unknowns. Thus far, I have argued for ways to reduce the likelihood of crises stemming from acts of commission. But we also have to address the possibility of crisis stemming from events and circumstances that no one was aware of or could anticipate; we must acknowledge that even with the best incentives in the world, a combination of mistakes, irrational beliefs, and sheer bad luck could plunge us into crisis again. We have to find ways to make the system more resilient to acts of omission—indeed, to make it robust no matter what the source of the problem. Almost certainly, the trigger will not be subprime mortgage-backed securities the next time around.[16] Put differently, we need not only to enforce the fire code to reduce the possibility of fires: we also need to install sprinklers.[17]

### Resources

Clearly, resources are important to deal with any crisis. In the current crisis, one reason industrial economies did not suffer the typical fate of emerging markets is that their governments could promise to guarantee bank liabilities to quell a panic, and those promises were credible. However, the crisis has stretched the finances of industrial countries, with a number of governments having lost their top ratings. To be prepared once again for emergencies, they have to restore government financial health by paying down debt, using some combination of tax hikes and expenditure cuts in a manner that does not have too adverse an impact on growth. I discuss U.S. policies on these issues in more detail in the next chapter.

Although it is important to have resources, making them readily available is not always a good thing. Proposals are currently being debated that would make resources easily available to the government and the central bank to carry out rescues, thus avoiding the kind of uncertainty that set off a near-panic in the weeks before Congress passed the Troubled Asset Relief Program in 2008.[18] Such a move would be a mistake because it would legitimize rescues. Would a treasury secretary ever let a large institution go under again if Congress had sanctioned rescues by providing ready access to funds? We should not make the process of appropriating resources to carry out rescues any easier. As Walter Bagehot rightly felt, systemic financial firms and markets should have some uncertainty about what will happen if they get into trouble. Having Congress debate rescues certainly adds uncertainty and some oversight, and Congress has shown an ability to act when needed—though it may have taken the treasury secretary going down on bended knee before the Speaker of the House to make it happen![19] Having one or two large firms experience severe distress, or even fail, before the cavalry comes to the rescue is not a bad idea *pour encourager les autres*.

## Redundancy

A system becomes fragile if it is overly reliant on any single institution, market, regulator, or regulation. We need real redundancy and variety—multiple pathways for providing any financial service, without too much reliance on any one path. For instance, as the subprime market heated up, too many investors started depending on ratings. It did not matter that different rating agencies provided those ratings or that the investors were diversified across a variety of mortgage-backed securities: what was compromised was the rating process itself. When suspicions rose about ratings, the entire market collapsed. To provide real redundancy and variety, we need not only multiple players at each level of the securitization process but also multiple ways of financing mortgages other than through securitization.

One way to obtain variety is to impose uniform regulation across institutional forms. For instance, banks in Europe issue covered bonds, which are essentially bonds issued against a pool of mortgages. They are similar to mortgage-backed securities, except that the investor in these bonds can ask the bank to pay what is owed if the pool of mortgages proves insufficient to cover the bonds. Banks in the United States chose to securitize mortgages instead and held many of them in off–balance sheet vehicles that came back on their balance sheets in times of trouble. In retrospect, covered bonds might have been a more transparent way of holding mortgages and might have given banks more incentive to be careful. But capital requirements favored off–balance sheet vehicles. Lighter, more uniform regulation across institutional forms would allow for greater institutional variety and more efficient, less regulator-determined, ways of undertaking activities.

We should, however, recognize that when more institutions come under the same regulatory umbrella, we open the door to a different mistake: if the regulator makes a mistake, she coordinates more institutions into following it. For example, because regulators around the world required very little capital to be held against super-senior mortgage-backed claims, banks around the world loaded up on them and took enormous losses together. By contrast, a number of large hedge funds stayed clear of these securities, partly because the hedge funds were not subject to capital regulation. Regulatory mistakes are particularly harmful because the regulator coordinates the regulated into following the mistake: the wider the ambit of the regulator, the more problematic the mistake.

There is, therefore, a trade-off. By spreading the regulatory net uniformly, we ensure that no institutions are favored or disadvantaged and that the institution most suited to an activity undertakes it. But we also increase the impact of regulatory mistakes. One way to mitigate this effect is to reduce the extent to which regulators embed what are essentially judgment calls—such as the amount of capital to be held against a certain activity—in regulations. Light, effective regulation is less liable to have serious consequences in the event of mistakes.

### Phasing Out Deposit Insurance

Finally, to ensure variety, we should not privilege any particular institutional form. An enormous source of privilege for banks is deposit insurance: if an institution happens to be funded with a certain form of demandable debt, that is deposits, the deposits are fully backed by the government's deposit insurer on payment of a nominal fee. No other institutional form has its short-term debt thus insured.

I asked earlier whether the activities of insured banks should be restricted. Perhaps a better question is whether banks should have deposit insurance at all. This may be a strange question to ask at a time when governments all over the world have guaranteed *all* the debt issued by their banks, not just the small, already insured deposits. But that is precisely the reason for my question. Deposit insurance is not meant to quell panics by preventing bank runs: the government, as we have recently seen, takes care of that. Instead, it merely protects individual banks from market discipline. Put differently, with implicit government guarantees all over the place, should we not strive to remove explicit government guarantees where we can?

One reason for insuring deposits was to provide a safe means of savings to households where none existed. Today, this rationale is archaic—a money-market fund invested in Treasury bills can provide that safety. A well-diversified money-market fund invested in highly rated commercial paper and marked every day to market is almost as safe and should not experience the kinds of runs experienced by funds that were not marked to market during this crisis.[20]

Another important reason for insuring deposits was to ensure that the payment system would be relatively safe: unregulated, unsafe, uninsured entities could not pollute it and cause the system to freeze. But now that technological advances, such as real-time gross settlement payments, make it possible to protect the payment system from the failure of any payer, even this rationale is weak.

Deposit insurance does help keep small, undiversified banks in business. To the extent that these small banks are important in making loans in the local community—to the local bakery or toy shop—they have some economic and social value. One possibility is to retain deposit insurance for small and medium-sized banks in return for their paying a fair insurance premium, but to reduce it progressively for larger banks until it is eliminated.

Clearly, if banks are seen as too big to fail, eliminating deposit insurance is moot, as the bank will be bailed out anyway. The United Kingdom deposit insurance system, which was partial, did not prevent Northern Rock from getting into trouble or the government from coming to the rescue. The point of eliminating deposit insurance, however, is to make depositors think before they make a bank too big. Unlike depositors in the United Kingdom (where all bank deposits were partially insured, and therefore depositing in a large bank was significantly safer), depositors in large banks under my proposal would have the choice between being fully insured in a small bank and largely uninsured in a large bank. Such a measure would place some constraints on the growth of seriously mismanaged larger banks while also leveling the playing field.

Phasing out deposit insurance does not mean doing away with regulation. Because the government will continue to step in when the financial sector gets into deep trouble, it will have to regulate financial institutions. But it can regulate large institutions more uniformly, based on their capital structure (their capital and short-term debt) and the nature of their assets (their holdings in illiquid securities and, in illiquid loans) rather than on the basis of whether they have a banking license.

It is not easy to contemplate doing away with deposit insurance. Few depositors today can recall a time when deposits were not insured. Yet uninsured banks existed for centuries. With alternative ways of ensuring the safety of household investments (such as money-market deposits) and safe payments, and with banks already protected enough from discipline because of recent events, perhaps it is time we did away with an archaic privilege.

## Caesar's Wife

Before concluding, I raise a final issue. I have focused on ways to ensure that the government is not easily drawn into supporting specific markets or private institutions. I have assumed that the government, like Caesar's wife, is above suspicion. The public has widespread concerns that it is not, as a quick survey of the blogosphere and cable news networks (admittedly not an unbiased sample of the public) suggests, and some of these concerns are justified. When a U.S. Treasury employee goes directly from running the biggest bailout fund in history to work for a company that runs the biggest bond fund in the world, and when another Treasury employee goes from organizing financial-sector rescues directly to running one of the banks that is most in need of rescue, the public's trust is strained. No matter how honorable the intentions of the individuals in question (and I have no doubt that they are honorable) or how careful the new employer in avoiding conflicts of interest, the deals, to put it mildly, stink.

Even as the private financial sector has displayed a tin ear for the political consequences of such behavior, its alumni in the government apparently fail to understand the difficulty. In normal times, the revolving door between government and the private sector has enabled governments around the world to attract tremendous talent, even while underpaying grossly. And in normal times, the conflicts of interest inherent in the revolving door are small. In downturns, however, they may be enormous: the government's coffers are fully open, and a stroke of a pen or a key can send billions of dollars of public money in one direction or another. The rules governing the revolving door have to be reexamined.

There is a broader question of whether government action is influenced excessively by Wall Street. I believe that when Wall Street alumni occupy powerful positions in the government or the Federal Reserve, they do what they think is best for the United States. But what they think accords with their Wall Street training and with the opinions of the people they talk to—and these people also are all largely from the Street. *Cognitive capture* is a better description of this phenomenon than crony capitalism.[21] The nexus needs to be broken, possibly by recruiting talent from outside Washington and New York, and even from outside finance, to staff critical positions in the Treasury—former career regulators, corporate executives with finance experience, and, dare I say, academics. Diversity will be key to improving trust.

## Summary and Conclusion

How do we preserve the benefits of the democratization of finance while ensuring that the system does not permit excessive risk? The answers I propose in this chapter are not so dramatic as doing away with the private sector or gagging and binding it, as suggested by Progressives, or doing away with all government and regulation, as suggested by the ideological Right. The problems emanated at the interfaces between the private sector and the government—the location of the fault lines—but since we cannot do away with either side, realistic reforms have to work on managing the interface. We are, however, in the position of someone asking for directions and getting the response, "Well, I wouldn't start from here."

The supercharged financial sector, having taken full advantage of the implicit guarantees embedded in the government's desire to push housing credit and promote employment growth, has ended up flat on its back. The government has then delivered on the guarantees to the best of its ability and, in fact, done more. It now has the task of convincing the financial sector that it will not do so again.

But the government has not withdrawn from housing finance: in fact, it is even more tightly enmeshed now. Even if it were to take care of the political compulsions that draw it in to supporting some markets and hence the financial sector, it still has to convince the financial sector that no entity is too systemically important to be allowed to fail. So the key question in financial sector reform is, How do we get the private sector to price risk properly again, without assuming government intervention? The proposals in this chapter offer a path.

The thrust has to be using transparency to draw the interested public into monitoring the relationship between the government or regulator and the financial sector. Much of what I propose falls short of the dramatic remedies that some desire. But the words of Justice Louis Brandeis, from a letter of 1922, are as apt for financial-sector reform as elsewhere: "Do not believe that you can find a universal remedy for evil conditions or immoral practices in effecting a fundamental change in society (as by State Socialism). And do not pin too much faith in legislation. Remedial institutions are apt to fall under control of the enemy and to become instruments of oppression."[22] His proposed alternative was what we would now call transparency, which he referred to as publicity: "Publicity is justly commended as a remedy for social and industrial diseases. Sunlight is said to be the best of disinfectants; electric light the most efficient policemen."[23]

I now turn to the reforms that are needed in the U.S. economy, focusing on how to improve access to quality education and how to strengthen the safety net.

# Improving Access to Opportunity in America

I ARGUE IN CHAPTER 1 THAT the pressures created by relatively stagnant incomes for many in the United States mirrored those in the typical developing country; they led U.S. politicians to push credit as a palliative. Subprime mortgage lending was the symptom, dwindling economic opportunity for many the cause.

Not all forms of income inequality are economically harmful. Higher wages serve to reward the very talented and the hardworking, identify the jobs in the economy that need the most skills, and signal to the young the benefits of investing in their own human capital. A forced equalization of wages that disregards the marginal contributions of different workers will deaden incentives and lead to a misallocation of resources and effort.

However, when the only pathways to high wages are seen to be birth, influence, luck, or cheating, wage differentials may not act as a spur to effort. Why bother when effort is not the route to rewards? Indeed, as the political economists Alberto Alesina and George-Marios Angeletos argue, perceptions in a democracy as to how high wages or wealth are obtained can create self-reinforcing patterns.[1] If society believes people earn high wages as a result of their training and hard work, it is less willing to tax high earners, thereby ensuring they have strong incentives to acquire skills and exert effort. If society believes people earn high wages because of connections, chance, or crookedness, then it will tax incomes more heavily, and since few of the honest will then bother to work hard, only those with influence, the lucky, or the cheats will flourish.

Indeed, one reason why the U.S. electorate today seems so receptive to proposals to make the rich pay much more in taxes is that perceptions of who is rich may have changed. Not so long ago, the prototypical rich person in the United States was the local self-made entrepreneur who owned the car dealership and the movie theater and who came from the same high school as everyone else. Today, it is the distant, overpaid CEO, the greedy banker, or the hedge-fund manager who thrives on insider trades. Stereotypes and perceptions matter: the rich are no longer us, they are *them*.

The United States needs to prevent further social polarization, both in reality and in perception. The precise way of doing this does matter. If the rise in the wage inequality most people experience stems from the relative scarcity of workers with more human capital, as I argue in Chapter 1, then the response has to be to improve the quality of human capital of the workforce. Heavy taxation solely to equalize wages will do little to tackle that problem and will reduce incentives to work or acquire human capital. This is why I will take as a given that the best way of reducing unnecessary income inequality is to reduce the inequality in access to better human capital.

Equalizing access can head off brewing conflicts. For instance, if rich parents can pay for better schools, extra tuition, and eventually good universities for their children while poor parents cannot, the poor will become more intolerant of high incomes and wealth. Apart from increasing conflict between the haves and the have-nevers, unequal access may also increase resistance to economic reforms that expand opportunity. For instance, the poor urban worker who does not have access to a university education may care little for reforms that make it easier to open small businesses, because she has no chance of obtaining the financing to open one.[2]

What we prefer politically depends on where we stand: if we stand at very different places, it is harder for us to come together as a society to make mutually beneficial decisions. And more than the quality of its institutions, what distinguishes a developed country from a developing one is the degree of consensus in its politics, and thus its ability to take actions to secure a better future despite short-term pain. Unequal access, and the resulting inequality, destroys consensus. And although this chapter focuses on the United States, the issues addressed here are relevant in many countries, including developing ones like China and India.

The problem is that the political and economic costs of any effort to improve access—for instance, providing quality preschool care for poor children—are incurred up front, whereas the benefits lie in the future. It is hard to get the public, and consequently politicians, excited about such undertakings, especially at a time of straitened public finances. But if nothing is done, inequality will feed on itself. The costs of redressing deficiencies will only increase, and many citizens will be left irremediably ill-equipped for a productive life in society. Put differently, the status quo entails unacceptable and growing costs, and avoiding those very visible costs has to be part of the cost-benefit calculus.

In arriving at solutions we should resist two seemingly attractive but dangerous notions. One is that government spending will fix all problems. The truth is that money is rarely the key missing ingredient, as we saw with the growth of developing nations. Indeed, government largesse can crowd out, if not corrupt, individual and community initiative. That does not mean, however, that all societal problems will be solved by spontaneous voluntary initiative, the second dangerous notion. Government effort (and sometimes money) is needed at key leverage points to coordinate individual and community action. Again and again, we see that successes involve a coming together of key players, a broader definition of the problem (and hence solutions) than what seems apparent initially, and a restructuring of incentives such that all players work together rather than at cross-purposes.

## Improving the Quality of Human Capital

Human capital, as described in Chapter 1, refers to the broad set of capabilities, including health, knowledge and intelligence, attitude, social aptitude, and empathy, that make a person a productive member of society. Schools and universities play a part, as do families and communities: it does take a village to create the values and attitudes that allow children to get the most out of their education! And once individuals complete their formal education, employers play an important role in training them further and encouraging them to continue building their human capital on the job. Such on-the-job development will become more important as the length of our working life increases: the typical knowledge worker may now work for nearly half a century after formal education ends. In what follows, I describe some of the important ways the quality of human capital can be improved in the United States.[3]

### Disadvantages Begin Early

The foundation for success in life is laid early. We cannot do anything about the genes a child is endowed with, but nutrition during pregnancy and in early childhood makes an enormous difference to a child's intelligence and health later in life. Poor nutrition in a child's early years seems to be associated with the early onset of the degenerative diseases of old age such as coronary heart disease and diabetes.[4] Poor habits of expectant mothers, such as drinking and smoking, also contribute to the long-term impairment of their children's health. Unfortunately, because these problems are likely to be more severe among the children of the poor and the poorly educated, they perpetuate the cycle of poverty. To break it, more resources have to be devoted to very young children in poor families, whether in the form of nutritional supplements, medical monitoring and treatment, or parental education.

Early education also seems to matter considerably. By age eight, intelligence, as measured by standard metrics, seems pretty well set.[5] Therefore it is critically important that young children have access to quality pedagogic resources. Studies show that early childhood learning programs tend to reduce the likelihood that a child will drop out of high school, increase the likelihood that the child will enroll in college, and increase earnings.[6] They also make it less likely that the child will become delinquent, a criminal, a drug addict, or a teenage mother.

Although evaluations of the government's Head Start program—a national program that promotes school readiness by enhancing child development through the provision of educational, health, nutritional, social, and other services—are still mixed, it is hard to believe that more attention to creating good day-care centers and preschool programs for poor children, funded by government resources, with scope for local experimentation and regular evaluation, will not produce benefits. Mexico has had tremendous success in encouraging poor parents to pay more attention to their children's nutrition, health, and education by making welfare payments conditional on parents meeting certain milestones.[7] Similar conditional cash transfers are being tried by Mayor Bloomberg in New York using donated funds, and although it is too early to tell whether they are effective, the success of similar programs around the world suggests that more experimentation is warranted.

Family matters. As far back as 1966, the influential Coleman report concluded that family background was a greater influence on school achievement than any measure of the school environment, including school districts' per-student expenditures.[8] Not only are the incomes of the parents important, but so is the relationship between them, as it influences the family's access to resources and the kind of environment it provides. Being born to teenage parents, or growing up with one or both parents absent, tends to be detrimental to a child's chances of success, as is divorce. Again, these problems tend to be more common among poorer families. Although the government has only a limited role, if any, to play in strengthening families (though it certainly should not tax married couples more, as it does now), greater community recognition of the harm done to the children by teenage pregnancies, absentee parents, and broken marriages can be a force for change.

More generally, as the Nobel laureate James Heckman from the University of Chicago has argued, many of the differences between children are set at an early stage: most of the gaps in abilities observed at age eighteen are already present at age five.[9] Furthermore, a child is most malleable when young: it becomes much harder and costlier to alter abilities and behavior as the child gets older. Early intervention is important for changing outcomes successfully.

*Noncognitive Skills*

Interventions are not just about improving the child's learning abilities. Success in school, as in work life, depends significantly on noncognitive abilities, such as perseverance, determination, and self-discipline.[10] And whereas cognitive abilities are relatively fixed early on, noncognitive abilities can be changed for considerably longer.

Good schools inculcate values that serve students well in later life. Past studies have shown that students from Catholic schools tend to do better than students from inner-city public schools, perhaps because they produce more disciplined and motivated students.[11] Substantial improvements to inner-city student performance seem to have been brought about by "paternalistic" schools that insist on discipline: students walk in an orderly way between classes, meet dress codes, sit up straight in class, do homework, use standard English, and are penalized for transgressions.[12] There is, however, little systematic evidence on the success of such schools, the key ingredients that make them work, or the environments in which they work best. Nevertheless, it seems a reasonable hypothesis that both the learning environment and the learning of noncognitive skills could be improved through attempts to teach behavior as well as impart knowledge.

As important as what happens in schools is what happens outside. Dysfunctional families and communities make it more difficult for a child to acquire the values that can help them succeed. After-school programs and mentoring programs—pairing students with successful and caring adults—have helped remedy some of the damage. So too has community leadership and a shared sense of parental responsibility. As a U.S. senator speaking at the 2004 Democratic convention, Barack Obama said: "Go into any inner-city neighborhood and folks will tell you that government alone can't teach our kids to learn; they know that parents have to teach, that children can't achieve unless we raise their expectations and turn off the television sets."[13] This kind of parental and community responsibility is needed to make full use of any government support.

More generally, careful longitudinal studies in Chicago suggest that failing schools can be transformed through collective effort: by leadership that creates an environment where the faculty work with one another to challenge students, where the faculty themselves are encouraged to develop their skills, where the school and other social service organizations work together to attempt to improve the student's entire learning environment and not just the one in school, and where parents and the community are drawn in to support this effort.[14]

## Amount of Schooling

Studies suggest that students from low socioeconomic groups who are enrolled in public schools make as much progress on math and reading exams during their elementary-school years as children from a high socioeconomic background, though they start at a lower level because of disadvantages inherited from early childhood. However, the gap in achievement scores grows over time, primarily because the achievement levels of children from low-income families fall or stagnate during the summer, while those of children from higher-income families continue to increase.[15] The learning environment in families differs, with children of high-income parents growing up with educational games, books, private tuition, and summer programs, all of which continue their learning outside school. Some economists have therefore suggested extending the school year: Japan's school year runs about 240 days, while the school year in the United States is 180 days.[16] Others have suggested offering vouchers to poor families so that they can enroll their children in summer programs. Both approaches are worth experimenting with.

## Quality of Teaching

Clearly, the quality of teaching also affects a child's educational experience.[17] Motivated, inspiring, knowledgeable teachers make an enormous difference, as many of us know from experience. So does class size.

Getting good teachers starts with hiring. When other opportunities for women and minorities were limited, many talented people went into teaching because it was a respectable occupation that was open to them. As opportunities for these groups have expanded, it has become more difficult to attract the talented into teaching. Pay has to be one component of a more attractive package. But pay increments should be tied to teacher performance in and outside the classroom, which should be measured in part by improvements in student performance. Additional increments should be given to those who teach difficult but required subjects such as math and science and to those who teach in difficult school environments, such as the inner cities. Teacher unions have resisted pay differentiation, especially on the basis of performance. However, they are slowly becoming more amenable to change.

As important as pay is a career path that makes full use of a teacher's experience. Only some teachers like, or are suited for, promotion to school administration. Others could play an important role as mentors to junior teachers, as master teachers conducting classes in pedagogy, or as subject-matter experts. These career paths need to be made clearer and rewarded appropriately.

Subject-matter expertise is important, but I am not persuaded that teachers need degrees in how to teach. Certainly, much of my own learning about teaching (admittedly only university students) has come from classroom experience and from mentoring by other colleagues. Requiring teachers to hold degrees in education or teaching tends to shrink the pool of candidates for teaching jobs substantially and likely deters many subject-matter experts who would otherwise become teachers. Instead, schools should create a more formal system of mentoring, with star teachers advising inexperienced teachers and sharing experiences. Furthermore, the school system should find ways to make use of those who are highly motivated and talented but are unlikely to see teaching as a long-term career. Both the young college graduate who wants to try out teaching, as in the Teach for America program, and more senior citizens, who want to give back to the community in a different role, should be welcomed.

Small classes help the learning experience because students get more attention. This is especially important in the early years, when children need help in developing focus and discipline. Resources will be needed to reduce class size. Resources are also needed for pedagogic aids, including computers, so trade-offs have to be made based on a careful cost-benefit analysis.

One way for the best teachers to reach more students is through technology. Technology can help teachers share experiences, lesson plans, and homework questions. I am a director of a company, Heymath, that is based in Chennai, India, and operates in three continents. The company helps teachers with the tools and templates needed to create math lessons and homework, as well as with the assessment process. It creates a community in which math teachers around the world share best practices. Heymath also offers students assistance with problems, to the extent permitted by the teacher. Technology can thus help upgrade the quality of teaching with relatively small investments.

Schools also need a system of accountability. A national standard of student achievement, coupled with testing at regular intervals to measure performance against those standards, is key to accountability. Because schools take in students at different levels of preparation and capability, performance assessments must take into account the quality of the intake: hence performance improvements as well as absolute performance levels should be measured. We also need to find ways of publicizing school-performance assessments in a manner that is both comparable across schools and easily understood by parents. Failing schools need to be given initial support to improve, but not multiple chances to do so. The No Child Left Behind Act of 2002 goes some way toward these goals but needs to be strengthened.

Finally, parental choice can help bring the discipline of competition to schools. School voucher programs, if properly administered, can allow students to vote with their feet and prevent failing schools from holding talented but poor students hostage. Charter schools can also help. These are quasi-public schools that have more freedom from regulation than public schools in return for greater accountability. They obtain tuition payments from school districts in proportion to the students they attract from them. Evidence suggests that such schools can lead to substantial performance improvement, especially relative to public schools that face little risk of closure.[18]

The poorest-performing public schools clearly need more time to change, since the problems in the school and the community are deeper. Organizational capital and community involvement need to be built up (much as in the developing economies). If everyone thinks the school is likely to be closed, collective action is unlikely. Therefore, a period in which resources are made available, change is encouraged, and the threat of closure is held in abeyance may be necessary. But if there is no requirement for improvements in performance at the end of the period, and a permanent guarantee of a quiet uncompetitive life, it will be equally hard to elicit collective effort. As with the developing economies, a combination of initial nurturing and protection followed by competition may work well.

The Obama administration has laid out a path for educational reform that involves a more detailed method of evaluating schools than the pass-fail system of the No Child Left Behind Act. It proposes nationwide testing standards, evaluation of teachers based on student test performance, and the entry of more charter schools, using the lever of additional cash for states and districts that adopt reforms.[19] These are important and useful ideas and, if implemented, would be a major step forward in improving education. We should not, however, underestimate the resistance to common standards, transparency on performance, and student choice from failing schools and underperforming teachers, even if these constitute the minority—the attractions of a quiet life are immense and worth fighting for.

## Help for and in College

Only 34 percent of youths from households in the bottom quintile of income distribution enroll in college, whereas 79 percent of those from households in the top quintile of family income do so.[20] Moreover, only 11 percent of youngsters from the bottom quintile graduate, whereas 53 percent from the top do so. The dropout rate is thus also disproportionately high among the poor.

Clearly, the cognitive and noncognitive skills acquired earlier are a significant source of such differences, and I discuss potential remedies above. In addition though, programs could help make it easier for disadvantaged youth to apply to, pay for, stay in, and succeed in college.

Students from better socioeconomic backgrounds have access to significant resources to aid the college application process, including school counselors and relatives who have been to college. Students from disadvantaged backgrounds do not. Although a number of remedial government programs exist, their effectiveness is questionable.[21] Recently, a number of programs have been established that link students with a disadvantaged background with undergraduate students who have recent experience with college applications.[22] These deserve further study and expansion if worthwhile.

Financial aid can also help. Studies suggest that $1,000 of subsidy increases college attendance rates by roughly 4 percentage points, improves graduation rates, and shifts students from choosing community colleges toward choosing four-year schools.[23] A substantial number of college aid programs are already in place. The key to their effectiveness is to target aid to those who would not otherwise go to college, to make the aid application process simple—currently there are a multiplicity of programs, many poorly advertised and each requiring different applications, all of which pose particular difficulties for poor children without Internet access or printers—and to make the continuation of aid contingent on student performance.[24]

## Job Apprenticeship and Training

Human capital can also be built through on-the-job training. Apprenticeships, especially in the private sector, can be important in inculcating work habits and behavior that can help disadvantaged youths hold a steady job. Because U.S. workers tend to change jobs a number of times in their careers, firms will have to be given incentives to offer these apprenticeships to compensate for the facts that they are unlikely to keep an apprentice in the long run and that such apprentices will require a fair amount of help and supervision.

*Determining What Works*

Many good ideas have been, and are being, proposed for improving human capital for the disadvantaged. However, ideas that make sense on paper often do not seem to work in practice. Although we should try ideas that evidence and common sense suggest stand a good chance of success, ideally, programs should also be subject to periodic evaluation. These evaluations will help identify ineffective programs, as well as modifications that could make a program work better.

As the quality of the human capital of the disadvantaged improves, wage inequality should diminish. There is no certainty, however, about whether any interventions will be implemented, whether they will work, and, if they do, how much time they will take. There could well be political pressure from those who have fallen behind to redistribute, either directly or by the extension of more easy credit. Countervailing pressure will come from those who have to pay the higher taxes or who do not believe in income redistribution. Political strife could well continue at an elevated level for a while. We must hope, however, that as the disadvantaged see the ladder of programs that will help their children climb to a better future, the prospective redistribution of opportunities will head off potential conflict and the associated costs to growth.

## Security and the Safety Net

As I argue in Chapters 4 and 5, the absence of a sufficient safety net to support workers who lose jobs in a prolonged downturn in the United States increases public anxiety and tends to generate a disproportionate monetary and fiscal response. The remedy is to improve workers' resilience to economic adversity. This issue is not unrelated to that of inequality. Low incomes give people little margin of safety or the ability to save enough to tide themselves over a period of unemployment.

In searching for remedies, we should recognize that the nature of firms and the employment relationship in the United States, which emphasize flexibility and mobility, may not sit well with the kind of long-duration safety nets available in continental Europe. In what follows, I examine the broad changes that could make the U.S. worker more resilient in downturns while preserving flexibility in the system.

*Contingent but Predetermined Unemployment Insurance*

The current unemployment safety net (beyond the minimum in place) is a contingent one whereby politicians respond to prolonged, massive unemployment by temporarily extending unemployment benefits. Workers experience tremendous uncertainty over whether benefits will be extended and the criteria for receiving them. Moreover, politicians exploit the public demand for action to push through all manner of pet projects without much scrutiny under the guise of emergency legislation.

If U.S. recoveries have indeed changed in nature and become more jobless, it is worth debating whether unemployment benefits need to be extended on a more permanent basis. Longer-duration unemployment benefits not only entail costs but also make some of the unemployed less anxious to find jobs. A less responsive labor market may alter the nature of the employment relationship in the United States as well as the ease with which firms can take up new opportunities. The United States may want to give up some corporate flexibility for greater worker security, but that decision, because of its long-term ramifications, can be more fruitfully addressed once we have a better analysis of whether recoveries have indeed changed, and, if so, why.

There are, however, two reforms of which the net benefits are clearer. First, the United States would benefit from predetermined, contingent extensions of unemployment insurance. In other words, instead of extending unemployment benefits on an ad hoc basis according to the politics of the moment, the decision could be tied to a formula. The formula could be some simple function of the extent of overall job losses (as already offered by some states), the proportion of jobs created to jobs lost, and the time elapsed since the recession began. More complicated formulas could take into account the sectors where jobs are lost (are these industries where output tends to be cyclical, or do the job losses indicate a more permanent transformation?), as well as the nature of jobs created (are these full-time, permanent jobs or part-time and temporary ones?). The virtue of keeping it simple is that extensions could be easier for workers to forecast and plan for, and such foreknowledge is central to reducing anxiety.

The second area requiring change is health care. Much of the anxiety surrounding unemployment has to do with employees' concerns about losing health insurance for themselves and their families. As I write, Congress has just passed a bill to create near-universal health care—near-universal because illegal immigrants will still be left uncovered even when the bill's provisions are fully implemented. The passage of the bill is just the first step in a long and arduous process to achieve effective universal health insurance. Indeed, with many of the provisions of the bill due to be implemented only years from now, with attempts by various state legislatures to opt out of the provisions of the bill, and with threats by conservatives to repeal the bill when they gain power, there is some small uncertainty still about whether even the main legislative hurdles have been overcome. Even if the legislation survives challenges, effective reform will have to make sure everyone is covered even while slowing or even reversing the rate of growth of health care costs. However, the political calculus, as reflected in this bill, is to emphasize the clear and immediate benefits of expanded coverage, while providing less detail about costs and controls. There are many good ideas in the bill (and some bad ones), but only time will tell which ideas gain momentum. The debate about universal health care and health care costs is far from settled, and it will be with us for many years to come; hence a closer look at the key issues is useful.

### Universal Health Care

There is little appetite in the United States for a radical overhaul of the largely private health care system. The key to universal health care, then, is to deal with the adverse-selection problem. If an insurance plan attracts a disproportionate number of those with preexisting health problems, which make them higher insurance risks, while attracting too few of the young and healthy whose premiums are necessary to subsidize the less healthy, the economics supporting insurance breaks down, and it becomes uneconomic.

Given that a number of the young and healthy prefer to stay uninsured—the young have a strong and misplaced sense of their own immortality—the key to successful universal insurance, in which no private plan can refuse those with preexisting conditions and premiums are kept at a reasonable level, is to ensure that the young and healthy pay in. Incentives can include a mix of carrots—such as rebates for not making claims—and sticks—penalties for not joining. These have to be high enough to deter healthy individuals from paying the penalty and joining the system only when the need arises. Moreover, plans that attract a disproportionate number of high-risk individuals need to be compensated with transfers from those that don't.

Universal health insurance will also require subsidies for the poor. This requirement clearly creates some tension with the American aversion to unconditional redistribution that I discuss in Chapter 4. Yet it is implausible that many Americans truly believe that their fellow citizens who have bad luck, or earn little, should pay with their health or the health of their children. Moreover, many of the uninsured sick eventually do receive treatment, but without any of the benefits of preventive care, thus exacerbating both health problems and treatment costs. Finally, there is a broader benefit to universal insurance. The reduction in anxiety among the population in downturns, and the associated reduction in the need for expansionary macroeconomic policies, will make the United States better able to calibrate fiscal and monetary policy to its actual needs, while serving notice on policy makers in the rest of the world that they need to become more expansionary.

The major problem in expanding coverage, once the adverse-selection problem is dealt with, is that U.S. health care does not seem cost-effective. The United States spent 15 percent of GDP on health care in 2006, compared to 11 percent in France and Germany, 10 percent in Canada, and 8 percent in the United Kingdom and Japan.[25] On a per capita basis, the United States spent $6,347, while Japan spent $2,474. The difference has been growing: in 1970 the United States spent 40 percent more on health care per capita than peer countries; in 2004 this difference had widened to 90 percent. But health outcomes have not improved commensurately: every country in the United States' peer group had a higher increase in life expectancy at age 65 over the period 1970–2004, except Canada, which experienced the same 3.7-year increase.[26]

Three factors seem important in driving up costs.[27] First, the United States has high prices for inputs: hip replacements in the United States, for example, cost twice as much as in Canada. Part of this difference is explained by higher compensation for doctors in the United States.[28] Second, because doctors and hospitals get paid for services provided rather than for outcomes, and because insurance picks up the bill, the system tends to promote overutilization of health care. Finally, the system tends to adopt innovations even when the evidence of effectiveness is weak. For instance, nuclear particle accelerators, costing more than $100 million, are very effective in treating rare brain and neck tumors; but they are also used to treat more common prostate cancers, with little additional benefit.[29] A good bill would encourage more competition, a move to paying for outcomes rather than inputs (as well as setting the per-visit deductible cost to each user at a level that encourages sound judgment about whether to visit the doctor), and a greater focus on using only proven treatments that offer significant improvements over cheaper alternatives.

Three other factors contribute to the high cost of health care in the United States but are not central. The first is administrative costs. These are notoriously difficult to estimate precisely, but one estimate indicates that the United States spent $465 per capita in 2006, while Japan spent only $52.[30] Clearly, given that the overall difference in health care costs between the United States and Japan is about ten times the difference in administrative costs, they are not the sole explanation. However, measures to improve cost efficiency are important. The information technology revolution could finally be brought to health care by, for example, standardizing electronic patient records so that they can be transferred easily among different providers.

The second is operational efficiency. Hospitals in the United States could learn more from each other, as well as from hospitals elsewhere, including India, where costs have been brought down by bringing mass-production techniques perfected in manufacturing to health care. Indian hospitals have found that error rates are reduced when their doctors specialize and perform many procedures of a similar kind. The time for operations is also cut down, with no loss of safety. A focus on eliminating unnecessary frills and on utilizing expensive resources like doctor time most effectively also helps: even though good surgeons in India earn about as much as surgeons in the United States, the cost of operations is often an order of magnitude lower. Regulations that force hospitals in the United States to be "full-service" hospitals rather than permitting specialization tend to drive up costs. Greater competition between hospitals could also bring down costs; an easy way of encouraging cross-border competition is to authorize Medicare and Medicaid reimbursements for procedures performed by authorized hospitals in other countries, like Mexico and Thailand.

The third factor contributing to the high cost of health care is the threat of malpractice suits, which cause physicians to recommend treatments that help protect them against future lawsuits, even if these treatments are strictly unnecessary for the patient's health. Expenditures for Medicare beneficiaries in states with larger malpractice awards are about 5 percent higher: this difference is significant, though not enough alone to explain why U.S. health care is so costly.[31] Nevertheless, these costs contribute to the overall cost of health care, and tort reform should be part of an effective bill.

It is easy to minimize the complex changes that need to happen. Doctors need to recommend necessary procedures to patients, including preventative ones, but should not have an incentive to undertake excessive treatment because of the associated fees. Flat doctor salaries and flat fees per patient enrolled in a health maintenance program or for treating a particular ailment seem attractive solutions, but they are not panaceas. For instance, without other sources of motivation, flat salaries can kill the incentive to exert effort. Similarly, with better public information about the effectiveness of specific doctors, hospitals, and procedures, people can make better decisions about where and how they want to be treated. Ultimately, though, most of us will make decisions based on the advice provided by the authority, our doctor. As with education, many experiments are under way on the right mix of incentives, transparency, competition, and organizational changes that can bring doctors, hospitals, insurance companies, patients, and the government together to create an effective health care system. We need to find out what solutions work, scale them up, and continue to evaluate them as they are rolled out, recognizing that a variety of approaches will make the system more resilient. All this needs to be done quickly. Effective change will not be easy, but the benefits of affordable universal health care go far beyond the physical and moral health of American society; they extend to the economic health of the country.

### Improving Portability of Benefits and Worker Mobility

An important element in promoting the resilience of the individual worker in downturns is the portability of savings and pension plans. Workers who are dependent on their employers for their long-run savings—for example, if they have underfunded defined-benefit pension plans, or hold large amounts of stock in the firm as part of their plans—tend to suffer a double blow when their employer gets into trouble; they lose both their jobs and their pensions. Theoretically, pension plans have to be kept fully funded, but troubled employers typically underfund their pension plans. Although the government picks up some of the tab through the Pension Benefit Guarantee Corporation, a better long-term solution is to make the workers' savings independent of the firm's health by ensuring that they invest in diversified defined-contribution pension plans (in which pension accumulations are invested by the employee in diversified mutual funds). More generally, making the moderately paid worker's long-term benefits, including health care, independent of a firm's health reduces both worker anxiety and the pressure on the government to intervene to bail out the firm to protect the workers.[32]

Restrictions on worker mobility also contribute to anxiety. The workplace increasingly demands credentials and certification: for example, doctors and lawyers need different licenses to practice in each state. It is important that the United States, and indeed the world, not be balkanized by requirements that professionals reestablish credentials whenever they move. Although there are indeed legitimate concerns that testing and certification requirements (and the quality of testing procedures) may differ across regions, as could the subject matter over which mastery is required, certification is sometimes used as a means of creating more profits for certified incumbents by keeping out competition. For instance, it is hard to believe that the practice of medicine differs widely in different U.S. states. This process should be carefully reexamined to harmonize requirements or promote cross-recognition of certificates wherever possible, and to facilitate easy testing and recertification where it is not. Rich professional organizations have little incentive to give up their rents, so public pressure may be required for them to reexamine their certification requirements.

Another factor restricting mobility, certainly in the current downturn, is home ownership. Anecdotal evidence suggests that hard-to-sell homes, and homes that are worth less than the debt that is owed, are weighing down workers and preventing them from looking elsewhere for employment. A number of financial innovations that would allow households to purchase insurance against home-price declines have been proposed, and in light of the recent crisis, demand for these instruments may increase.[33] This is also a reason why the government's focus on encouraging home ownership needs to be revisited.

Although the modern economy needs some workers to specialize, workers like Badri, encountered in Chapter 4, may tend to grow overly specialized in one industry. Robert Shiller of Yale University has argued for "livelihood" insurance —insurance that would protect workers against a decline in incomes or jobs in their particular areas of specialization. In a sense, long-term unemployment insurance is a form of livelihood insurance provided by society. The downside of such insurance is that it reduces worker incentives to keep their human capital relevant. Having an unproductive underclass that lives off their insurance payments is better than having a destitute underclass, but it is best if such payments simply help sustain them while they retool to become productive members of society again.

An alternative is for the worker to retain mobility by building flexible human capital. Clearly, firms have little direct incentive to encourage workers to acquire general skills that their employers cannot use. Yet greater potential mobility would make workers feel more secure. In order to attract good workers, firms should offer more opportunities for human capital development. Some firms already do, but many don't. Perhaps the problem is that young, good workers don't fear for their future, and firms don't want to attract less-secure workers by offering opportunities for career development. Perhaps workers themselves, once they are in the firm, delay developing portable skills—going back to school is not easy—until it is just too difficult to do so.

Whatever the reason, as the length of working lives increases and as technology changes rapidly, more and more workers, especially in knowledge-based industries, are likely to find themselves with outdated and excessively specialized human capital. Academics typically get a sabbatical year once every seven years to renew their knowledge. (University of Chicago faculty are an exception: there is a presumption that we could not possibly learn more anywhere else on earth, so we don't have sabbaticals.) As more workers come to resemble academics, perhaps employee sabbaticals should become more widespread. As the government could well benefit from the renewal of worker human capital, it could contemplate offering tax credits for workers who have worked for a number of years and decide to take a break to study or retool. Such a move would also put pressure on employers to allow such sabbaticals.

Universities also need to do their bit. In the United States, life expectancy has increased by about 30 years since 1900, almost the span of an entire working career.[34] Although more people today acquire advanced degrees, most still stop their formal education early in life, much as they did a hundred years ago. Education is still geared toward the first job, even though technological change, competition, and greater job mobility means that for most people, that first job, or even that first career, will not be the last.

A system of formal education that terminates when one is twenty-five probably provides too much information related to the first few years of one's career and too little knowledge for the half-century that follows. Would it not make more sense to deemphasize early specialization and offer more doses of formal education later on, so that individuals can cope with changes in environment and preferences?

Business schools have taken a lead here by offering open-enrollment refresher courses to senior executives who feel the skills obtained during their MBA training need updating. But there may be a reason to rethink the entire structure of U.S. higher education, a system designed when students typically left university for a lifelong career with one employer. We need more modular degrees and lifelong admission to higher education (at least for general programs) so that students can pick and choose what they want when they need it.

Advances in distance education using the Internet will help individuals keep up to date even while working full time and help reduce the cost of higher education. A few universities already offer a full MBA degree that requires only a few weeks of in-person attendance, with much of the necessary communication and instruction provided through online discussion groups, e-mail, and lectures. These kinds of programs will expand. One important tool, therefore, in helping citizens cope with the greater uncertainty in their lives will be a revolution in higher education.

### Savings

Finally, workers are more resilient in the face of adversity when they have adequate savings. For too many American workers, growing house prices created an illusion of increasing wealth. It was an illusion even before the current crisis —after all, you have to live somewhere, so if the value of the home you live in is rising, you really do not have extra disposable wealth—and it became even more illusory as house prices collapsed and borrowers were left staring at a mountain of debt.

Americans need to save more, and the government should be far less eager to encourage them to spend. Savings rates are increasing as households dig themselves out of this crisis. A number of interesting ideas have been proposed to encourage savings and are worth exploring. For instance, my colleague Richard Thaler at the University of Chicago has suggested innovative ways by which households can be nudged into saving more. In his "Save More Tomorrow" plan, devised with Shlomo Benartzi, workers sign an agreement with their employer and their financial services provider that they will place some portion of future salary raises into savings plans. The idea is that when they commit to doing so, the extra amount saved does not shrink their budget and requires no sacrifice of current consumption. Thus they are "tricked" into saving more, a decision they are perfectly willing to respect over time—for they have the ability to tear up the agreement any time they want.[35]

Perhaps the most important source of future security for most Americans is social security. Unfortunately, the social security system, a pay-as-you-go system whereby current payers fund the payments made to current recipients, is currently projected to become insolvent in the long run, as the population ages and the number of retirees swamps the number of payers. Current workers will have to work until a later age, and future retirees will receive fewer benefits. These real changes cannot be wished away, and we should not pretend there are painless ways to reform social security (for example, by investing its assets in corporate equities). The system needs to be reformed, most obviously by extending the age of retirement and slowing the rate of increase of benefits; the sooner it is done, the more equitably the costs can be spread across generations.

### Government Capacity

Finally, the government's finances have to be restored to health after the enormous toll taken by this crisis. The government's capacity to spend is always a source of resilience for both banks and the public in downturns. Perhaps the largest unfunded liabilities of the U.S. government have to do with Medicare and Medicaid. This is one more reason why controlling the growth of health care costs has to be high on the government's agenda.

Reducing deficits by curbing unnecessary expenditures and increasing taxes in an equitable and efficient way must also be part of the answer. We will need a bipartisan effort that looks at all possible options—including a value-added tax (a kind of national sales tax) and a carbon tax, options that have been off the table so far. The very poor can be protected from the effects of these taxes on their consumption through higher earned-income tax credits. However, the notion that only the rich need be taxed to restore government finances to health has to be set against the fact that the incentive effects on dulling the desire to work may well be higher for the rich (because they do not work to live), and they are also probably better able to avoid taxes by moving to tax havens or through tax planning. In all likelihood, all of us will have to tighten our belts.

## Summary and Conclusion

American overconsumption is driven by policies that were framed in reaction to growing public perceptions of inequality and insecurity, and these policies have contributed to financial-sector excess. The remedies are not easy and will require further government intervention. Given the propensity for government action to go wrong, we should approach interventions with care and some skepticism. Yet inaction will make matters considerably worse.

For the young, the answers lie in broadening the pathways that allow them to build human capital. For those who are older, we have to improve ways people can remake themselves to stay competitive even as their old skills become obsolete. For those who cannot change, we need to understand how to keep them involved as productive, valuable members of society while providing necessary support. These are not easy tasks. American society will have to balance compassion and understanding against the risk of creating a dependent and resentful underclass.

Some of the changes that are needed today may seem to go against the grain of America's self-image of entrepreneurial achievement unbridled by the heavy hand of government. Yet central to that self-image have been a sense that anyone who tries hard can succeed and the confidence that tomorrow will be better than today. Inequality of access to education and health care, and mounting insecurity, especially during prolonged downturns, strike at that self-image.

An anxious America is a cause of concern for the rest of the world, for it ultimately means a more inward-looking, fractious world. The world needs America to reform. The United States has always been able to remake itself in adversity, and there is no reason why it cannot do so again. It is in America's past that we should see hope for its future. But what of the world itself? This is the question I turn to now.

# CHAPTER TEN

# The Fable of the Bees Replayed

I N 1714, BERNARD MANDEVILLE, a Dutchman living in England, wrote *The Fable of the Bees: Or Private Vices, Public Benefits*. Part verse, part prose, the tract was an indictment of the sharp practices, extravagance, and hypocrisy of the rich ruling class. For example, his portrait of lawyers in his fictitious bee-hive, a thinly disguised allegory for the England of his time, is one that should strike a chord with people in many countries today:

> The Lawyers, of whose Art the Basis
> Was raising Feuds and splitting Cases, . . .
> They kept off Hearings wilfully,
> To finger the retaining Fee;
> And to defend a wicked Cause,
> Examin'd and survey'd the Laws;
> As Burglars Shops and Houses do;
> To find out where they'd best break through.[1]

But after criticizing them, Mandeville went on to make an important economic point: the luxurious living of the rich and powerful, their changing fashions and tastes, had the one enormous benefit of providing work for the many. So

> whilst Luxury
> Employ'd a Million of the Poor,
> And odious Pride a Million more
> Envy itself, and Vanity
> Were Ministers of Industry;
> Their darling Folly, Fickleness
> In Diet, Furniture, and Dress,

That strange, ridic'lous Vice, was made
The very Wheel, that turn'd the Trade.[2]

Indeed, when the voices of opposition grow loud enough in the beehive for Jove to put an end to the corruption and excessive consumption, the bee economy collapses. Mandeville thus makes the simple point that an economy full of thrifty savers cannot flourish for long because nobody can earn income if no one else spends money. We exalt frugality and excoriate borrowing, but in a vibrant economy, you cannot have one without the other.

In recent years, the world economy has come to resemble Mandeville's beehive. The United States (and a few other rich industrial countries like Spain and the United Kingdom) have been spending more than they produce or earn and thus borrowing to finance the difference. Poorer countries like China or Vietnam have been doing the opposite.

Energy use is a good indicator of actual consumption of goods. Each person in the United States used 7.8 tons of oil in 2003, which was about twice the amount used per person in France, Germany, and Japan; about 7 times the amount used in China; and 15 times the amount used in India. Of course, per capita income in the United States is among the highest in the world, but its consumption is disproportionately high relative to other rich countries. And because its savings are commensurately low, the United States financed its spending in 2006 by borrowing 70 percent of the world's excess savings.

This pattern of spending emerged, in part, because U.S. policies encouraged debt-fueled spending, both in normal times and as a way out of recessions, and because international financial markets were willing to accommodate the United States' needs. Countries like Chile, China, Germany, Japan, Malaysia, Saudi Arabia, and South Korea supplied the United States by following a pattern of growth that emphasized exports and financed it by being willing to hold U.S. debt, much as the tradesmen held the IOUs of the spendthrift lords of Mandeville's time. For many of these countries, supplying foreign needs was a more stable path to growth than creating their own.

This mutually beneficial but ultimately unsustainable equilibrium has been disrupted by the financial crisis and the subsequent downturn. Like many a developing country before it, the United States has come to recognize that the spending financed by a populist credit expansion is typically unproductive. Indebted U.S. households, weighed down by houses that are worth less than the mortgages they owe, have started saving more. To ensure that spending does not collapse, the U.S. government has stepped in to spend, but there are limits to how much it can do effectively. Consensus forecasts today suggest the United States will have to settle for a period of relatively slow growth. Forecasting is always difficult (especially about the future!), but if these forecasts are correct, sustained high unemployment will compound uncertainty for a middle class already hit by stagnant wages. They will have to face all this without the opiate of rising house prices and illusory wealth. Households in Spain and in the United Kingdom are in a similar situation, while smaller countries like Greece are on the verge of crisis.

Prudent macroeconomic management suggests that large-deficit countries should be more careful about spending and save more. If the world economy is not to slow considerably, the countries with trade surpluses will have to offset this shift by spending more. Ideally, the richer among them—Germany and Japan—should improve productivity in domestically oriented sectors like banking and retailing so that the added growth leads to greater incomes and more spending, while poorer but fast-growing developing countries like China and Vietnam should gradually reduce their emphasis on exports and promote domestic consumption.

There is even some hope that developing countries will start running large trade deficits once again and pull the industrial countries out of their growth slump, especially if multilateral lending institutions are reformed to be more supportive of borrowing. Such a hope is unrealistic and even dangerous, because developing countries have historically found it difficult to safely expand domestic demand financed with foreign borrowing. The problem is that domestic demand typically expands rapidly at times when the government has political aims or the financial sector has skewed incentives. In such situations, the fundamental allocation of resources is distorted. Anticipated financial support from multilateral organizations only increases wasteful spending before the inevitable crisis. Irresponsible foreign lenders get a larger subsidy, and the size of the hole that taxpayers eventually have to fill increases. There is, of course, some room for multilateral organizations to improve the availability of loans to countries with responsible policies, if nothing else so that countries do not run trade surpluses only to build up foreign exchange reserves. But in the foreseeable future, the response to the sustained reduction in industrial-country trade deficits should not be a commensurate sustained expansion of developing-country deficits and debts. Instead, it should require a narrowing of trade surpluses around the world, among both industrial and developing countries.

In practice, any such shift will be politically painful in the short term both for deficit and for surplus countries. Even as I write, the Federal Reserve is holding interest rates artificially low (especially in the housing market) in the hopes that households will start consuming more again—after all, household consumption has been the primary source of growth in recent years. China is actively intervening to stabilize the value of the renminbi against the dollar so that its exports do not suffer. These myopic actions will help entrench a longer-term pattern of behavior that will make it harder to move away from the current unsustainable equilibrium.

Of course, as Herbert Stein, the chairman of Richard Nixon's Council of Economic Advisors, once said, "If something is unsustainable, it will stop." Foreign investors have become increasingly wary about the amount of debt the U.S. government has had to issue to finance its deficits. With the majority of U.S. taxpayers believing they have benefited little from the boom years, the battle over who will bear the burden of additional taxes could turn ugly. Unlike the typical emerging-market country, the United States has not suffered a "sudden stop" of capital inflows during this crisis, because it has still been able to attract capital on easy terms from the rest of the world. However, if foreign investors fear that the United States will be unlikely to achieve the political consensus needed to set its government finances in order, they could start worrying that the government will follow the time-honored path of reducing the real value of its public debt through a bout of high inflation. If they take fright, they will sell their holdings of U.S. government bonds, causing the value of the dollar to slide more quickly. U.S. interest rates might have to go up substantially to retain foreign investor interest, thereby reducing U.S. growth even further than anticipated. That shift will bring down the U.S. trade deficit and spending, but in a way that maximizes pain all around.

Even if the status quo does persist for longer than we expect, there are longer-run consequences of maintaining the current pattern of imbalances. One is the issue of environmental sustainability around the world. Undoubtedly, as developing countries grown richer, their households will look to consume more. At current levels of technology, it is simply infeasible for the world to aspire to consume as much, and waste as much, as the average suburban American household does: as the former Indian finance minister Yashwant Sinha put it, we would then have no world to live in.[3] No doubt technology will improve over time, making a unit of consumption progressively less destructive to the environment. Nevertheless, if sacrifices are to be evenly spread across the world, it makes sense for consumption growth to shift from rich deficit countries to developing ones.

It is also in the exporters' long-run self-interest to alter their strategies. Although the reliance on exports has been very successful at both promoting rapid growth and ensuring stability, the Japanese experience raises questions about whether countries should follow it until they become rich—and risk subsequent stagnation—or turn to a more balanced path long before then. For a number of exporters, like China and Malaysia, the initial phase of building capabilities is long over. The challenge now is to broaden their sources of growth, withdrawing implicit and explicit subsidies to exporters gradually while extending the discipline of competition to the sectors focused on domestic production. Large countries like China may have no alternative but to wean themselves off dependence on global demand, because the world's ability to absorb Chinese exports will be limited if China does not import more goods from them. Of course, the world's political tolerance for buying Chinese goods may wear out long before its economic capacity to buy them does.

Change will therefore help global stability and sustainability and will be beneficial for each country in the long run. But change does upset the cozy status quo and the interests that benefit from it. For instance, the real estate lobby in the United States has no desire to see government support for housing diminish, even though the United States probably has far more housing stock than it can afford. Similarly, the export lobby in China has no interest in seeing the renminbi strengthen significantly. So we are caught between the rock of a financially and environmentally unsustainable pattern of global demand and a hard place of a politically difficult change in domestic policies.

These issues are not new. The political scientist Jeffry Frieden of Harvard University writes of the 1920s, when there was a macroeconomic imbalance between a great power running a sustained current-account deficit and a rising power that financed the deficits.[4] The rising power was the United States, and the great power was Germany, which had borrowed heavily from abroad

> to fuel a consumption boom that, among other things, dampened some of the underlying social tensions that beset the Weimar Republic. This was no small matter: without American financing to sustain the dynamism of the German economy, Weimar social and political instability might have caused serious problems for the rest of Europe. . . .
>
> The German-American financial relationship rested on weak political foundations, as neither country was really prepared for the implications of the capital flows. The United States was not willing to provide an open market for German goods that would facilitate debt service, or any government measures to deal with eventual financial distress, and the Germans were unwilling or unable to make the sacrifices necessary to provide prompt debt service.[5]

As the Depression hit, each country looked inward, ignoring the consequences for other countries. The Smoot-Hawley Act passed by the U.S. Congress in June 1930 raised trade tariffs on imports in an attempt to protect U.S. jobs, making it still more difficult for debtor countries around the world to service debts. These countries either defaulted on their debt or overthrew governments that tried to adopt the austerity measures required to service it. Hitler was carried to power on the coattails of economic distress, and one of his first acts after taking power in January 1933 was to declare that Germany would not pay its foreign creditors. His message of hate and revenge fell on receptive ears in a Germany that felt ill-treated by the global economy.

The United States does not have the political weaknesses of the Weimar Republic, but the broader point is that without global economic cooperation when change is needed, countries could descend into opportunistic nationalism to the detriment of the global economy and the global political environment. Nationalism, coupled with great faith in the power of the government to enact domestic bargains between labor and capital, has been seen before: it was called fascism then. It is a development to be avoided at all costs.

Our existing global institutions, like the IMF and the World Bank, will likely prove ineffective in fostering global cooperation if they continue to operate as they have in the past. They will have to make radical changes in how they function, appealing more directly to the people than to their leaders, to soft power rather than to hard power. I discuss how such an approach dovetails well with the reforms that are needed in China. Clearly, the soft power of multilateral organizations can also be used to promote the reforms, discussed in the previous chapter, that are necessary in the United States.

## The G-20 and the IMF

In September 2009, the leaders of the world's largest economies met in Pittsburgh and designated their group, the G-20, as the primary forum for global economic cooperation. Much like its predecessor organization, the G-7, the new self-proclaimed guardian of the world economy excludes many countries—almost a necessity in order to get dialogue rather than a cacophony, but undemocratic nevertheless. Who is in and who is out is also somewhat arbitrarily decided: Argentina is a member, while Spain, with a GDP that is nearly five times the size of Argentina's, is a member only indirectly, through the European Union. Be that as it may, the leaders of the G-20 patted themselves on the back for a "coordinated" fiscal and monetary stimulus in response to the crisis and had an unusually brief (for an official communiqué) description of the result: "It worked." They went on to say: "Today we are launching a Framework for Strong, Sustainable, and Balanced Growth. To put in place this framework, we commit to develop a process whereby we set out our objectives, put forward policies to achieve these objectives, and together assess our progress. We will ask the IMF to help us with its analysis of how our respective national or regional policy frameworks fit together.... We will work together to ensure that our fiscal, monetary, trade, and structural policies are collectively consistent with more sustainable and balanced trajectories of growth."[6]

So the G-20, having successfully coordinated responses to the crisis, is now taking on the bigger challenge of making sure national growth strategies fit together to rebalance global growth. This is precisely what I have argued must be done. Given its recent achievements during the crisis, however, can we have any confidence that the G-20, working through the IMF, will be effective?

Unfortunately not. It is very easy to get politicians to spend in the face of a crisis and to get central banks to ease monetary policy. No coordination is required, as every country wants to pump up its economy to the extent possible: the G-20 leaders were pushing on an open door when they called for coordinated stimulus. The real difficulties emerge when countries need to undertake politically painful reforms, reforms that might even seem to be more oriented toward helping other countries in the short run rather than the reformer itself. Politics is always local: there is no constituency for the global economy.

I know, because we have been through an attempt at global policy coordination before, precisely to deal with the problem of large global trade imbalances. That effort failed, and it is instructive to understand why.

In 2006, as the U.S. current-account deficit broke record after record and as China's current-account surplus soared, the IMF became deeply concerned. The managing director, Rodrigo de Rato, decided a new approach was warranted. We at the Fund (I was still the chief economist then) called on the five entities most responsible for the imbalances—the United States, the Euro zone, China, Japan, and Saudi Arabia—to come together to discuss how they would jointly bring the imbalances down. To prepare for the meetings, I jointly headed an IMF team, which traveled around the world in the summer of 2006, trying to secure some agreement among the countries that had been called together for the consultation. We were following the adage that nothing of substance is settled at most international meetings; all important issues are usually settled beforehand.

The weather ranged from 122 degrees in the shade in Riyadh, Saudi Arabia, to unseasonably cool in Tokyo. The response from our interlocutors was, however, pretty uniform. Countries agreed that the trade imbalances were a potential source of instability, and economic reforms were needed to bring them down before markets took fright or politicians decided to enter the fray with protectionist measures. But each country was then quick to point out why it was not responsible for the imbalances and why it would be so much easier for some other country to push a magic button to make them disappear.

For instance, the United States authorities argued that it was not their fault that the rest of the world was so eager to put their money in the United States: imbalances were the fault of the Chinese, who were buying dollars to restrain the appreciation of the renminbi. It was the pressure of these enormous inflows that led the United States to consume. The Chinese argued that if they allowed the renminbi to appreciate faster, exports from China to the United States would fall, while exports from Cambodia or Vietnam would pick up, and the U.S. trade deficit would remain unchanged. In their view, the real problem was that the U.S. consumer had no self-restraint. Moreover, their trade surplus was so large only because the United States limited Chinese purchases of high-tech equipment. And so it went. Everyone pointed the finger at someone else. The truth was that everyone contributed in some way to the problem, but no one wanted to be part of the solution.

At the end of 2006, I returned from the Fund to the University of Chicago, dejected that we had accomplished so little. When the consultations eventually concluded in 2007, the Fund declared that they had been a success: there had been a free and frank exchange of views, which is bureaucratese for total disagreement. Every country agreed to do what it had always intended to do, which was very little. The consultations had failed to produce concrete action. A few months later, born partly from the actions that created the imbalances, the crisis began.

The IMF did not fail because our arguments were not convincing. The reason everyone pointed a finger at everyone else was not that they did not understand their own responsibility but because no one we spoke to could really commit to the actions that were needed. Indeed, these were decisions that even the head of government could not take. For instance, no U.S. president can commit to reining in the budget deficit: that is a decision that only Congress can take. Similarly, no Chinese president can unilaterally agree to allow the renminbi to appreciate: that is a decision deliberated for months by various echelons of the

State Council and the Communist Party. Moreover, the needed changes went beyond reining in the budget deficit or letting the currency appreciate. They required deeper fundamental changes to the economy. And the global good counts for little among the politicians in the U.S. Congress or the Chinese Communist Party when it comes to contemplating fundamental change.

This is why, despite hoping for the best, I have deep skepticism that anything will come of the ambitious G-20 declaration. Nor is it likely that the IMF will achieve anything more than it did in the multilateral consultations that ended in 2007, crisis notwithstanding. Change will come only when countries are forced to change, or decide it is in their best interest to do so, but that process may be too costly, or too slow, for the global economy.

If doing nothing is not a viable option, how can we get global cooperation? I think any answer lies in a fundamental remake of multilateral institutions like the IMF and the ways they interact with sovereign countries.

## Multilateral Institutions and Their Influence

Multilateral institutions have hitherto worked in two ways. One approach is the quasi-legal one followed by the World Trade Organization (WTO), which regulates trade between participating countries. The WTO bases its actions on a set of agreements that limit barriers to trade. These agreements have been signed and ratified by member governments after long and arduous negotiations. The WTO has a dispute-resolution process aimed at enforcing participants' adherence to the agreements, and because the rules are relatively clear, adherence can be judged in a quasi-legal setting. Penalties against violators, usually in the form of sanctions on their trade, are easily imposed. Countries do give up some sovereignty, such as the freedom to set import tariffs or subsidize favored industries, in exchange for others doing the same, and these concessions promote mutually beneficial trade. When industry presses national politicians to protect them, the politicians can simply throw up their hands and blame the WTO.

A second approach, one that is far less effective because of the nature of the task, is the way the IMF goes about international macroeconomic management and coordination: essentially through a process of exhortation that fails to move anyone except those who need the Fund's money. The problem here is that the rules of the game are not clear at all. When does a pattern of actions by a country create global harm? When the Fed cuts interest rates to the bone, and thus sets off a global wave of risk taking, do countries elsewhere have the right to protest? Could the Fed not say it is focused solely on U.S. economic conditions, which is its primary remit? When China intervenes in exchange markets to hold the value of the renminbi against the dollar, is it using unfair means to gain a competitive advantage? Some have argued that China's huge buildup of reserves is evidence of an unfair policy.[7] But unlike developed countries, China restricts its citizens and private firms from holding foreign assets, so it is almost inevitable that its holdings of foreign assets will show up as central bank reserves. And even if it were proved that it had a policy of deliberate undervaluation, could it not claim it is a poor country, using exchange-rate undervaluation to offset its other natural disadvantages?[8]

Unlike the WTO, therefore, the IMF cannot frame a careful and universally agreed-upon set of rules. And there is some virtue to rules. Although establishing such rules requires an enormous amount of negotiation and bargaining, many of the parties who would be adversely affected by specific aspects of them also see broad long-term gains from the framework. As a result, in the WTO, disagreements can typically be papered over during the long and tortuous trade-negotiation rounds, with some give-and-take possible in setting the detailed rules. The problem with trying to secure an agreement on policy reforms across a set of countries on a case-by-case basis, as the Fund has to do if it is to bring down trade imbalances, is that winners and losers are clearly identified, both across countries and within countries. Each agreement is sui generis, and the Fund cannot make commitments across agreements to try to appease those who feel they may lose out in a particular instance.

Of course, countries could dispense with rules or agreements and give discretion to one agency, such as the IMF, to judge disputes and identify policy violations that cause international harm on a case-by-case basis, with some penalties for noncompliance. But because macroeconomic policy covers such a broad area, this would require countries to give up a tremendous amount of sovereignty to an international bureaucracy, an unlikely scenario. Historically, the world's great powers have been reluctant to see independent, strong multilateral organizations emerge. When strong, multilateral organizations have not been independent; and when independent, they have been largely irrelevant. The growing power of developing countries like China and India is unlikely to change this situation because they too have little desire for their policies to be scrutinized.

Even if an organization like the IMF could be independent of the big powers, it has a limitation: a mindset driven by a particular experience. Almost inevitably, organizations like the IMF recruit students trained in industrial countries, especially the United States. Most of the macroeconomic principles that are taught derive from the experiences of industrial countries, where organized markets typically function fairly well. So it is natural for the staff to favor certain kinds of intervention in the functioning of markets, such as monetary policy, while being critical of other kinds of intervention, such as those in the foreign exchange market. Of course, developing countries, where fewer markets work well and a broader set of interventions may be warranted, may be at a disadvantage when their policies are scrutinized by the Fund.

Also, economic growth happens in mysterious ways. If all countries had followed the prevailing economic orthodoxy in the 1950s and 1960s, we would never have had the Japanese or East Asian growth miracles. If countries did allow their macroeconomic policies to be policed by an international organization with the power to impose penalties for deviation, it could lead to a lack of diversity in policies that could limit learning and greatly dampen world growth.

Finally, even if the IMF could come up with a set of recommendations that were theoretically acceptable, not all countries would be willing to implement them. The WTO's rules not only are backed by the possibility of sanctions but can also be quietly implemented by governments through executive order: the commerce ministry can reduce a tariff here or remove a subsidy there. The IMF's recommendations are not backed by any power of enforcement: most industrial countries and large emerging-market countries do not need IMF funding, which constitutes its main means of persuasion. Moreover, the kind of reforms recommended are typically the kind that go against a ruling party's electoral calculus, making it impossible for a finance minister or head of state to commit to implementing them.

In sum, the IMF's role in macroeconomic policy coordination is quite different from the WTO's role in trade facilitation because, first, there are no clear rules on what is permissible and what is not, and any attempt to formulate such rules is likely to be unacceptable to many countries. Second, and in consequence, reforms have to be agreed to on a case-by-case basis, and governments typically do not have the domestic political support to commit confidently to the reforms they would have to undertake as part of an international agreement. Third, the inability to commit means that grand international agreements requiring fundamental reform by each country are hard to pull off, even when the reforms are in each country's long-term interest.

Even though the Fund is not always right, its prescriptions often hit the mark simply because the Fund is apolitical. However, the Fund will not gain WTO-like powers of sanction over something as amorphous as macroeconomic policy. Nor is "naming and shaming" violators in front of the community of nations likely to have much effect. Finance ministers care primarily about domestic con-stituencies, which typically pay little attention to the workings of the IMF. That has made finance ministers pretty shameless, at least to date.

But these observations suggest an alternative. Rather than try to impose its will over nations by fiat, which the IMF will never have the authority to do, it should strive for influence by appealing more directly to a country's citizens. This would facilitate the government's task in building support for reforms. Put differently, instead of trying to be like the WTO and using hard power, it should emulate Oxfam's methods and use soft power.

## Obtaining Global Influence

Consider the impetus to do more about mitigating climate change. This is a quintessential example of an issue with short-term costs and long-term gains. Politicians would shy away from such issues were it not for the grassroots move-ments in their constituencies. The pressure on governments to do something has increased not just because of mounting evidence that climate change is a real threat but also because a variety of organizations, from local to international, have mobilized people to press their representatives for action. Similarly, a pop-ular movement led by rock stars like Bono pushed rich-country governments into forgiving debt to poor countries and into pledging to give more aid at the 2005 Gleneagles Summit.

Of course, governments have not signed up yet to binding commitments on emissions, and they have backtracked on aid commitments, but the point is that these movements gained influence by convincing political leaders that there was domestic support for international agreement. As the power of the Internet in-creases through social and political networking sites, and as virtual democracy spreads, public influence is likely to be as much bottom-up—leaders adopting popular positions—as top-down—leaders convincing the public of the merit of their views. Those who would influence the calculations of politicians must do so not by appealing to their better instincts but by convincing their masters, the people, directly.

Multilateral organizations like the IMF and the World Bank need to do far more to expand their reach—to speak for the world to the world. In addition to trying to persuade finance ministers and heads of state, they should go directly to the public, including political parties, nongovernmental organizations, and influential personalities in each country and explain their position. They need to become much more sophisticated about using Web-enabled networks to reach the connected citizen and find ways to enter school and university class-rooms, where students can be most receptive to ideas about global citizenship.

The public has a longer-term horizon than the government in power and typically more idealism and concern for the global good. It is also likely to be more receptive to persuasion, especially when it is less anxious than in the current times. Of course, reforms whose benefits for a country over time swamp the costs are much more likely to be acceptable than ones that ask the country to make sacrifices for the world's good, but even the latter should not be ruled out: after all, aid in its purest form requires one-sided sacrifices, and the thinking active public in rich countries has pushed for it. The knowledge that citizens in other countries are being asked to pitch in at the same time—that solutions are truly intended to be global and multilateral—should be important in making persuasion easier. Moreover, to the extent that a domestic constituency develops that cares about a country's multilateral responsibilities, politicians will no longer feel it politically costless to violate international obligations; thus naming and shaming may have more force.

This sort of campaigning is not something multilateral organizations are currently well equipped to carry out. The IMF, for example, views its primary audience as finance ministries and central bankers. After years of trying to not offend anyone in member countries, IMF staff have developed a special way of writing reports that ensures that everything important can be inferred by those who know how to read between the lines (typically IMF staff and bureaucrats from the member countries), and anyone else falls asleep reading the turgid prose. The IMF has had long practice in communicating with bureaucrats or ministers, but far less in speaking to nongovernmental organizations (NGOs) or the press. The World Bank is better, but not by much.

Moreover, it is not clear that powerful member-country governments want an international organization speaking within their borders on a message they cannot control, even if it is strictly on economics. It is not just undemocratic countries that repress free speech; democratic countries that preach in public about the need for transparency and honest appraisals are often the ones that lean most heavily on international organizations in private to alter their message.

I recall a Washington press conference held to release the semiannual IMF World Economic Outlook in the spring of 2005. Campaigning was under way for the British elections. In response to the anticipated question from a reporter from the *Financial Times,* I remarked that the United Kingdom would need to do more to raise revenues or cut costs to meet its own fiscal rules, thus implying that it might have to raise taxes. My comments were based on impeccable analysis by the IMF's staff, but Gordon Brown, then chancellor of the exchequer, was furious because they contradicted his own public statements during the campaign. The Fund stood by its analysis despite immense pressure from the British treasury. Gordon Brown was also chairman of the IMF's governing committee and had a press conference scheduled the next day. With the IMF's managing director, Rodrigo de Rato, sitting embarrassed by his side, he launched into a broadside (prompted again by the inevitable question) against the Fund and how it was wrong once again about the United Kingdom. The managing director politely said nothing, but in doing so, he implicitly backed his staff's views. The data since then suggest the Fund was right.

On the one hand, the very fact that governments are concerned about the possible public influence of an impartial commentator on government policies suggests that this avenue is grossly underexploited. On the other hand, such action will require a change in how multilateral organizations see themselves— as WTO wannabes hankering after hard power that they will never get, or those who respect the sovereignty of each country and work for the global good, country by country, through soft power and persuasion.

## Reforms to Global Economic Governance

If multilateral organizations are to change their strategies of persuasion, fundamental reform is required. These include changes to the organizations as well as to the way they operate in countries. Their governance structure needs to be reformed so that they are seen to be independent of undue influence by any country, and some of these changes are under way. They should also make a conscious effort to broaden their intellectual frameworks by recruiting personnel trained outside the United States. Some of this will happen as universities across the developing world strengthen their research capabilities and produce high-quality graduates. Multilateral organizations should see engagement in the public debate in member countries as one of their most important tools in encouraging domestic policies that foster the global good. And finally, the rules governing membership of these organizations should force members to accept such engagement, facilitate it, and protect it when carried out in good faith. This may indeed require important revisions to the articles of agreement signed by members of the IMF, perhaps even a new historic agreement like the one at Bretton Woods that created the IMF and the World Bank.

This last point is important. No large power, especially but not exclusively countries that are undemocratic, will be happy giving multilateral organizations a platform to sound off on anything they want. Countries have to understand that there are important collective benefits from adopting sounder policies, and that if they want a platform from which to influence the policies of others, they have to allow others a platform to influence theirs. It should be understood that the multilateral organization will confine itself to economic and socioeconomic issues, with its views arrived at through a fair, deliberative process within the organization, based primarily on convincing economic research and data analysis. Its views should then be protected by international agreement, much as embassies and their activities are. Of course, a transparent and fair process will be essential to convincing citizens in each country that the multilateral organization has their interests at heart. Put differently, instead of an international agreement about economic policies à la WTO, we need an international agreement about how domestic policies can be influenced by multilateral agencies to incorporate the global good.

I have raised the issue of reform in the context of trade imbalances. But there are many other issues on which the world needs to come together on which it is currently being dragged apart. For example, whenever food prices rise, a number of countries start banning food exports. Although in the very short term such measures ensure that their citizens have access to cheap food, they deprive domestic farmers of higher prices and make them less eager to grow food. They also make other countries feel insecure and attempt to grow their own food, even if it is grossly inefficient for them to do so: the fields of grain that now appear in the middle of the Arabian desert are unlikely to be the best use of water in that location. The net outcome is that the myopic actions by governments to protect their citizenry in the short run result in global food insecurity and inefficient methods of production in the long run. We need a global agreement to ensure that international food markets will not be disrupted by government action—but no government today will risk being accused by the opposition of signing away its ability to ensure that its citizens have food. The multilateral organizations need to create the necessary awareness and momentum for agreement.

I have no illusions about how easy change will be. The instinct of global bureaucrats is to press for clear rules, but even in the European Union, which has some rule-making power and some ability to constrain the domestic policies of members, relatively homogenous countries have proved unwilling to accept strong external constraints on their policy making. Over time, rulings from Brussels have come to be seen as an imposition by citizens of EU countries, because domestic politicians blame them for everything unpleasant that has to be done and take credit for all the successes. It is no surprise, then, that when the people are asked if they want a stronger Brussels, they vociferously respond, "No!"

We must remember that even Keynes worried about global imbalances and proposed the radical idea of penalizing countries that ran persistent trade surpluses.[9] Such ideas are unlikely to be acceptable to independent nations today. A diverse world will not accept any forceful global coordination of policies to bridge the fault line between nations. I do not advocate a halt to the many international meetings that attempt to coordinate reforms, which have produced much talk and little action thus far. Perhaps the G-20 will pull off a miracle. But because the issues are too important to be left to the bureaucrats and politicians, I have advocated opening a second track, a track that the smaller, non-G-20 countries of the world should back, to bring the policies of the big powers into line. Multilateral organizations like the IMF should present countries with a course of action that is individually and collectively beneficial and that can avoid the political and economic risks of inaction. The multilateral organizations will have to make the persuasive case in country after country that the gain is worth the short-term pain. If there is domestic political momentum, it will make it easier for leaders to conclude an acceptable pact at the international level. Put differently, global policy discussions have to be introduced into the political debate in every country and thereby make their way back into the closed-door meetings of global leaders. Global multilateral organizations will have to work with global democracy rather than avoid it.

## China and the World

The most important economy in the world in the next decade, other than the United States, is likely to be China. Many policy makers outside China are concerned with the Chinese currency's peg to the dollar. From July 2005, the People's Bank of China (PBOC) allowed the renminbi to appreciate steadily against the dollar, but with the onset of the financial crisis in October 2008, it halted the appreciation and pegged the currency to the dollar again. Accusations of unfair trade are being heard in Washington corridors, and with U.S. unemployment touching 10 percent and Chinese growth also touching 10 percent, the disparity seems obvious. The momentum for Congress to impose some form of trade barrier is increasing, and even a renewed appreciation of the renminbi may not quell it.

Is Chinese currency intervention unfair? And if so, to whom? In one sense, the answer is obvious. Chinese exporters already enjoy subsidies such as cheap capital, land, and energy. With their goods made even cheaper by an under-valued currency, Chinese exporters can outcompete firms in industrial countries. This situation seems blatantly unfair. But this view assumes equivalence between countries in many other respects: the infrastructure in each country, the quality of its legal and contractual system, its regulatory structure, the education of its workers, and so on. Thus when one country intervenes to give itself a leg up, it seems to be violating the rules.

But there are other ways of looking at competition. Most outsiders contemplating China think of the swanky new parts of Beijing and Shanghai, not the interior and western provinces where conditions are far more backward. The infrastructure in a developed country is typically much better; its legal system is more effective at enforcing contracts; its regulatory structure is far more predictable and less corrupt; and its schools, no matter how downtrodden the area they are located in, at least have basic facilities.

An analogy may be useful. In an international athletic race, one of the participants is found to have taken an energy booster. He is disqualified for violating the rules. But on closer investigation, we find that when the race began, one set of participants had the latest, specially designed aerodynamic equipment, specifically allowed by the rule-making body, which is dominated by representatives of this set of countries, whereas the participant who took the energy booster used ordinary, off-the-shelf, cheap equipment. Who is competing unfairly now? Under the rules of the game, it is still the competitor who took the energy booster. But the rules themselves entrench disadvantages.

The term *unfair* takes a lot as given, including the framework of evaluation, and it is a term that cuts little ice with the leaders of developing countries. Dani Rodrik at Harvard University, for example, has argued that currency undervaluation may be the way for developing countries to offset their institutional disadvantages. Clearly, undervaluation is unfair once they fix their deficiencies (and the Chinese athletes today do have state-of-the-art equipment). It is also unfair to the poorer countries that do not have even China's advantages but have to compete with it to export. Nevertheless, judging what is unfair is not easy.

A stronger argument against persistent undervaluation is based on China's own interests. Undervaluation of the currency is a form of subsidy to a country's export sector that is financed by taxing those who import and those who finance the mechanism of exchange-rate intervention. The argument against continued Chinese intervention is that the subsidy does not help those who receive it and is becoming increasingly burdensome on those who pay for it.

Many of China's industries are beyond the stage where they need infant-industry protection. Also, because of fierce competition among Chinese firms, any subsidies they get are passed on to industrial-country buyers in the form of lower prices. Because other Asian economies also intervene in their currency's exchange rates and subsidize their exporters to remain competitive with China, poor households across Asia are effectively taxed to transfer benefits to exporters and are thus subsidizing the consumption of rich households in industrial countries. This situation is neither efficient nor fair.

Moreover, firms that invest on the basis of the competitive advantage obtained from an undervalued currency are creating an additional inefficient base of production that will remain competitive only if undervaluation persists. These firms will eventually join those that already lobby for undervaluation. Like many inefficient distortions, undervaluation is creating its own constituency in China, which will fight hard to preserve the status quo because its existence depends on it. Continued undervaluation is increasing China's dependence on traded goods while reducing its room to maneuver.

Most important, though, the effort to keep the currency undervalued is creating enormous distortions in the economy, holding down consumption, making all forms of production extremely capital intensive in a country with an abundant supply of labor, and leaving the financial sector underdeveloped.[10]

## The Costs of Undervaluation

If China's central bank, the PBOC, buys dollars from Chinese exporters so as to keep the renminbi from appreciating, it has to give them renminbi in exchange. If it intervenes a lot, the abundance of renminbi in circulation will push up inflation. To avoid inflation, the PBOC issues its own debt at the same time as it buys dollars, so as to mop up and thereby "sterilize" the excess renminbi. Put differently, exporters effectively exchange dollars for renminbi-denominated claims on the PBOC—a process that is known as *sterilized intervention*. The PBOC uses the exporter's dollars to buy interest-earning U.S. assets, including the agency bonds discussed in Chapter 1, thus earning interest on dollar assets while paying interest on renminbi claims.

If the interest paid on dollar assets is low, while renminbi interest rates are high, the central bank will effectively be holding a low-yield asset while issuing a high-yield liability—which means it will incur a loss. If this negative spread were multiplied by the $2 trillion worth of foreign reserves (not all dollars, of course) that China has, it would blow a gigantic hole in the Chinese budget. Moreover, a high renminbi interest rate would attract yet more foreign capital inflows. In order to sterilize without making huge losses, the PBOC fixes the economywide interest rate at a lower level than the dollar interest rate, both by forcing banks to pay households a low rate on their deposits and by paying a low rate on its own borrowing.

A direct effect of such a policy is that China mirrors the United States' monetary policy. If interest rates in the United States are very low, China also has to keep interest rates low. Doing so risks creating credit, housing, and stock market bubbles in China, much as in the United States. With little freedom to use interest rates to counteract such trends, the Chinese authorities have to use blunt tools: for example, when credit starts growing strongly, the word goes out from the Chinese bank regulator that the banks should cut back on issuing credit. Typically, private firms without strong connections bear the brunt of these credit crunches. Chinese industry goes from credit feast to credit famine, which disrupts long-range planning.

The low interest rate has other adverse effects: it reduces household income and, somewhat perversely, may force households to save more in order to build a sufficient nest egg for retirement.[11] It thus depresses household consumption and makes China yet more dependent on foreign final demand. More problematic, it keeps the cost of capital unnaturally low. So when banks are willing to lend, firms borrow to the hilt to finance capital-intensive projects (and to keep some reserves for when lending stops), with machinery substituting for jobs. So a country with a labor surplus invests a tremendous amount in capital-intensive industries, creating far fewer jobs than needed.

Last, but not least, despite lending at rates that are very low in real terms to industry, the even lower rate they pay on deposits gives banks an enormous profit spread. This cushion, accumulated at households' expense, allows them to make gigantic lending mistakes without going under. It also allows them to exclude other competing sources of finance, such as corporate bond markets. All a bank has to do is to cut its spread a little to persuade firms not to issue in the bond market, thus keeping those markets illiquid and unattractive.

There are other, related, distortions. One of the dangers of having an inefficient, bank-dominated financial system, as we have seen, is that firms with good connections in the system get loans, while others do not. In China, the dominant state-owned banking system typically lends to state-owned companies— no loan officer risks being accused of corruption if he lends to a state-owned firm—and starves the private sector of funds. The Chinese private sector is thus squeezed between a state-owned sector, which gets cheap local funds, and foreign companies investing in China, who can raise cheap money outside. No wonder so few large private Chinese companies exist, as they do, for example, in India.[12] Far from being the brains of the economy, which it will increasingly need to become if China is to allocate capital and resources better, the Chinese financial sector is becoming the inefficient tool of state policy. This cannot be good for China in the long run.

China's undervalued exchange rate, driven by a strong exporter lobby, is likely to be detrimental to China's development. The export-led path also takes it down the same road as Japan, and that road, as we have seen, leads in a dangerous direction.

## Persuading China

Whenever I broach the subject in China of whether the renminbi will be allowed to appreciate, my hosts remind me how Japan made the mistake of agreeing to U.S. pressure in 1987 and allowed the yen to appreciate sharply. Japan's woes, according to the Chinese, date from that period, for they slowed the growth of the successful export sector without replacing it with anything else. The Chinese would prefer to proceed more slowly and deliberately, "crossing the river by feeling the stones," as they put it.

What they don't see is that the Japanese may have left the transition from export-oriented growth to more balanced growth until too late, and now have to contend with both that problem and that of a rapidly aging population. China can move to a more balanced growth path while its population is still relatively young (albeit aging as a result of the one-child policy).

The needed reforms are likely to be attractive to households, which is why multilateral institutions might find an attentive audience if they explained to the Chinese people what needs to be done and why. A stronger renminbi will allow the Chinese middle class to import cheaper foreign goods and enjoy less expensive foreign holidays. Higher and more market-driven interest rates should give them higher incomes. And a more broadly based pension or social security scheme, strengthened by allocating the shares of state-owned enterprises to the scheme, should give them greater confidence to spend.

When financial institutions have to pay higher interest rates on their borrowing, their margins will shrink, and they will have less room to offer attractive deals to favored state-owned enterprises. Some of these will raise money directly from bond markets and equity markets, forcing these firms to raise transparency, improve governance practices, and increase dividend payouts.

Corporate bond markets could become a viable alternative to banks, creating funding channels outside the relationship system. If they lose their best clients, the banks will have to go beyond their comfort zone. They may start lending to small and medium-sized private enterprises, thus giving them the resources to grow. They may also expand retail credit, thus reducing the need for households to save before they can buy. China could become less of a producer-oriented, capital-intensive economy and become both more private-sector-oriented and far less dependent on foreign demand.

Such a transition is not easy, but the time is right. Because food prices are high, farmers, still the most numerous constituency in China, will not be hurt significantly by an appreciation of the renminbi that will bring in competing food imports. State-owned firms are flush with cash, so this powerful group can sustain the loss of profits as inputs like capital, energy, and land are subsidized less. They have invested a lot recently, and a slowdown in investment may not be entirely bad. However, reforms will have to depart from the path of steady experimentation and incrementalism and will require bold moves into the un-known on multiple fronts—freeing exchange rates, interest rates, and some prices, for example. Regulators will have to be extremely vigilant that the bank-ing system does not go berserk during the process of change: this is a very im-portant lesson from the failed Japanese transition.

There are two important reasons why China may be more open to strength-ening multilateral organizations and agreements at this juncture. First, it is ex-tremely dependent on exports, and the growing protectionist mood in developed countries has it worried. To the extent that it can ward off such moves through the persuasive efforts of multilateral organizations, it has an incentive to sup-port them. Second, China has more than $2 trillion worth of reserves that are fully exposed to the bad macroeconomic policies of the countries whose debt it holds. More than any other country, it would benefit from a strong international economic arrangement that scrutinizes country policies. This also means that in order to persuade China of the value of change, industrial countries should show that they themselves can also be persuaded.

In sum then, this would be a good time for multilateral organizations to ob-tain a mandate to make the case more directly to the thinking middle class in China—to explain their research, analysis, and recommendations in under-standable prose directly to the Chinese intelligentsia via articles, in conferences, and on the Internet. If the role of the multilateral organizations can be appro-priately circumscribed, the Chinese leadership might possibly accept such a mandate, especially if a similar case for change is being made elsewhere and the alternative is a disintegration of the global economy into protectionism. Indeed, the G-20 should agree to permit the multilateral organizations like the IMF substantial leeway to foster broader discussion within their countries in an attempt to achieve the grand objectives of global adjustment laid out earlier. If it is to gain wide acceptance, the IMF should also be evenhanded in making a case for policy change in other countries, above all in the United States. In going beyond their own comfort zone, multilateral organizations have little to lose but their irrelevance in addressing perhaps the most important global macroeconomic problem of our time.

## Summary and Conclusion

The fault lines that have led to the global trade imbalances and created today's Mandevillean world are deep. Moreover, because the imbalances are the result of deeply embedded strategies, change will be painful. It is not just a matter of raising an interest rate here, a tax there, or an exchange rate somewhere else. It is tempting for the international establishment to treat adjustment as a simple matter and then express continuous surprise that change does not occur. It also gives politicians the dangerous impression that change is easy for the other side, so punitive trade sanctions can help persuade. We should have no illusions: change is difficult for all countries, though they all stand to gain in the long term, not just from a more stable world economy but also from a more sustainable domestic growth strategy.

Given that actions to reduce sustained trade surpluses or deficits require domestic political momentum, it is not surprising that nothing really happens at these international meetings. Platitudes are rolled out, but everyone knows nothing will be done. I have argued that multilateral institutions like the IMF and the World Bank should take a cue from the movements promoting action against climate change and supporting aid to poor countries. They should expand beyond making their case to the top leaders to creating more political momentum within countries, using all the modern methods of contact that technology has put at our command. They should speak directly to the influential and the connected, explaining why change is necessary and how it can be beneficial despite the pain of adjustment. The multilateral agencies should help bridge the fault lines between nations and help each one see what it needs to do.

This is not a task that the private or nonprofit sector will undertake. Cuddly koalas, rain forests, and destitute children inspire hearts, minds, and donations. Causes such as global trade imbalances, exchange rates, and even food scarcity are unlikely to have the same public appeal and will not be taken up by NGOs. This is precisely why the well-funded multilateral organizations have to get involved. Unlike the NGOs, they do not have to choose exciting or emotional issues that attract funding: they can focus on the drier issues that are every bit as important to the future of our globe.

Finally, change, whether attempting to enforce global discipline with a stick or encouraging citizens to push for it from below, will not come easily for the multilateral organizations. Nor will it be easy for countries to contemplate giving multilateral organizations the freedom to influence domestic opinions. China has not shown much tolerance for domestic discussion, and even as I write, is embroiled in a dispute with the search giant Google over censorship. But even China is finding it increasingly difficult to control discussion on the Web. There is more democracy in China than is reflected in its elections. Its growing Web-connected middle class is obtaining more influence over the Communist Party and the Chinese leadership. The recent ham-fisted attempt by the authorities to limit the viewing of the worldwide hit movie *Avatar,* and the subsequent furious public reaction prompting (an admittedly rare) policy reversal, may be indicative of things to come. At any rate, draconian attempts to limit outside contact may work for a while but will eventually hurt the Chinese economy, a key concern of the Communist Party. Moreover, pressure will build both from inside and from outside for China to be a responsible global citizen.

In sum, multilateral organizations should play a greater role in defining what global economic citizenship means and appeal directly to thinking people around the world, using not obscure, unread papers but modern technological tools. Because my proposal does not preclude the holding of those frenetic international meetings and conferences that achieve little, why not try it?

# Epilogue

**W**E LIVE IN AN AGE OF PLENTY. If I reflect on just the changes I have experienced as an academic over the past three decades or so, they boggle my mind. My first experience with a computer came only in the second year of my undergraduate degree in electrical engineering. I say *experience* because we never actually saw or touched the computer. It was housed in a mysterious air-conditioned room that only the privileged were allowed to enter. We hoi polloi used to write our programs on punch cards and submit them to the computing services desk. When the computer was free of more urgent tasks, the cards would be fed into it. When, pregnant with hope, we got the strangely thin output a few days later, we would realize to our chagrin that we had misplaced a comma on some card in the deck. A simple program that would take a few minutes to debug today took us weeks of hard labor then.

The advent of the personal computer made an enormous difference to the productivity of academic work. Early word processors let us dispense with typewriters and correction fluid, but they were difficult to use, especially when it came to formulating mathematical equations: I spent many nights as a PhD student trying to make equations look right on the screen, only to find on further analysis that they were technically wrong. Of course, computer games were ubiquitous even then, though far less sophisticated. At least one fellow student took an additional year to finish his PhD because he got hooked on a game called Tetris. I escaped addiction only because I was so bad at the game to start off with.

Research collaborations across any distance were extremely difficult when I was starting out. The cost of international phone calls was prohibitive, and documents had to be shipped by snail mail, adding enormously to the time taken to complete projects. The search for relevant papers involved hours in the library, and typically we knew only of papers that had already been published, not those in the pipeline. Because of the long lead times for publication, papers in the latest journals had typically been written years before. Imagine my dismay when I found a paper in the *Journal of Finance,* a few weeks before I went out onto the academic job market, that contained the central idea in my thesis. (Luckily, there were enough points of differentiation that it was clear I had made a contribution, but the experience was still very demoralizing.)

Today everything has changed. Indeed, the notebook computer on which I am writing this book has thousands of times the processing power of the room-sized mainframe I started out with not so long ago, and costs about one-thousandth the price. To my children, my student life occurred BIE—before the Internet era. They cannot imagine anybody could be that ancient! Technology has changed their lives, and mine, dramatically. The magnitude of the change I have experienced over just the past three decades gives me hope that we will be able to solve many of the problems that seem intractable today.

Those problems are many. Abject poverty is still a scourge in many developing countries. The poor seem especially damned by nature. The recent earthquake in Haiti killed hundreds of thousands of people. Equally strong earthquakes occur in other parts of the world without killing so many, possibly because buildings are built to withstand shocks. Perhaps the roots of poverty and the cause of nature's seeming lack of compassion for the vulnerable are the same: the inability in many parts of the world to create the basic governance structures that will allow people to create decent livelihoods—and safe buildings—for themselves.

Industrial countries have their own problems. Even as government debt mounts in the aftermath of this crisis, populations in many countries are aging rapidly and coming to the realization that their government's earlier promises of security and health care in old age are likely to be reneged on. As they tighten their belts to provide for the difficult present, the future, if anything, looks bleaker.

As if this were not enough, the sins of our past are catching up with us. The evidence for climate change, with potentially disastrous environmental and economic consequences, seems compelling. Although there is always a possibility that we will overreact, the richest countries need to think of ways of reducing unnecessary consumption of energy and materials, and developing countries need to consider more sustainable pathways to growth.

These problems can and will be solved, provided we retain faith in human ingenuity and give it space to express itself. Economic reforms in China and India have unleashed the creative energies of more than a third of humanity. Millions of highly trained Chinese and Indian engineers are putting their brains to work to meet the challenges. Companies in China are now leaders in developing electric car batteries, and companies in India are producing affordable electric cars. When these developments are coupled with the advances in nuclear, solar, and wind energy that are taking place in industrial countries, we should be able to reach the goal of zero auto emissions at a viable cost in the not too distant future. If China and India can reverse centuries of decline in the space of decades, perhaps even Haiti may be able to use the ferment created by its recent tragedy to overcome the greater tragedy of its history.

Collaboration between countries can help in other areas: health management practices in developing countries could show the way to making health care more affordable in developed countries. "Medical tourism," whereby patients from rich countries can undergo much-needed medical procedures at significantly lower costs in developing countries, or "retirement migration," whereby the elderly migrate to retirement communities in salubrious but less expensive countries, helps bring incomes to developing countries while making treatment and old-age assistance affordable. Conversely, the migration of younger workers from developing to industrial countries can provide the tax base to help support aging industrial-country populations while also equalizing incomes globally. Remittances from migrants can help their relatives back home live better lives: entire areas in India, Mexico, and the Philippines have been transformed by remittances. Two-way flows of people can, if properly managed, be an answer to some of the world's most pressing problems.

Vibrant financial markets can provide the risk capital needed by the innovators across the world as well as the savings instruments needed by the aging and the currency-transfer facilities needed by migrants. But finance is in disrepute. Calls to shackle it are being heard from every quarter. More dangerous is the possibility that industrial countries, especially the United States, could lose faith in the financial system that has made them what they are. A misbegotten sense of the inadequacy of markets and competition is leading to ever more faith being placed in the government. Although there are certain things government can (and must) do, leading dynamic change and innovation is not among them.

It is an easy step for countries whose governments fail to meet the now-heightened expectations to seek to keep what they have by means of assertive nationalism and protectionism. Instead of embracing the growth of developing countries and keeping their domestic markets open, industrial countries could turn inward, to the detriment of all. According to polling by the Pew Foundation, 49 percent of Americans think their country should mind its own business internationally, a proportion 30 percentage points higher than when the question was first asked in 1964.[1] Equally, instead of accepting greater responsibility as their economic might grows, developing countries could prompt a stronger reaction by behaving as if their policies continue to have little effect on the world. We could yet convert hope into conflict, then despair, as the world has done many times before.

Economic stagnation is the breeding ground for conflict. To prevent history from mimicking itself, we have to understand the causes of the recent crisis and act on that understanding. Financial markets and democratic government are not incompatible. The role of financial markets is to allocate resources to those most capable of using them, while spreading the risks to those most capable of bearing them. The role of democratic government is to create a legal, regulatory, and supervisory framework within which financial markets can operate. However, democratic government has other roles, including limiting the most inequitable consequences of the market economy through taxes, subsidies, and safety nets. It is when democratic government uses these other tools inadequately, when it tries to use modern financial markets to fulfill political goals, when it becomes a participant in markets rather than a regulator, that we get the kind of disasters that we have just experienced.

Some argue that it was laissez-faire ideology that led us to this pass: regulators became enamored of the ideal of the self-regulating market and stood on the sidelines as it self-destructed. They are only partly right. Although it ought to be the duty of regulators to lean against the prevailing winds of optimism (and sometimes pessimism), regulation in the United States was driven by the misplaced view that markets would take care of themselves, a view that time and time again makes the ideological Right play into the hands of the ideological Left. Yet the bulk of the damage was done as the sophisticated financial sector tried to seek an edge that the U.S. government, driven by political compulsions, was only too willing to provide.

Progressives in the United States blame the bankers, while conservatives blame the government and the Federal Reserve. The worrying reality is that both are to blame, but neither may have been fully cognizant of the fault lines guiding their actions. Changing the actors, or trying to change their incentives directly, may have limited effect: we need to bridge the deeper fault lines. Unless we reestablish the proper role of the government and the financial sector, as well as fix the imbalances between nations, what happened may happen again.

The financial sector needs to know that it will bear the full consequences of its actions, which means that it, and not the taxpayer, will have to bear the losses it generates. The U.S. government has to re-create the access and opportunity for all its people that has historically been the hallmark of its economy while helping those who fall behind. This will reduce the pressure on the government to intervene in financial markets or to stimulate the economy excessively.

Other countries have to implement reforms that will help rebalance the world economy while reducing their own dependence on global growth. In this, as with the other challenges that the world faces, we will need international cooperation. The world's great powers, both the established ones and the emerging ones, have to recognize that their policies do not add up to a coherent whole. They have been reluctant to create strong global institutions that might impose constraints on their policies. To counter this reluctance, we need to broaden the policy debate across the world, persuading civil society in each country to push its government to enact policies that further the global good.

I write these last lines in a Lufthansa Airbus, flying back to the United States from a conference in Moscow. It is late in the evening, and the gentle rays of the wintry setting sun, toward which we are headed, glint magically off the plane's giant engines. The venue of the conference reminds me how far we have come. Three decades ago, Moscow was virtually closed to academics from the West. When I landed yesterday, the main problem was getting from the airport to the city, because the road was clogged, seemingly with all the millions of cars Muscovites have acquired since the fall of communism. That is progress, though clearly progress has brought new problems.

Such scenes should remind us that the past three decades have brought immense improvements to countries around the world, as they have harnessed the power of global markets and finance while obtaining economic freedom. Unfortunately, we have allowed political imbalances to develop within countries and economic imbalances to grow between countries. In many rich countries, insecurity and despair have replaced hope. We should not let what has gone wrong obscure all that can go right, or reverse the progress we have made. But to preserve and rebuild trust in the market system, we have to make fundamental changes. Governments have to do more to help their citizens build capabilities that will allow them to be productive. But they also have to step back in other areas to allow the market to function effectively. This crisis has resulted from a confusion about the appropriate roles of the government and the market. We need to find the right balance again, and I am hopeful we will.

# NOTES

## Introduction

1 For examples, see Paul Krugman, "How Did Economists Get It So Wrong?" *New York Times,* September 6, 2009, www.nytimes.com/2009/09/06/magazine/06Economict .html; John H. Cochrane, "How Did Paul Krugman Get It So Wrong?" University of Chicago Booth School of Business, http://faculty.chicagobooth.edu/john.cochrane/ research/Papers/krugman_response.htm, accessed March 5, 2010.

2 J. Lahart, "Mr. Rajan Was Unpopular (but Prescient) at Greenspan Party," *Wall Street Journal,* January 2, 2009.

3 See C. Reinhart and K. Rogoff, *This Time Is Different: Eight Centuries of Financial Folly* (Princeton, NJ: Princeton University Press, 2009) for an excellent study delineating the commonalities between crises through history.

4 For surveys, see M. Brunnermeier, "Deciphering the Liquidity and Credit Crunch, 2007–2008," *Journal of Economic Perspectives* 23, no. 1 (Winter 2009): 77–100; G. Gorton, "Information, Liquidity, and the (Ongoing) Panic of 2007," NBER Working Paper 14649, National Bureau of Economic Research, Cambridge, MA, 2009; D. Diamond and R. Rajan, "The Credit Crisis: Conjectures about Causes and Remedies," *American Economic Review* 99 (2009): 606–10. A number of very good books have been written on the crisis, including Gillian Tett, *Fool's Gold* (New York: Free Press, 2009); Richard Posner, *A Failure of Capitalism* (Cambridge, MA: Harvard University Press, 2009); Andrew Ross Sorkin, *Too Big to Fail* (New York: Viking, 2009); and David Wessel, *In Fed We Trust* (New York: Crown Business, 2009).

5 A. Atkinson, T. Piketty, and E. Saez, "Top Incomes in the Long Run of History," NBER Working Paper 15408, National Bureau of Economic Research, Cambridge, MA, 2009.

6 J. Anderson, "Wall Street Winners Get Billion-Dollar Paydays," *New York Times,* April 16, 2010, www.nytimes.com/2008/04/16/business/16wall.html.

7 See Stacey Schreft, Aarti Singh, and Ashley Hodgson, "Jobless Recoveries and the Wait-and-See Hypothesis," *Economic Review,* Federal Reserve Bank of Kansas City (4th quarter, 2005): 81–99.

8 Ibid.

## Chapter One. Let Them Eat Credit

1 See, for example, Richard Florida, *The Rise of the Creative Class: And How It's Transforming Work, Leisure, Community and Everyday Life* (New York: Basic Books, 2004).

2 See Claudia Goldin and Lawrence Katz, *The Race between Education and Technology* (Cambridge, MA: Belknap Press, 2009), 231.

3 Ibid., 330–31.

4 On educational attainment, see U.S. Census Bureau, "Educational Attainment in the United States: 2008," www.census.gov/population/www/socdemo/education/cps2008 .html, accessed March 5, 2010.

5 Brink Lindsey, "Paul Krugman's Nostalgianomics: Economic Policies, Social Norms, and Income Inequality," Cato Institute working paper, Washington, DC, 2009.

6 Author's calculations based on Goldin and Katz, *The Race between Education and Technology*, 52.

7 U.S. Census Bureau, "Educational Attainment: People 25 Years Old and Over, by Total Money Earnings in 2008," www.census.gov/hhes/www/cpstables/032009/perinc/ new03_001.htm, accessed March 5, 2010.

8 See Goldin and Katz, *The Race between Education and Technology*, 327.

9 Ibid., 249–50.

10 Ibid., 326–28.

11 T. Piketty and E. Saez, "Income Inequality in the United States, 1913–1998," NBER Working Paper 8467, National Bureau of Economic Research, Cambridge, MA, 2001.

12 Ross Douthat and Reihan Salam, *Grand New Party* (New York: Doubleday, 2008), 55.

13 See Lindsey, "Paul Krugman's Nostalgianomics."

14 See P. Gottschalk and R. Moffitt, "The Growth of Earnings Instability in the U.S. Labor Market," *Brookings Papers on Economic Activity* 25, no. 2 (1994): 217–72.

15 See Goldin and Katz, *The Race between Education and Technology*; Lindsey, "Paul Krugman's Nostalgianomics."

16 See, for example, Nolan McCarthy, Keith Poole, and Howard Rosenthal, *Polarized America: The Dance of Ideology and Unequal Riches* (Cambridge, MA: MIT Press, 2008).

17 See Lindsey, "Paul Krugman's Nostalgianomics," 10.

18 See, for example, A. Alesina and E. LaFerrara, "Preferences for Redistribution in the Land of Opportunities," NBER Working Paper 8267, National Bureau of Economic Research, Cambridge, MA, 2001.

19 See Alberto Alesina and Edward Glaeser, *Fighting Poverty in the US and Europe: A World of Difference* (Oxford: Oxford University Press, 2004), 61.

20 Ibid.

21 Alexis de Tocqueville, *Democracy in America* (New York: Doubleday, 1959), 53.

22 Robert J. Samuelson, "Indifferent to Inequality," *Newsweek*, May 7, 2001, 45.

23 The quote is from a description by Jennifer Hochschild on what her survey respondents believe, from *What's Fair? American Beliefs about Distributive Justice* (Cambridge, MA: Harvard University Press, 1981).

24 See Robert Frank, *Falling Behind: How Rising Inequality Harms the Middle Class* (Berkeley: University of California Press, 2007).

25 McCarthy, Poole, and Rosenthal, *Polarized America.*

26 Aristotle, *Politics*, book V, parts 1–5 (New York: Cambridge University Press, 1988). Indeed, Abhijit Banerjee and Esther Duflo argue in "Inequality and Growth: What Can the Data Say?" (NBER Working Paper 7793, National Bureau of Economic Research, Cambridge, MA, 2000) that changes in inequality in either direction tend to be associated with reduced growth.

27 See R. Green and S. Wachter, "The American Mortgage Market in Historical and International Context," *Journal of Economic Perspectives* 19, no. 4 (2005): 93–114.

28 See, for example, James R. Barth, S. Trimbath, and Glenn Yago, *The Savings and Loan Crisis: Lessons from a Regulatory Failure* (Los Angeles: Milken Institute, 2004).

29 Bethany McLean, "Fannie Mae's Last Stand," *Vanity Fair*, February 2009.

30 Steven Holmes, "Fannie Mae Eases Credit to Aid Mortgage Lending," *New York Times*, September 30, 1999.

31 Wayne Barrett, "Andrew Cuomo and Fannie and Freddie: How the Youngest Housing and Urban Development Secretary in History Gave Birth to the Mortgage Crisis," *Village Voice*, August 5, 2008.

32 *National Home Ownership Strategy* (Washington, DC: Department of Housing and Urban Development, 1995), Chapter 4. I thank Professor Joseph Mason of Louisiana State University for bringing my attention to this document and for first highlighting these issues.

33 See Lawrence McDonald and Patrick Robinson, *A Colossal Failure of Common Sense: The Inside Story of the Collapse of Lehman Brothers* (New York: Crown Business, 2009).

34 Neil Bhutta, "Giving Credit Where Credit Is Due? The Community Reinvestment Act and Mortgage Lending in Lower-Income Neighborhoods," Federal Reserve Board Working Paper 2008–61, Washington, DC, 2008. Also see Peter Wallison, "Deregulation and the Financial Crisis: Another Urban Myth," American Enterprise Institute, www .aei.org/outlook/100089, October 2009.

35 George W. Bush, "America's Ownership Society: Expanding Opportunities," June 17, 2004, http://georgewbush-whitehouse.archives.gov/news/releases/2004/08/ 20040809-9.html.

36 George W. Bush, "Remarks by the President on Homeownership," speech at the Department of Housing and Urban Development, Washington DC, June 18, 2002.

37 Ibid.

38 See Peter J. Wallison and Charles W. Calomiris, *The Last Trillion Dollar Commitment: The Destruction of Fannie Mae and Freddie Mac* (Washington, DC: American Enterprise Institute, September 2008).

39 Edward Pinto, "Sizing Total Exposure to Sub-Prime and Alt-A Loans in U.S. First

Mortgage Market as of 6.30.08," American Enterprise Institute, www.aei.org/docLib/ Pinto-Sizing-Total-Exposure.pdf, accessed March 10, 2010.

40 Edward Pinto, "High LTV, Sub-Prime and Alt-A Originations over the Period 1992–1997 and Fannie, Freddie, FHA, and VA's Role," American Enterprise Institute, www.aei.org/docLib/Pinto-High-LTV-Subprime-Alt-A.pdf, accessed March 10, 2010.

41 Ibid.

42 Atif Mian and Amir Sufi, "The Consequences of Mortgage Credit Expansion: Evidence from the U.S. Mortgage Default Crisis," *Quarterly Journal of Economics* 124, no. 4 (November 2009): 1449–96.

43 Peter Wallison, "Barney Frank, Predatory Lender," *Wall Street Journal,* October 16, 2009.

44 Ibid.

45 Of course, some of the change is also accounted for by the greater willingness of lenders to accept higher loan-to-value ratios as the credit market boomed. See James MacGee, "Why Didn't Canada's Housing Market Go Bust?" Federal Reserve Bank of Cleveland website, www.clevelandfed.org/research/commentary/2009/0909.cfm, December 2, 2009.

46 Nicolas P. Retsinas and Eric S. Belsky, eds., *Borrowing to Live: Consumer and Mortgage Credit Revisited* (Washington, DC: Brookings Institution Press, 2008), 14.

47 Tim Landvoigt, Monika Piazzesi, and Martin Schneider, "The Housing Market(s) of San Diego," presentation at Stanford University, 2009.

48 See, for example, *IMF World Economic Outlook* (Washington, DC: International Monetary Fund, September 2004), 76.

49 See, for example, Joseph Stiglitz, *Free Fall* (New York: Norton, 2010).

50 See Seymour Lipset, *Agrarian Socialism: The Cooperative Commonwealth Federation in Saskatchewan; A Study in Political Sociology* (Berkeley: University of California Press, 1951). I thank Rodney Ramcharan for this reference.

51 Shawn Cole, "Fixing Market Failures or Fixing Elections: Agricultural Credit in India," Harvard Business School working paper, www.hbs.edu/research/pdf/09-001.pdf, 2008.

52 U.S. Census Bureau, "Homeownership Rates for the U.S. and Regions: 1965 to Present," www.census.gov/hhes/www/housing/hvs/historic/index.html, accessed March 10, 2010.

53 See, for instance, Raghuram G. Rajan and Arvind Subramanian, "Aid and Growth: What Does the Cross-Country Evidence Really Show?" *Review of Economics and Statistics* 90, no. 4 (2008): 643–65.

## Chapter Two. Exporting to Grow

1 See Angus Maddison, "Monitoring the World Economy, 1820–1992," University of Groningen, Faculty of Economics, www.ggdc.net/maddison, accessed February 2010.

2 R. E. Lucas Jr., "Why Doesn't Capital Flow from Rich to Poor Countries?" *American Economic Review* 80, no. 2 (May 1990): 92–96.

3 Lant Pritchett, "Where Has All the Education Gone?" *World Bank Economic Review* 15, no. 3 (2001): 367–91.

4 There are many antecedents to this view, though not necessarily in the precise way I have formulated it. One of the early formulations is by Albert Hirschman in *The Strategy of Economic Development* (New Haven, CT: Yale University Press, 1958).

5 See Angus Maddison, "The Economic and Social Impact of Colonial Rule in India," Chapter 3 of *Class Structure and Economic Growth: India and Pakistan Since the Moghuls* (New York: Norton, 1971).

6 E. Glaeser, R. La Porta, F. Lopez-de-Silanes, and A. Shleifer, "Do Institutions Cause Growth?" NBER Working Paper 10568, National Bureau of Economic Research, Cambridge, MA, 2004.

7 See, for example, David S. Landes, *Dynasties: Fortunes and Misfortunes of the World's Great Businesses* (New York: Viking, 2006).

8 For instance, according to a recent study, 50 to 60 percent of restaurants survive less than three years: see H. Parsa, J. Self, D. Njite, and T. King, "Why Restaurants Fail," *Cornell Hotel and Restaurant Administration Quarterly* 46, no. 3 (2005): 304–22.

9 "Historical Tables: Budget of the U.S. Government—Fiscal Year 2010," Office of Management and Budget, www.whitehouse.gov/omb/budget/fy2010/assets/hist.pdf, accessed February 2010.

10 From Daniel Defoe, *A Plan of the English Commerce* (1728), described in Ha-Joon Chang, *Kicking Away the Ladder* (London: Anthem Press, 2002), 20–21.

11 Speech by Shri Syed Masudal Hossain in the Indian Parliament, Lok Sabha website, http://parliamentofindia.nic.in/lsdeb/ls11/ses5sp/0227089716.htm, accessed February 2010.

12 See Daniel Yergin and Joseph Stanislaw, *The Commanding Heights: The Battle between Governments and the Marketplace That Is Remaking the Modern World* (New York: Simon and Schuster, 1998), 12.

13 See Michael Reid, *The Forgotten Continent: The Battle for Latin America's Soul* (New Haven, CT: Yale University Press, 2007), 127.

14 See Yergin and Stanislaw, *The Commanding Heights*.

15 See Robert Wade, *Governing the Market: Economic Theory and the Role of Government in East Asian Industrialization* (Princeton, NJ: Princeton University Press), 79–80.

16 See Yergin and Stanislaw, *The Commanding Heights*, 176–77.

17 See Wade, *Governing the Market*, 80.

18 Ibid., 81.

19 See, for example, Alice Amsden, *Asia's Next Giant* (New York: Oxford University Press, 1989), 143–45.

20 For Korea's main exports in 1970, see Mark L. Clifford, *Troubled Tiger: Businessmen, Bureaucrats, and Generals in South Korea* (Armonk, NY: M. E. Sharpe, 1994), 60.

21 See Robert Brenner, *The Economics of Global Turbulence* (London: Verso, 2006).

22 See Hiroko Tabuchi, "Japan Strives to Balance Growth and Stability," *New York Times*, September 15, 2009.

23 Quoted in T. Taniguchi, *Japan's Banks and the "Bubble Economy" of the Late 1980s* (Princeton, NJ: Center for International Studies, Program on US-Japan Relations, 1993), 9. Also quoted in Brenner, *The Economics of Global Turbulence,* 219.

24 Why did the dot-com boom not do more to pull Japan out of its slump? In part, Japan was held back by its banking sector, which was in deep trouble. It was only after the banks were recapitalized and had cleared their balance sheets of bad loans in the early 2000s that they were in a position to resume lending.

25 See Hiroko Tabuchi, "Once Slave to Luxury, Japan Catches Thrift Bug," *New York Times,* September 21, 2009.

26 Marcos Chamon and Eswar Prasad, "Why Are Savings Rates of Urban Households in China Rising?" Brookings Global Economy and Development Paper 31, Brookings Institution, Washington, DC, 2008.

27 Peter Evans makes this point forcefully in *Embedded Autonomy: States and Industrial Transformation* (Princeton, NJ: Princeton University Press, 1995).

## Chapter Three. Flighty Foreign Financing

1 Through much of the 1990s, Germany ran current-account surpluses because of the economic consequences of reunification. By the early 2000s, it was back to running surpluses.

2 For an excellent introduction to foreign financing, see Barry Eichengreen, *Globalizing Capital: A History of the International Monetary System* (Princeton, NJ: Princeton University Press, 1996).

3 I owe the term "boom in busts" to Gerry Caprio of Williams College.

4 Martin Feldstein and Charles Horioka, "Domestic Saving and International Capital Flows," *Economic Journal* 90 (1980): 314–29.

5 Marc Lacey, "Kenyan Parliament Unites, for More Money," *New York Times,* May 22, 2005, www.nytimes.com/2006/05/22/world/africa/22iht-kenya.html.

6 See, for example, R. Rajan and L. Zingales, "Which Capitalism? Lessons from the East Asian Crisis," *Journal of Applied Corporate Finance* 11, no. 3 (1998): 40–48; R. Rajan and I. Tokatlidis, "Dollar Shortages and Crises," *International Journal of Central Banking* 1, no. 2 (September 2005): 177–220; D. Diamond and R. Rajan, "Banks, Short-Term Debt and Financial Crises: Theory, Policy Implications and Applications," *Carnegie-Rochester Conference Series on Public Policy* 54, no. 1 (June 2001): 37–71.

7 Tarun Khanna and Krishna Palepu, "Is Group Affiliation Profitable in Emerging Markets? An Analysis of Diversified Indian Business Groups," *Journal of Finance* 55, no. 2 (April 2000): 867–91.

8 The description of Alphatec is drawn from Mark L. Clifford and Peter Engardio, *Meltdown: Asia's Boom, Bust and Beyond* (Paramus, NJ: Prentice-Hall, 2000), 136–38.

9 See Shalendra D. Sharma, *The Asian Financial Crisis: Crisis, Reform, and Recovery* (Manchester, U.K.: Manchester University Press, 2003), 42.

10 The photograph is widely accessible, for example on the website of the International Political Economy Zone, http://ipezone.blogspot.com/2007/09/flashback-camdessus-suharto-pic.html, accessed March 10, 2010.

## Chapter Four. A Weak Safety Net

1 I have concealed real names here.

2 The ideas in this chapter evolved out of an initial office conversation with Martin Wolf of the *Financial Times*, to whom I owe thanks.

3 Stacey Schreft, Aarti Singh, and Ashley Hodgson, "Jobless Recoveries and the Wait-and-See Hypothesis," *Economic Review*, Federal Reserve Bank of Kansas City (4th quarter, 2005): 81–99.

4 R. Haskin and I. Sawhill, *Creating an Opportunity Society* (Washington, DC: Brookings Institution Press, 2009), 111.

5 Erica Groshen and Simon Potter, "Has Structural Change Contributed to a Jobless Recovery?" *Current Issues in Economics and Finance*, Federal Reserve Bank of New York, 9, no. 8 (August 2003): 1–7.

6 Kathryn Koenders and Richard Rogerson, "Organizational Dynamics over the Business Cycle: A View on Jobless Recoveries," *Federal Reserve Bank of St. Louis Review* 87, no. 4 (July–August 2005): 555–80.

7 Schreft, Singh, and Hodgson, "Jobless Recoveries."

8 Louis Uchitelle, "Labor Data Show Surge in Temporary Workers," *New York Times*, December 20, 2009.

9 Study by the U.K. National Council for Volunteer Organizations and United for a Fair Economy, cited in Alberto Alesina and Edward Glaeser, *Fighting Poverty in the US and Europe* (Oxford: Oxford University Press, 2004), 45.

10 See, for example, Joe Peek and Eric S. Rosengren, "Unnatural Selection: Perverse Incentives and the Misallocation of Credit in Japan," *American Economic Review* 95, no. 4 (September 2005): 1144–66; Takeo Hoshi and Anil Kashyap, *Corporate Financing and Governance in Japan: The Road to the Future* (Cambridge, MA: MIT Press, 2004).

11 See "A Fork in the Road," *Financial Times*, December 11, 2009.

12 See, for example, Clayton Christensen, *The Innovator's Dilemma* (New York: Harper Paperbacks, 2003).

13 National Science Foundation, *Science and Engineering Indicators*, Chapter 5, Appendix Table 5–43, National Science Foundation, www.nsf.gov/statistics/seind10/c5/c5s4.htm, accessed March 10, 2010.

14 Alesina and Glaeser, *Fighting Poverty*, 19.

15 *Talkin' 'bout My Generation: The Economic Impact of Aging U.S. Baby Boomers*, McKinsey Global Institute, Washington, DC, 2008.

16 See, for example, Louis Hartz, *The Liberal Tradition in America* (San Diego, CA: Harvest HBJ, 1991).

17 Alesina and Glaeser, *Fighting Poverty*, 197.

18 See Theda Skocpol, *Protecting Soldiers and Mothers: The Political Origins of Social Policy in the United States* (Cambridge, MA: Belknap Press, 1992), 50.

19 See Raghuram Rajan and Luigi Zingales, *Saving Capitalism from the Capitalists* (Princeton, NJ: Princeton University Press, 2004).

20 See Alesina and Glaeser, *Fighting Poverty*.

21 See Jacob S. Hacker and Paul Pierson, "Business Power and Social Policy: Employers and the Formation of the American Welfare State," *Politics and Society* 30, no. 2 (June 2002): 277–325.

22 See chart "Unemployment during the Depression," MSN Encarta, http://encarta.msn.com/media_461546193/unemployment_during_the_depression.html, accessed December 20, 2009.

23 See Hacker and Pierson, "Business Power and Social Policy."

24 See Peter A. Swenson, "Varieties of Capitalist Interests: Power, Institutions, and the Regulatory Welfare State in the United States and Sweden," *Studies in American Political Development* 18 (Spring 2004): 1–29.

25 See John B. Taylor, "The Lack of an Empirical Rationale for a Revival of Discretionary Fiscal Policy," *CES Info Forum* 10, no. 2 (Summer 2009): 9–13.

26 Elizabeth Drew, "Thirty Days of Barack Obama," *New York Review of Books,* March 26, 2009, www.nybooks.com/articles/22450.

27 Gerald Seib, "In Crisis, Opportunity for Obama," *Wall Street Journal,* November 21, 2008.

## Chapter Five. From Bubble to Bubble

1 Ben Bernanke, testimony before the Senate Banking Committee, Washington, DC, September 23, 2008, http://banking.senate.gov/public/index.cfm?FuseAction=Hearings.Testimony&Hearing_ID=7a41ae9e-30b2-4d7f-8f1b-4ef2e8ae28f7&Witness_ID=c52a9dcc-1eb1-474c-a493-461c8fef9afd, accessed March 28, 2010.

2 Ben Bernanke, "Asset Price Bubbles and Monetary Policy," speech made at the New York Chapter of the National Association of Business Economists, October 15, 2002.

3 See Ben Bernanke, "An Unwelcome Fall in Inflation," remarks made at the Economics Roundtable, University of California, San Diego, La Jolla, California, July 23, 2003.

4 See "Lessons for Monetary Policy from Asset Price Fluctuations," Chapter 3, *World Economic Outlook* (Washington, DC: International Monetary Fund, October 2009).

5 John Taylor, *Getting Off Track: How Government Actions and Interventions Caused, Prolonged, and Worsened the Financial Crisis* (Stanford, CA: Hoover Institution Press, 2009).

6 See Alan Blinder, "Monetary Policy Today: Sixteen Questions and about Twelve Answers," in *Central Banks in the 21st Century,* ed. S. Fernandez de Lis and F. Restoy (Madrid: Banco de Espana, 2006), 31–72, which cites evidence indicating that the Greenspan Fed was more focused on output and unemployment than inflation. The Fed may be more conscious about unemployment than, say, the European Central Bank. For example, see Joseph Lupton, "The Central Bank Bucket List" (JP Morgan Economic Research Note, Global Data Watch, JP Morgan, New York, September 11, 2009), which shows that the U.S. Federal Reserve started raising rates 20 months after peak unemployment in the 1990–91 recession and 12 months after peak unemployment in the 2001 recession. By contrast, the euro area not only cut rates less but also was quicker to raise rates, doing so 7 months after peak unemployment on average in the 1991 recession and 9 months after peak unemployment in the 2001 recession.

7  See David Backus and Jonathan Wright, "Cracking the Conundrum," New York University Working Paper, New York, 2007.

8  See Claudio Borio and Haibin Zhu, "Capital Regulation, Risk-Taking and Monetary Policy: A Missing Link in the Transmission Mechanism?" Bank of International Settlements Working Paper 268, Basel, 2009; Raghuram Rajan, "Has Financial Development Increased Risk Taking?" *Proceedings of the Jackson Hole Conference* (Kansas City, MO: Federal Reserve Bank of Kansas City, August 2005), 313–69.

9  I thank Rakesh Mohan, former deputy governor at the Reserve Bank of India, for pointing out this trend to me.

10  P. Gourinchas and H. Rey, "From World Banker to World Venture Capitalist: US External Adjustment and the Exorbitant Privilege," NBER Working Paper 11563, National Bureau of Economic Research, Cambridge, MA, 2005.

11  B. Bernanke, M. Gertler, and S. Gilchrist, "The Financial Accelerator and the Flight to Quality," *Review of Economics and Statistics* 78, no. 1 (February 1996): 1–15.

12  Studies using detailed banking data now show that low interest rates cause riskier lending. See G. Jimenez, S. Ongenga, J. Peydro, and J. Saurina, "Hazardous Times for Monetary Policy: What Do Twenty-Three Million Bank Loans Say about the Effects of Monetary Policy on Credit Risk?" CEPR Discussion Paper No. 6514, Center for Economic Policy Research, London, 2007; V. Ionnadou, S. Ongenga, and J. Peydro, "Monetary Policy, Risk Taking and Pricing: Evidence from a Quasi-Natural Experiment," paper presented at IMF Annual Research Conference, Washington, DC, November 2008.

13  See Raghuram G. Rajan, "Investment Restraint, the Liquidity Glut, and Global Imbalances," remarks presented at the Conference on Global Imbalances, Bali, Indonesia, November 16, 2006.

14  See. A. Shleifer and R. Vishny, "The Limits of Arbitrage," *Journal of Finance* 52, no. 1 (1997): 35–55, for a theory as to why arbitrageurs may find it difficult to bring asset prices back in line even without short-sales constraints.

15  See Claudio Borio and Philip Lowe, "Asset Prices, Financial and Monetary Stability: Exploring the Nexus," BIS Working Paper 114, Bank for International Settlements, Basel, July 2002.

16  See, for example, Bernanke, "Asset Price Bubbles and Monetary Policy."

17  Alan Greenspan, speech at the American Enterprise Institute, December, 5, 1996.

18  Alan Greenspan, *The Age of Turbulence: Adventures in a New World* (New York: Penguin Press, 2007), 176–78

19  Alan Greenspan, "Opening Remarks," Federal Reserve Bank of Kansas City symposium, Jackson Hole, WY, August 2002.

20  Ben Bernanke, "Monetary Policy and the Housing Bubble," speech delivered at the annual meeting of the American Economic Association, January 3, 2010.

21  Marek Jarocinski and Frank Smets, "House Prices and the Stance of Monetary Policy," *Federal Reserve Bank of St. Louis Review* 90, no. 4 (July–August 2008): 319–65.

22  However, studies have identified a clear relationship between the level of interest rates and the level of house prices across countries.

## Chapter Six. When Money Is the Measure of All Worth

1 This example relies on Peter Hoffman, Gilles Postel-Vinay, and Jean-Laurent Rosenthal, *Surviving Large Losses: Financial Crises, the Middle Class, and the Development of Capital Markets* (Cambridge, MA: Belknap Press, 2007), 149–51.

2 Adam Smith, *An Inquiry into the Causes of the Wealth of Nations* (Chicago: University of Chicago Press, 1976), 18.

3 Dan Ariely, Emir Kamenica, and Dražen Prelec, "Man's Search for Meaning: The Case of Legos," *Journal of Economic Behavior and Organization* 67, no. 3 (September 2008): 671–77.

4 See James Chanos, "Prepared Statement: U.S. Securities and Exchange Commission Roundtable on Hedge Funds," U.S. Securities and Exchange Commission, www.sec.gov/spotlight/hedgefunds/hedge-chanos.htm, accessed March 10, 2010.

5 Jill Riepenhoff and Doug Haddox, "Risky Refinancings Deepen Financial Hole," *Columbus Dispatch*, June 2, 2008.

6 See Allen Frankel, "The Risk of Relying on Reputational Capital: A Case Study of the 2007 Failure of New Century Financial," BIS Working Paper 294, Bank for International Settlements, Basel, 2009.

7 James R. Hagerty, Ruth Simon, Michael Corkery, and Gregory Zuckerman, "Home Stretch: At a Mortgage Lender, Rapid Rise, Faster Fall," *Wall Street Journal*, March 12, 2007.

8 Riepenhoff and Haddox, "Risky Refinancings."

9 For arguments and evidence along these lines, see U. Rajan, A. Seru, and V. Vig, "The Failure of Models That Predict Failure: Distance, Incentives and Defaults," University of Chicago working paper, 2009.

10 Even the credit score of a borrower could be "managed," with arrangements sometimes being made for a borrower to piggyback, for a fee, on the loan of a stranger with higher credit quality. See Frankel, "The Risk of Relying on Reputational Capital"; David Streitfeld, "In Appraisal Shift, Lenders Gain Power and Critics," *New York Times*, August 19, 2009.

11 Riepenhoff and Haddox, "Risky Refinancings."

12 Bradley Keoun and Steven Church, "New Century, Biggest Subprime Casualty, Goes Bankrupt," Bloomberg.com, www.bloomberg.com/apps/news?pid=20601087&refer=home&sid=aXHDSbOcAChc, accessed March 10, 2010.

13 See Atif Mian and Amir Sufi, "The Consequences of Mortgage Credit Expansion: Evidence from the U.S. Mortgage Default Crisis," *Quarterly Journal of Economics* 124, no. 4 (November 2009): 1449–96.

14 For a model of how volume can swamp incentives, see Andrei Shleifer and Robert Vishny, "Unstable Banking," NBER Working Paper 14943, National Bureau of Economic Research, Cambridge, MA, 2009.

15 See Frankel, "The Risk of Relying on Reputational Capital."

16 Peter Wallison, "Barney Frank: Predatory Lender," *Wall Street Journal*, October 16, 2009.

## Chapter Seven. Betting the Bank

1  This example borrows from Joshua Coval, Jakub Jurek, and Erik Stafford, "The Economics of Structured Finance," Harvard Business School Working Paper 09–060, Cambridge, MA, 2008.

2  Tim Rayment, "The Man with the Trillion Dollar Price on His Head," *Sunday Times,* May 17, 2009.

3  Ibid.

4  *Shareholder Report on UBS's Writedowns,* UBS, Zurich, April 18, 2008.

5  See the colorful account in Lawrence McDonald and Patrick Robinson, *A Colossal Failure of Common Sense* (New York: Crown Business, 2009).

6  Eric Dash and Julie Creswell, "The Rush to Riches that Undid Citigroup: Banking Giant's Management Failed to Monitor the Risks Tied to Its Deals," *International Herald Tribune,* November 24, 2008.

7  Andrew Ellul and Vijay Yerramilli, "Stronger Risk Controls, Lower Risk: Evidence from U.S. Bank Holding Companies," Indiana University working paper, Bloomington, 2010. Available at Social Science Research Network, http://ssrn.com/abstract=1550361.

8  Rudiger Fahlenbrach and Rene Stulz, "Bank CEO Incentives and the Credit Crisis," NBER Working Paper 15212, National Bureau of Economic Research, Cambridge, MA, July 2009.

9  McDonald and Robinson, *Colossal Failure.*

10  Calvin Trillin, "Wall Street Smarts," *New York Times,* October 14, 2009.

11  Ibid.

12  Thomas Philippon and Ariell Reshef, "Wages and Human Capital in the U.S. Financial Industry: 1909–2006," NBER Working Paper 14644, National Bureau of Economic Research, Cambridge, MA, 2009.

13  See R. Rajan, "Why Bank Credit Policies Fluctuate: A Theory and Some Evidence," *Quarterly Journal of Economics* 109, no. 2 (May 1994): 399–441.

14  Andrew Ross Sorkin, *Too Big to Fail* (New York: Viking, 2009), 145.

15  Michiyo Nakamoto and David Wighton, "Citigroup Chief Stays Bullish on Buyouts," *Financial Times,* July 9, 2007.

16  Gillian Tett, *Fool's Gold* (New York: Free Press, 2009), 144–45.

17  Ibid., 112–13.

18  I. Cheng, H. Hong, and J. Scheinkman, "Yesterday's Heroes: Compensation and Creative Risk Taking," working paper, Princeton University, 2009.

19  Steve Fishman, "Burning Down His House: Is Lehman CEO Dick Fuld the True Villain in the Wall Street Collapse?" *New York* magazine, November 30, 2008, http://nymag.com/news/business/52603/index3.html#ixzz0XFCXEyhZ.

20  Sorkin, *Too Big to Fail,* 273.

21  Andrea Beltratti and Rene Stulz, "Why Did Some Banks Perform Better during the Credit Crisis? A Cross-Country Study of the Impact of Governance and Regulation," NBER Working Paper 15180, National Bureau of Economic Research, Cambridge, MA, July 2009.

22  See editorial, " 'No Line Responsibilities': What Robert Rubin Did for His $115 Million," *Wall Street Journal,* December 3, 2008, http://online.wsj.com/article/SB1228266 32081174473.html.

23  See Viral V. Acharya, Thomas Cooley, Matthew Richardson, and Ingo Walter, "Manufacturing Tail Risk: A Perspective on the Financial Crisis of 2007–09," working paper, New York University Stern School of Business, 2009.

24  Caroline Baum, "Fed Should Read Its Own Memo on Rising-Rate Risk," Bloomberg .com, January 19, 2010, www.bloomberg.com/apps/news?pid=20601039&sid=aygo_ Qm9sZ9I.

25  See Tom Braithwaite, "Banks Face Probe over Trading in Tarp Frenzy," *Financial Times,* February 1, 2010.

26  Ibid.

27  Henry Paulson, *On the Brink: Inside the Race to Stop the Collapse of the Global Financial System* (New York: Business Plus, 2009), 293.

28  D. Diamond and R. Rajan, "Fear of Firesales and Credit Freezes," NBER Working Paper 14925, National Bureau of Economic Research, Cambridge, MA, 2009.

## Chapter Eight. Reforming Finance

1  Matt Taibbi, "Inside the Great American Bubble Machine," *Rolling Stone,* July 2, 2009.

2  See the discussion in Donncha Marron, *Consumer Credit in the United States: A Sociological Perspective from the 19th Century to the Present* (New York: Palgrave Macmillan, 2009), 3–5.

3  Benjamin Franklin, *The Way to Wealth,* Wealth Reader, http://wealthreader .com/book/the_way_to_wealth/1, accessed March 10, 2010 (italics in original).

4  See Robert Higgs, *Crisis and Leviathan: Critical Episodes in the Growth of American Government* (Oxford: Oxford University Press, 1987), 179.

5  For an excellent paper on tail risk, see Viral V. Acharya, Thomas Cooley, Matthew Richardson, and Ingo Walter, "Manufacturing Tail Risk: A Perspective on the Financial Crisis of 2007–09," working paper, New York University Stern School of Business, 2009.

6  Raghuram Rajan, "Bankers' Pay Is Deeply Flawed," *Financial Times,* January 9, 2008.

7  Dennis Berman, "Where Was Lehman's Board?" *Wall Street Journal,* September 15, 2008, http://blogs.wsj.com/deals/2008/09/15/where-was-lehmans-board/.

8  The ideas on disclosure are based on a working paper by the Squam Lake Working Group on Financial Regulation, "A New Information Structure for Financial Markets," Council on Foreign Relations, www.cfr.org/publication/18568/new_information _infrastructure_for_financial_markets.html, February 2009.

9  See Andrew Ross Sorkin, *Too Big to Fail* (New York: Viking, 2009), 304.

10  See D. Diamond and R. Rajan, "Illiquidity and Interest Rate Policy," NBER Working Paper 15197, National Bureau of Economic Research, Cambridge, MA, 2009.

11 This is a proposal made by the Squam Lake Group in its forthcoming report, to be published by Princeton University Press.

12 Banks should benefit by committing to their clients that they will not trade using their information or against their interests. Some boutique investment banks use the fact they have no conflicts of interest as a selling point. Perhaps this trend will catch on, in which case regulation will be unnecessary.

13 For a detailed explanation of why equity capital is costly in banks, those familiar with the Modigliani-Miller theorem can consult D. Diamond and R. Rajan, "A Theory of Bank Capital," *Journal of Finance* 55, no. 6 (December 2000): 2431–65.

14 See the proposal "An Expedited Resolution Mechanism for Distressed Financial Firms: Regulatory Hybrid Securities," Council on Foreign Relations, www.cfr.org/publication/19002/expedited_resolution_mechanism_for_distressed_financial_firms.html, April 2009.

15 See A. Kashyap, R. Rajan, and J. Stein, "Rethinking Capital Regulation," paper prepared for the Federal Reserve Bank of Kansas City symposium "Maintaining Stability in a Changing Financial System," Jackson Hole, WY, August 21–23, 2008.

16 See Aaron Wildavsky, *Searching for Safety* (New Brunswick, NJ: Transaction Books, 1988).

17 See Thomas Hoenig, president of the Federal Reserve Bank of Kansas City, "Perspectives on the Recent Financial Market Turmoil," speech at the 2008 Institute of International Finance Membership Meeting, Rio de Janeiro, Brazil, March 5, 2008.

18 See, for example, the proposed House Financial Regulatory Reform Bill of 2009.

19 See Sorkin, *Too Big to Fail*, 490.

20 Prime Reserves, a money-market fund, suffered losses on its Lehman debt holdings after the Lehman collapse. Because it paid out $1 for every dollar invested instead of the $0.97 or so that the investments were now worth, investors rushed to the exit to avoid being forced to bear the losses. If the fund had marked its assets to market and paid out only $0.97, there would have been less of a panic. Again, in a crisis, perhaps no asset is safe without a government guarantee, including money-market funds that are invested in anything other than Treasury bills.

21 I thank Viral Acharya for suggesting this term.

22 Louis D. Brandeis to Robert W. Bruere, *Columbia Law Review* 31 (1922): 7.

23 Louis D. Brandeis, *Other People's Money: And How the Bankers Use It* (Washington, DC: National Home Library Foundation, 1933), 62.

## Chapter Nine. Improving Access to Opportunity in America

1 Alberto Alesina and George-Marios Angeletos, "Corruption, Inequality and Fairness," working paper, Harvard Institute of Economic Research, Harvard University, 2005.

2 See R. Rajan, "Rent Preservation and the Persistence of Underdevelopment," *American Economic Journal: Macroeconomics* 1, no. 1 (January 2009): 178–218.

3 This section relies extensively on R. Haskin and I. Sawhill, *Creating an Opportunity Society* (Washington, DC: Brookings Institution Press, 2009), and J. Heckman and A. Krueger, *Inequality in America* (Cambridge, MA: MIT Press, 2005).

4 David Barker, "In Utero Programming of Chronic Disease," *Clinical Science* 95, no. 2 (1998): 115–28; David Barker, "Maternal and Fetal Origins of Coronary Heart Disease," *Journal of Royal College of Physicians* 28, no. 6 (1994): 544–51; David Barker, "The Fetal Origins of Adult Hypertension," *Journal of Hypertension* Supplement 10, no. 7 (1992): S39–44.

5 James Heckman, "Lessons from the Bell Curve," *Journal of Political Economy* 103, no. 5 (1995): 1091–120.

6 Haskins and Sawhill, *Creating an Opportunity Society,* 134.

7 See Santiago Levy, *Progress against Poverty: Sustaining Mexico's Progresa-Oportunidades Program* (Washington, DC: Brookings Institution Press, 2006).

8 James S. Coleman, *Educational Equality of Opportunity,* U.S. Department of Health, Education, and Welfare, 1966.

9 James Heckman, "Schools, Skills, and Synapses," NBER Working Paper 14064, National Bureau of Economic Research, Cambridge, MA, 2008.

10 Heckman and Krueger, *Inequality in America,* 95; S. Bowles and H. Gintis, *Schooling in Capitalist America* (New York: Basic Books, 1976).

11 J. Coleman and T. Hoffer, *Public and Private High Schools* (New York: Basic Books, 1983).

12 See Haskin and Sawhill, *Creating an Opportunity Society,* 144–45.

13 Barack Obama, speech at Democratic National Convention, quoted in *Washington Post,* July 27, 2004, www.washingtonpost.com/wp-dyn/articles/A19751-2004 Jul27.html.

14 Anthony Bryk, Penny Bender Sebring, Elaine Allensworth, Stuart Luppescu, and John Easton, *Organizing Schools for Improvement: Lessons from Chicago* (Chicago: University of Chicago Press, 2009).

15 Doris Entwisle, Karl Alexander, and Linda Olsen, *Children, Schools, and Inequality* (Boulder, CO: Westview, 1997).

16 Alan Krueger, "Inequality: Too Much of a Good Thing," in Heckman and Krueger, *Inequality in America.*

17 Much of what follows is based on the report of the Teaching Commission, a private nonpartisan group chaired by Lou Gerstner, former CEO of IBM. Their 2004 report "Teaching at Risk: A Call to Action" can be found at www.csl.usf.edu/teaching%20at% 20risk.pdf.

18 See Atila Abdulkadiroglu, Joshua Angrist, Susan Dynarski, Thomas Kane, and Parag Pathak, "Accountability and Flexibility in Public Schools: Evidence from Boston's Charters and Pilots," NBER Working Paper 15549, National Bureau of Economic Research, Cambridge, MA, 2009.

19 See Sam Dillon "Obama to Seek Sweeping Change in 'No Child' Law," *New York Times,* February 1, 2010.

20 See Haskin and Sawhill, *Creating an Opportunity Society,* 149.

21 Ibid., 153.

22 Ibid., 158.

23 This paragraph is based on David Deming and Susan Dynarski, "Into College and Out of Poverty? Policies to Increase the Post-Secondary Attainment of the Poor," NBER Working Paper 15387, National Bureau of Economic Research, Cambridge, MA, 2009.

24 Susan Dynarski, *The Economics of Student Aid,* NBER Reporter Research Summary 2007, no. 1, National Bureau of Economic Research, Cambridge, MA, 2007.

25 OECD, *Health Data 2008: Statistics and Indicators for 30 Countries* (Paris: Organization for Economic Co-operation and Development, 2008).

26 The peer group consisted of Canada, France, Germany, Japan, Switzerland, and the United Kingdom. See Alan Garber and Jonathan Skinner, "Is American Healthcare Uniquely Inefficient?" *Journal of Economic Perspectives* 22, no. 4 (Fall 2008): 27–50.

27 This and the next paragraph rely on Garber and Skinner, "Is American Healthcare Uniquely Inefficient?"

28 Chris Peterson and Rachel Burton, *US Healthcare Spending: Comparison with Other OECD Countries* (Washington, DC: Congressional Research Service, 2007).

29 Andrew Pollack, "Hospitals Look to Nuclear Tool to Fight Cancer," *New York Times,* December 26, 2007.

30 See Garber and Skinner, "Is American Healthcare Uniquely Inefficient?"

31 Katherine Baicker, Elliott S. Fisher, and Amitabh Chandra, "Malpractice Liability Costs and the Practice of Medicine in the Medicare Program," *Health Affairs* 26, no. 3 (May–June 2007): 841–52.

32 For the highly paid workers in the financial sector, I argue that having a stake in the firm can improve incentives. However, some reasonable portion of their savings should be independent of the health of their firms.

33 See, for instance, Robert Shiller, *The New Financial Order* (Princeton, NJ: Princeton University Press, 2003), 118–19.

34 The next few paragraphs draw on my previous book with Luigi Zingales, *Saving Capitalism from the Capitalists* (Princeton, NJ: Princeton University Press, 2004).

35 Shlomo Benartzi and Richard Thaler, "Save More Tomorrow: Using Behavioral Economics to Increase Employee Savings," unpublished manuscript, University of Chicago.

### Chapter Ten. The Fable of the Bees Replayed

1 Bernard Mandeville, *The Fable of the Bees* (1714) (Oxford: Clarendon Press, 1957).

2 Ibid.

3 Yashwant Sinha, speech at World Economic Forum, Davos, Switzerland, January 2001.

4 Jeffry Frieden, "Global Imbalances, National Rebalancing, and the Political Economy of Recovery," working paper, Council on Foreign Relations, New York, 2009.

5 Ibid.

6 "Leaders' Statement: The Pittsburgh Summit," Pittsburgh Summit, www.pittsburgh summit.gov/mediacenter/129639.htm, September 25, 2009.

7  M. Goldstein and N. Lardy, *The Future of China's Exchange Rate Policy* (Washington, DC: Peterson Institute for International Economics, 2009).

8  See Dani Rodrik, "The Real Exchange Rate and Economic Growth," working paper, Kennedy School of Government, Harvard University, 2008.

9  See George Monbiot, "Keynes Is Innocent: The Toxic Spawn of Bretton Woods Was No Plan of His," *Guardian,* November 18, 2008.

10  See Eswar S. Prasad, "Is the Chinese Growth Miracle Built to Last?" *China Economic Review* 20 (2009): 103–23.

11  Economists will see that I am arguing here that the income effect swamps the substitution effect.

12  See Tarun Khanna and Yasheng Huang, "Can India Overtake China?" *Foreign Policy* (July–August 2003): 75–81.

## Epilogue

1  Cited in "Counting Their Blessings," *Economist,* January 2, 2010.

INDEX

consumption in, 203; exchange-rate intervention by, 106, 205, 209–10, 211, 217–21; export-led growth strategy of, 65–66, 206; exports of, 58, 106, 218; foreign reserves of, 211, 219–20, 222; interest rates in, 220, 221–22; investment in, 66; middle class in, 224; one-child policy of, 65; reforms in, 221–22, 224, 226–27; savings in, 65, 220; state-owned enterprises in, 65, 220–21, 222

Chrysler, 91

Citigroup: board members of, 147, 152; CEO of, 143; off–balance sheet assets of, 150–51, 161; risk managers of, 140; risks taken by, 139, 145–46; salaries in, 144; stock price of, 152

climate change, 213, 226

Clinton, Bill, 36, 39, 85

Clinton administration, 35–37, 43

CLOs. See collateralized loan obligations

cognitive capture, 181

Cole, Shawn, 43

collateralized debt obligations (CDOs), 142, 160

collateralized loan obligations (CLOs), 110

colleges. See higher education

Community Reinvestment Act (CRA), 36–37, 131

conglomerates, 74–75

consumption: in China, 65–66, 220; in developing countries, 205; discouragement of, 46, 57–58; of energy, 203; excess, 157, 206; in Japan, 64; of middle class, 8–9; political pressure for economic stimulus to, 13–16; in United States, 5, 6, 9–10, 16, 203, 205, 209

contingent capital, 174–75

corruption, 57, 170

CRA. See Community Reinvestment Act

credit: benefits and costs of easy, 31, 44; definition of, 157; democratization of, 156–58

credit card debt, 41

credit default swaps, 3, 135–36

credit markets: access to, 5–6, 156–58; in developing countries, 70–72; expansion of, 109, 111, 118; government intervention in, 43, 148; informal, 71; microcredit, 44–45; political pressure for easy credit, 8–9, 23–24, 39, 42–43. See also subprime mortgage market

credit ratings, of mortgage-backed securities, 128, 130, 134–35, 136, 177

crises. See financial crises

crony capitalism, 56, 78–79, 170

currencies. See exchange-rate policies

current-account balances, 69–70, 73

debt: consumer, 41; government, 72–73; household, 71; negative views of, 157. See also credit markets; foreign debt; mortgages

Defoe, Daniel, A Plan of the English Commerce, 52

demand: in housing market, 5–6, 16; interest rate levels and, 105; in United States, 84. See also consumption

democracies, 214–15, 228

democratization of credit, 156–58

Dennis, William, 88

deposit insurance, 149, 178–80

deregulation, 28, 33, 142, 155, 158

developing countries: central banks of, 109, 111; consumption in, 205; current-account surpluses of, 69–70; economic growth of, 69–70; excess savings of, 5, 16; exchange-rate policies of, 13, 109, 218; financial systems of, 12, 70–71, 80–81; foreign debt of, 47, 68, 72–73, 79–80, 204; foreign exchange reserves of, 13, 82; foreign investment in, 12–13, 68; microcredit in, 44–45; organizational capital in, 49–50; poverty in, 226; trade deficits of, 47, 204; trade surpluses of, 70, 209